THE BIBLE SOCIETY OF
HIS IMPERIAL MAJESTY (BSHIM)
PUBLISHED BY: H.H. RAS IADONIS TAFARI,
& H.H. WOIZERO TEHETENA GIRMA-ASFAW
OF THE LION OF JUDAH SOCIETY (LOJS)
IMPERIAL PUBLISHERS TO THE H.I.M. UNIVERSITIES, COLLEGES & CHRISTIAN [TEWAHEDO] CHURCHES

©1991-2015 BSHIM-LOJ

©2015 by LION OF JUDAH SOCIETY PUBLISHERS & IYOBELYU [JUBILEE] PRINTING PRESS

We are the CHURCH OF RASTAFARI, and therefore a noncommercial interest that may reproduces portions of books or entire volumes for *the Education and Fine-Arts* development of Our people, the ETHIOPIAN-HEBREWS at home and abroad. We ask only that, when reproducing text from this book, please include the following credit line: "From ***The Queen Of Sheba & Biblical Scholarship*** " by Bernard Leeman, 2005" now herein reprinted and re-published in a new edition by THE LION OF JUDAH SOCIETY. *Imperial permission granted in advance.*"

The faithful intent of this Society of HIS IMPERIAL MAJESTY, HAILE SELLASSIE FIRST, whose divine utterances are contained elsewhere, according to His Selected Speeches foreword and Imperial note, is also herein likewise affirmed, *namely that*: **"*Any portion of this Book could be reproduced by any process without permission.*"**

All English-language scripture quotations, unless otherwise noted, are taken from the King James Version of the 1611 A.D. Holy Bible [KJV].

All Amharic-language scripture quotations, unless otherwise noted, are taken the *Emperor's Bible*, the 1961/2 A.D. Authorized H.I.M. HAILE SELLASSIE I Revised Amharic Bible [RAB].

Published by THE LION OF JUDAH SOCIETY, *www.lojsociety.org*

Our mission is to bring good tidings, that publisheth peace; that bringeth good tidings of good, that saith to Zion, Thy God reigneth. – Isaiah 52:7

Printed in the United States of America.

PREFACE TO OUR ETHOPIC MSS LIMITED EDITION PRINTINGS:

here are a number of rare and recently re-discovered books, manuscripts and documents, including Ancient MSS of highly significant value, especially to all of us who are diligent students and faithful disciples of THE REVELATION OF THE RAS TAFARI. In particular, these reprints may be of interest to those persons, irrespective of race, class and creed who are sincerely interested in furthering their studies into many of the related subject matters that often embraces a wide range of topical and academic themes, *namely* – the ETHIOPIC [GE'EZ] and AMHARIC languages, Ancient manuscripts, biblical, apocryphal and even so-called "pseudepigraphal," or early translations of the history, culture and origins of the uniquely and indigenous Ethiopian [*Tewahedo*] Orthodox Church and their evident Black Jewish [or, Beta Israel], i.e. Ethiopian-Hebraic roots and culture of the Highland civilization located at, what one early African traveler termed – the *"Source of the Nile"* – just to briefly name a very few of the more generally defined categories into which these topics are often classified arbitrarily, here and there. We, for our part, have inquired, searched and re-discovered a host of these documents and found it necessary to the Society of His Majesty to present them to the new and future generations for their possession, benefit and knowledge of self.

Over time, it has been noted, many of the older, in some cases better and definitely earlier writings, translations and Scholarly researches have been taken off of the library shelves, subsequently buried, purposely misplaced, hidden from public view and not easily accessible to the great majority of those, like ourselves, who have sought them everywhere we could. It is chiefly due to the new technology, that is the internet and the increased distribution of postscript document files online that serves as ready resources of redistribution of these original facsimiles of these, our stolen heritages, here again restored to a new, wider audience and present readership.

If knowledge is power, then we must deduce that any lack of the same is virtually tantamount to slavery of the spirit and soul to ignorance; and in its due course the body suffers. History bears witness to all this; it is without controversy. Thus in order to remedy this current "lack of information" that too often leads to an increase of ignorance, error and envy, we have decided at our own expense to prioritize the reprinting and republishing of the various texts, books and manuscripts in our archives and collection, many of them for the very first time. The bulk of these books have not seen the light of day since they were originally printed by their initial authors and respective printing presses; and, often only limited run of copies were formerly put into circulation to begin with, mostly exclusively deposited in university libraries, scholarly archives and private collections.

Thus, for now, this brief foreword and similar introductory statements will be prefaced to all of our new series of publications and attached to the newer reprints of the selected books and documents being made available by the Lion of Judah Society Publishers. May the Almighty bless and prosper the works of our hands and the intent of our heart for the gospel of Christ in His Kingly character, our Divine Heritage and in the furtherance of the dissemination of the "ancient Ethiopian culture" to our sisters and brothers, at home and abroad. Amen.

RAS IADONIS TAFARI [1]
Chairman, LOJS
MINISTRY OF EDUCATION & FINE-ARTS
c. 13th *February*, 2014

የዮሐንስ ራእይ ምዕራፍ፡ 5 ቁጥር 5

«ከሽማግሌዎቹም አንዱ። አታልቅስ፤ እነሆ፤ ከይሁዳ ነገድ የሆነው አንበሳ እርሱም የዳዊት ሥር መጽሐፉን ይዘጋ ዘንድ ሰባቱንም ማኅተም ይፈታ ዘንድ ድል ነሥቶአል አለኝ።»

REVELATION CHAPTER 5, VERSE 5 *"And one of the elders saith unto me, Weep not: behold, the **Lion of the tribe of Juda**, the Root of David, hath prevailed to open the book, and to loose the seven seals thereof."*

---

[1] *Alius dictus*, **Debtera: Rasiadonis Tafari,** *A Sometime Scholar of LOJS' Black Christ College;* H.I.M. HAILE SELLASSIE I University in Exile [USA], *An Ethiopian-Hebrew Scholar;* and Keeper of the *Department of Ethiopic & Amharic Antiquities* in the Black Lion Museum, USA-ET.

የዮሐንስ ራእይ። ምዕራፍ ፭፥ቁጥር ፭።

«ከሽማግሌዎቹም አንዱ፡ እታልቀስ፤ እነሆ፡ ከይሁዳ ነገድ የሆነው አንበሳ አርሱም የዳዊት ሥር መጽሐፉን ይዘረጋ ዘንድ ሰባቱንም ማኅተም ይፈታ ዘንድ ድል ነሥቶአል አለኝ።»

REVELATION CHAPTER 5, VERSE 5

"And one of the elders saith to me, Weep not: behold, the **Lion of the tribe of Juda,** the Root of David, hath prevailed to open the book, and to loose the seven seals thereof."[2]

---

[2] According to the best and most accurate interpretation, to date, proposed by Ras Iadonis Tafari, this scripture was fulfilled by THE CONQUERING LION OF THE TRIBE OF JUDAH: HIS IMPERIAL MAJESTY, H.I.M. HAILE SELLASSIE I, ELECT OF GOD, KING OF KINGS OF ETHIOPIA; *initially* beginning when He, Our Kinsman Redeemer, who was known as 'Ras Tafari Makonnen,' plenipotentiary and Heir to the Davidic Throne of Solomon. At His own expense and goodwill, RAS TAFARI, purchased and brought the first modern Printing Press into Ethiopia for the expressed purpose of dissemination of Our Ancient culture, education, and in the strengthening of the *Tewahedo* True Faith by way of the translations and printing of rare and very ancient Judeo-Christian manuscripts and scrolls from the old Ethiopic, or GE'EZ, into the Amharic language, culminating in the First Haile Sellassie Bible (1936) and later the 1961 A.D. Authorized Revised Amharic Bible, also called and known as the Emperor's Bible. For more, refer to the recently published *Rastafari Preliminary Notes to the H.I.M. Haile Sellassie I Amharic Bible: An Introduction to the Book of the Seven Seals.*

Queen of Sheba and Biblical Scholarship

©2005 by Bernard Leeman
All rights reserved

Queensland Academic Press
PO Box 227
Darling Heights
Queensland 4350
Australia

www.queensland-academic-press.com

First published November 2005
Second Edition January 2006
Third Edition January 2007

Readers have full permission to copy, distribute, and sell this book either in print or as a CD.

CONTENTS

Maps	*iii*
Introduction	*iv*
Acknowledgements	*vii*
CHAPTER 1 Sheba, Zionism, and the Old Testament	1
CHAPTER 2 The Search for Evidence	23
CHAPTER 3 Writing the Old Testament	39
CHAPTER 4 The Queen of Sheba	54
CHAPTER 5 The Kebra Nagast	84
CHAPTER 6 Western Arabia and the Sheba-Menelik Cycle	119
CHAPTER 7 The Ark of the Covenant and Israelite Influences	168
REFERENCES AND NOTES	191

APPENDIX A 201
Comparison of Subject Material Describing
the Queen of Sheba's Visit to Solomon's Court

APPENDIX B 203
1. The Jewish Torah
2. The Israelite Torah of the Sheba-Menelik Cycle

APPENDIX C 208
The Ge'ez (Ethiopic) Alphabet

APPENDIX D 209
The Ge'ez (Ethiopic) Numerals

APPENDIX E 210
Ge'ez transcript of sections of the Sheba-Menelik
Cycle of the Kebra Nagast

BIBLIOGRAPHY 221

INDEX 237

Map 1 viii
    Major locations mentioned in the text

Map 2 ix
    The Promised Land according to the Salibi Hypothesis

Map 3 x
    Solomon's Kingdom according to the Salibi Hypothesis

Map 4 xi
    Ethiopian and Eritrean languages

Map 5 xii
    Major Middle Eastern and N.E. African Land and Sea Trade
Routes in Antiquity

Map 6   *xii*
   Archaeological sites in Palestine/Israel

Map 7   *93*
   Menelik's journey with Jerusalem sited in Palestine

Map 8   *141*
   Arabic dialects of Western Arabia

Map 9   *164*
   Menelik's journey with Jerusalem in Arabia

Introduction

This book is designed to introduce college-level students to Old Testament history and to show that in western Arabia and in the Horn of Africa evidence relating to the Queen of Sheba indicates that the Promised Land was more likely in western Arabia, not in Palestine.

My research on the Queen of Sheba was originally inspired by the legend in my home region of Kilimanjaro, Tanzania, that Menelik, son of Solomon and the Queen of Sheba, was buried in the crater of Kibo, the highest of Kilimanjaro's three peaks. The local Chagga word for God is *Ruwa/Looa*, adopted from a Cushitic people who settled there around 1000 years B.C.E. These Cushitic speakers, although later absorbed by Bantu-speaking settlers, nevertheless maintained their own separate Mbulu identity south of Arusha. Ruwa/Looa is a feminine noun and phonetically identical to the Hebrew word for *Holy Spirit*, also a feminine noun.

My research produced nothing more than legends that long ago a great king was buried on the mountain and that a sacred book had been placed in the crater. My interest did however lead me to the *Kebra Nagast,* the ancient Ge'ez manuscript, which, from ca. A.D. 1314 until 1974, served as one of the most important documents in Ethiopian constitutional history. The *Kebra Nagast* is a combination of three ancient manuscripts, written at different times, and finally intertwined in a single document, edited in the first years of the fourteenth century A.D. The oldest section of the *Kebra Nagast* is the *Sheba-Menelik Cycle,* which tells the story of the meeting ca. 950 B.C.E. of King Solomon and the Queen of Sheba, the birth of their son Menelik, and the establishment of an Israelite state in Ethiopia. The second part of the *Kebra Nagast* is the *Caleb Cycle*, which deals with sixth-century A.D. Byzantine, southern Arabian, and Aksumite (early Ethiopian) political and religious issues. The third part is a brief account of how the *Kebra Nagast* was finally edited in Aksum ca. A.D. 1314.

After reading the *Sheba-Menelik Cycle,* my initial reaction was one of disappointment, for its geographical references made no sense. Consequently, I rejected it as having no historical merit.

From 1974 to 1975, I taught in Jizan in southwestern Saudi Arabia and was puzzled by the remains of substantial but uninvestigated ancient urban settlements scattered about that region. I found that there is very little literature on the pre-Christian history of the region between Jeddah and the

Yemen. Arab legends about an ancient Israelite presence in the region were not at that time taken seriously by Western academics.

My interest in the *Sheba-Menelik Cycle* revived following the 1985 publication of Kamal Salibi's *The Bible Came from Arabia*. I sent Professor Salibi the list of locations mentioned in the *Sheba-Menelik Cycle*. He replied, confessing he was not conversant with the *Sheba-Menelik Cycle's* content; nevertheless he provided a map marking the place names. This map convinced me that the *Sheba-Menelik Cycle* was a true story, for its narrative matched Old Testament locations in western Arabia not Palestine.

Place names, Arabian traditions, and the lack of archaeological remains in Palestine/Israel did not offer sufficient proof to argue the case of a western Arabian location for the Old Testament, and it would take much more research to uncover more convincing evidence. I had already spent several years in the most unpromising circumstances undertaking research for a Ph.D. in modern southern African politics. I had never received any financial assistance for my doctoral research, and much of my work was undertaken clandestinely in Southern Africa during military service against the apartheid regime. Research on the *Sheba-Menelik Cycle* presented similar problems, mostly because of the Saudi government's hostile attitude, the Ethiopian civil war, and the Eritrean war of independence.

I eventually immigrated to Australia and was fortunately able to utilize the excellent facilities of the Australian National University during my service in Canberra for the Australian Army, the Commonwealth Department of Education, and as Australian Capital Territory representative of the African Studies Association of Australasia and the Pacific (AFSAAP). In 1994, I presented my views at the AFSAAP Conference at La Trobe University, Australia. As a consequence Professor Ashenafi Kebede of Florida State University invited me to join the Ethiopian Research Council. In 1996 I went to Asmara University, Eritrea, as assistant professor and deputy head of the History section, as well as lecturer in phonetics and phonology in the English Department. During my stay at Asmara I copied out the entire Ge'ez text of the *Kebra Nagast* and also checked Bezold's German translation against Wallis Budge's English version. I shall always be grateful to all those who encouraged my work, particularly students at Asmara University who asked for repeat lectures; and Dr Desmond Thomas of the School of Oriental and African Studies,

London University, for using a 2003 video of my lecture on the Queen of Sheba as part of the academic oral presentation training course.

This book evolved from the AFSAAP conference paper, and lectures I gave at Asmara and at universities, schools, and public meetings in Ethiopia, Tanzania, Kenya, Australia, the USA, South Korea, China, Thailand, Vietnam, Morocco, and England. In my continuous work on this project, what strikes me most is how the story of the Queen of Sheba evokes enthusiasm even in societies with little or no Biblical tradition. She was young, beautiful, loved learning more than position and wealth, and symbolizes a long lost gentler more tolerant world that continues to inspire idealists today.

Introduction to the Third Edition January 2007

Readers should be warned that possession of this book has led to arrest in Saudi Arabia. There has been also been a strong clandestine campaign to block its sales. Internet sites falsely claim it was published by Africa World Press at more than $100 a copy but is now "not available."

Acknowledgements

I should like to thank the following for their help and encouragement:

Elizabeth Abebe, Fessehaye Abraham, Sofia Abraham, Peter Alexander, Laetitia Amon-Tanoh, David Appleyard, Douglas Archer, Antonio Arnazi-Villena, Letebrehan Assefaw, Tekie Asyhun, Seife Berhe, Lin Boyle, Mike Brownhill, David Deaton, Jane Delahunty-Goodman, John Distefano, David Dorward, Rodolpho Fattovich, Tigisti Fesshaye, David Fisher, Stephanie Fitzpatrick, Asmeret Ghebreizgiabiher, Richard Gibson, Bill Glanzman, Wolfgang Graßmann, Richard Greenfield, Bjoerne Grimsrud, Bink Hallum, Harald Hammarström, Janet Hanley, Moktar Hassan, Bernd Heine, David Hubbard, Grover Hudson, Miri Hunter-Haruach, Ararat Iyob, Debbie Jordan, Will Kabaruka, Ed Keall, Ashenafi Kebede, Aubine Kirkley, Michael Kirkley, Ernst Knauf, Sergey Kotelnikov, Asli Kylemariam, Kim Hang Eui, Kim Kyong Hyo, Mumbua Kioko, Potlako Leballo, Lee Hyang Joo, Lee So Young, Margaret Leeman, Nicholas Leeman, Sarah-Louise Leeman, Trilas Matesha Leeman, Wolf Leslau, Yoseph Libsekal, Alf Lindberg, Marcia Marsh-Hinds, Ntsukunyane Mphanya, Nigel Mullally, Stuart Munro-Hay, Julius Nyang'oro, Gerald Obermeyer, Aileen Page, Richard Pankhurst, Tudor Parfitt, Park Kyoung Ran, Roy Pateman, Rosey Peacock, Tony Peacock, Elisabeth Pfützner, Helmut Pfützner, Pham Thi Huan, James Quirin, Ken Rook, Eric Ross, Kamal Salibi, Michael Sanders, Gordon Sato, Nicole Saulsberry, Peter Schmidt, Huda Seif, Kay Shelemay, John Shoup, Neil Silberman, Zecarias Russom, Stephen Tavener, Tiberh Tesfamariam, Donica Tesfamariam, Desmond Thomas, Thomas Thompson, Enzio Tonini, Edward Ullendorf, Simona Vitale, Elvie Weldon, Else Yttredal, Selamawit Zewolde.

MAP 1

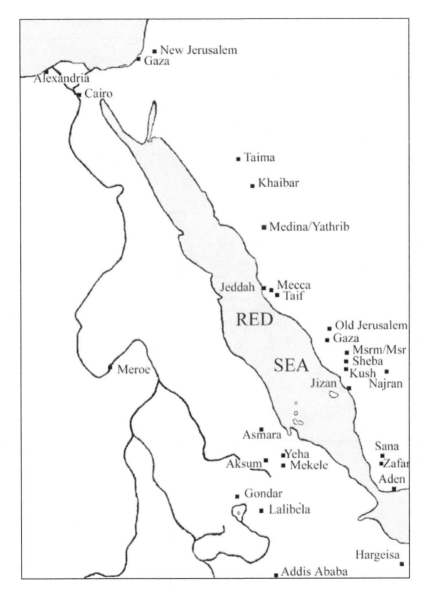

Major locations mentioned in the text

MAP 2

The Promised Land according to the Salibi Hypothesis

MAP 3

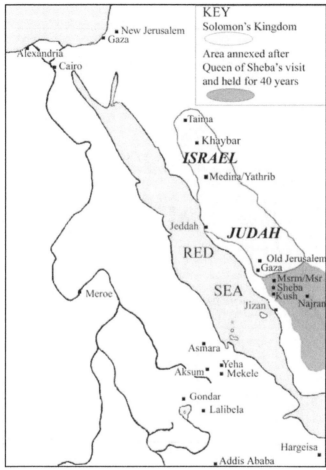

The shaded area is the region that contains the "Hebrew-isms" recorded by Chaim Rabin in "Ancient West Arabian", the Old Testament place names noted by Kamal Salibi, iron deposits, and an ancient ark culture. It also straddles the lucrative incense, gold, precious stones, and luxury goods trade routes from Sabaea (Sheba). This area was temporarily abandoned by Egyptian and Assyrian imperial control ca. 1000-920 B.C.E., the same years as the zenith of the Israelite states under David and Solomon.

MAP 4

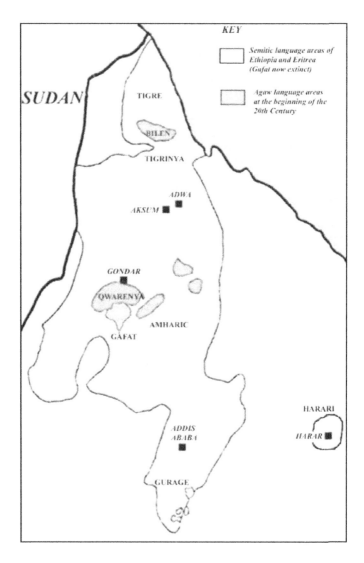

The Semitic Languages of Ethiopia and Agaw (Central Cushitic) remnant isolates

MAP 5

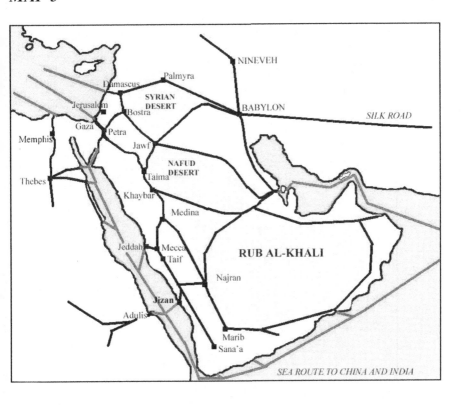

Major Middle Eastern and North East African Land and Sea Trade Routes in Antiquity

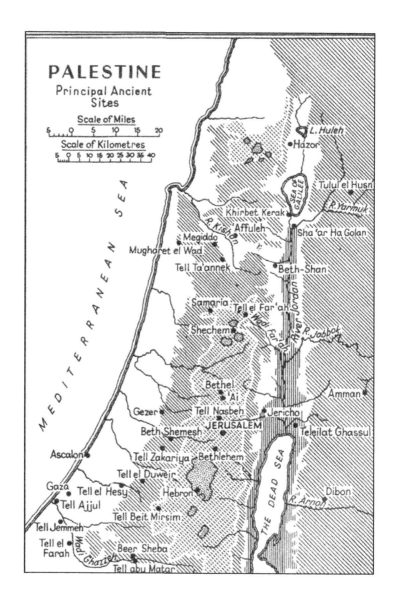

CHAPTER ONE

Sheba, Zionism, and the Old Testament

According to ancient texts and oral traditions the Queen of Sheba was a beautiful and brilliant young monarch who controlled the immensely wealthy incense trade of southern Arabia around 1000 years B.C.E. She made a state visit to King Solomon, ruler of the united kingdoms of Judah and Israel. Jewish and Christian sources say she came to seek wisdom; Islamic sources say she was forced.

The Queen of Sheba was the only major figure in the Old Testament who simply wanted to know the truth. The queen, declared Christ with some exasperation (Matthew 12:42 and Luke 11:31), was a great deal smarter than the members of the Jerusalem religious establishment a thousand years later. She, unlike them, recognized greatness when she saw it. Having heard wonders about Solomon's wisdom, she made an epic journey to meet him. Although Christ was eminently greater than Solomon, the priests and scribes refused to accept it. Come Judgment Day the Queen of Sheba would be able to testify that they had made a terrible mistake.

Though it is hoped that Judgment Day will be a long way off, the Queen of Sheba has returned in a literary if not literal sense to testify that two thousand years later the interpreters of Hebrew holy writ have again refused to recognize the obvious.

Interest in the Old Testament is not merely a literary exercise. Whereas Britons may speculate whether stories about King Arthur and Robin Hood are fantasies or exaggerations, the Old Testament account is the *raison d'être* of the state of Israel. Belief in Friar Tuck, Camelot, and Merlin is one thing; Moses, Solomon's Jerusalem, and Ezra another. If biblical testimony is false, modern Israel could no longer present itself as the fulfilment of divine will but more as an embattled colonial settlement comparable with French Algeria or apartheid South Africa.

The Zionist movement, which has seen the establishment in 1948 of the State of Israel and the consequent regional and global crises thereafter, takes its theological and political inspiration from twenty references in the Old Testament books of Genesis, Exodus, Leviticus, Numbers, and Deuteronomy concerning divine assurances to the Hebrew patriarchs Abraham and Moses that their followers would inherit a Promised Land "flowing with milk and honey."

The Old Testament is a theological and historical account that begins with the wanderings of the Hebrew people. They appear originally to have been a group of several tribes, but in the Old Testament they are only mentioned seventeen times by name (`bry/`brym/`bryym/`bryt), which comes from the name of their common ancestor, `brm h-`bry, or Abraham the Hebrew, who lived ca. 1800 - 1400 B.C.E. The original language of the Hebrew is unknown because they adopted Canaanite after they conquered the Promised Land ca.1200 B.C.E. Canaanite/Hebrew was written without vowels, so the word "Hebrew" would appear as `br, which in general Semitic can mean "those who crossed over."

The Hebrew were a nomadic people seeking permanent settlement. It is generally accepted that they were a technologically skilled people who quickly adopted ironworking. The exact date of the true Iron Age, when Middle Eastern peoples began forging iron rather than merely smelting and hammering it, is unknown, but it was probably around 1500 B.C.E. The Hittites appear to have attempted to guard the secret of forging, but after the downfall of their empire ca. 1200 B.C.E. many other peoples developed the technique. Iron tools made it easier to establish permanent agricultural settlements. Forests could more easily be cleared and iron ploughs used to cultivate heavier soils. Increased food production fostered larger families, and more children survived infancy. Population explosions followed, and large groups of Iron Age peoples began to migrate. For the first time in history ordinary people had access to powerful weapons, and they used them to overrun Bronze Age peoples. This led to the formation of strong centralized states, as the ruling elites developed organizational skills to control the new situation and thus preserve their privileges. It was not until ca. A.D. 1000 that societies in Asia and Europe stabilized after 2000 years of dislocation resulting from the Iron Age migrations.

The Hebrew were unusual among these migrating peoples in that they kept an oral record of their experiences which they eventually committed to writing, a text that would thereafter dominate their existence, giving them an allegedly divine but demanding code of behavior and political-religious objectives. Because of the nature of their experience they had an egalitarian outlook that recalled their failures as well as their successes, unlike the practices of court-sponsored scribes elsewhere whose existence depended on continual praise of their royal benefactors. However, although the Hebrew intermarried with other peoples, they periodically reverted to a strict fundamentalism that demanded separation in accordance with a divine destiny.

Nearly everything we know about the Hebrew has reached us through hundreds of years of Old Testament editing by priests and scribes associated with the traditions of the Zadokites, so named after Zadok, the high priest of Solomon's first temple (His theological legacy will be discussed in the next chapter). Even those who opposed the Zadokites, like the Samaritans, have accepted their edition of the first five books of the Old Testament, which deal with the early history of the Hebrew and the Law of Moses (Torah). According to the Old Testament the first known Hebrew was the patriarch Abraham, who is believed to have lived ca. 1800-1400 B.C.E. The Old Testament states that he came from R, which is generally taken to be either an unknown city *(ir)* or Ur in Mesopotamia, 300 kilometers southeast of modern Baghdad.

Although the Hebrew were most probably a Semitic people, it is also worth considering the outside possibility that some were Cushitic. While in the remote past such terms were ethnic as well as linguistic, today they should be treated overwhelmingly as linguistic, otherwise it would be like saying English-speaking Inuit of northern Canada and African Americans are Indo-Europeans because they speak a Germanic language. The most widely accepted theory is that Semitic-speaking peoples belong to a very large linguistic group that includes Berber, Chadic, Egyptian, Omotic, and Cushitic languages, all of them descended from an ancestral language known as Afro-Asiatic, which is sometimes also called Hamito-Semitic or Erythraic (after the Greek word for the Red Sea). About 5000 years ago Afro-Asiatic began to splinter into the six separate groups listed above, and as time passed they splintered further into other groups. Semitic probably developed in the Nile valley region and is the only member of the Afro-Asiatic group to have spread to Asia from its African homeland, although it is conceivable that Cushitic may have once had a limited presence in southwestern Arabia.

Most authorities believe that Semitic speakers crossed into the Middle East through the Sinai peninsula. Some pressed to the north, settling in Syria and Mesopotamia; others went south, settling in Yemen. The pre-Classical Arabic dialects of Arabia testify that there is a distinct East-West linguistic division reflecting these migration patterns. Until recently it was assumed that Semites from South Arabia introduced the Semitic languages of Ethiopia and Eritrea. However this view is increasingly being challenged. It is possible that the Semitic speakers of Ethiopia and Eritrea, such as the Tigrinya, Tigré, Amhara, and Gurage, are descendants of a Semitic population that never left Africa but later were augmented by small influxes from Southern Arabia.

Biblical tradition maintains that Abraham recognized the existence of a special unknown true God and rejected all other gods, but from his time until about 400 B.C.E. the Hebrew/Israelite communities frequently deviated from this path. Abraham was given divine assurance that he would father nations, that he would enter a Promised Land, and that his descendants would inherit the earth. Despite his advanced age Abraham responded by quitting his city for the nomadic life. Recent evidence suggests that a meteorite shower devastated Mesopotamia, Egypt, and Greece in about 2350 B.C.E. initially causing famine, flooding, and fires on a vast scale that dramatically altered climatic conditions and forced people to move to new areas.[1] Perhaps similar disasters afflicted the Hebrew ca. 1800 - 1400 B.C.E.

Whatever the reason for Abraham's migration, tradition says he spent some time in modern Turkey before passing on to Canaan (Palestine), probably via Syria. Abraham is supposed to have settled near Hebron and to have had dealings with Egypt. He fathered a son, Isaac, with his wife Serai/Sarah; and another son, Ishmael, with Sarah's servant Hagar. Isaac's son Jacob fathered the leaders of the twelve tribes of Israel, while Ishmael was the ancestor of the Arabs. The Arabs contend that Abraham was responsible for the establishment of the Ka'bah in Mecca, now Islam's holiest shrine.

Jacob's son Joseph became a powerful advisor to the court of an unnamed Egyptian pharaoh, but later the Hebrew became slaves in Egypt for a period of 430 years. The reasons for this captivity are not clear. The story of Joseph speaks of famine, and a later Islamic account speaks of a volcanic eruption that dispossessed "the Israelites" of their land. In such circumstances the Hebrew may have been forced to accept servitude in Egypt in order to survive. If their captivity occurred in Egypt they may well have arrived during the lengthy period of drought that forced much of the Palestinian population in late eighteenth century B.C.E. to migrate and to settle in the northeast area of the Nile Delta. This supports the theory that the Exodus took place in 1440 B.C.E. during the reign of Pharaoh Thutmose III (ca. 1479-1426 B.C.E.). Thutmose overran Palestine, Syria, the Upper Nile (Nubia), and perhaps parts of Arabia. Part of his imperial policy was to take the children of local rulers, raise them as Egyptians, and then return them as Egyptian vassal rulers with Egyptian garrisons to oversee their own people. This practice is reflected in the story alleging that Moses was brought up as an Egyptian prince. However, some authorities date the Exodus to the reign of Ramses II (ca. 1279-1213 B.C.E.), builder of vast public works to assuage his failure against the Hittites; but they give the reason for the Exodus as discontent with the harsh demands of Ramses' father, Seti I (ca. 1318-1304 B.C.E.) during his public works program. There may also have been ideological disputes between an Egyptian bureaucracy extending a uniform code of administration and theology on a subject people who, as in later times in Babylon and elsewhere, were held together by a hereditary priesthood that interpreted the imposition of central control as a threat to their own interests. Lastly, a skilled but alien artisan class may have resented being denied concomitant political power under a demanding but technologically backward ruling class. Commentators who oppose linking the Exodus to the period of Seti's reign point out that both his capital and his building program were in the Luxor area, whereas Ramses II's new capital and public works program were in the eastern Delta.

Accounts of Moses may not have been based on a single man. The Old Testament has two versions of his childhood: one, his being rescued from the river; the other, being brought up with his brother Aaron and sister Miriam in the Levi priestly clan. After killing an Egyptian overseer and fearful of denunciation from his fellow Hebrew who resented his privileged status, Moses fled and became a military commander, reputedly leading the Egyptian army against Ethiopia and taking an Ethiopian wife. This version is based on unvocalized place names *msrm* and *kws* that probably do not refer to Egypt and Ethiopia at all but (certainly in the case of *kws*) to a location far from Egypt. Moses' career and other early episodes in the Old Testament are associated with volcanic activity and monotheism, indicating that the Israelite god Yhwh may originally have been a volcano deity, linked, like the Roman god Vulcan, to metal working. Yemen is the most likely place for volcanoes, and evidence found there indicates a very early form of monotheism that would profoundly influence Islam later. While Moses' career was so remarkable that he may well have been responsible for actions ascribed to him in the Old Testament, many authorities still believe that the Old Testament account is probably based on more than one person. Especially difficult is reconciling the Egyptian prince of unknown parentage turned nationalist military commander with the monotheist religious leader who had a known family and led the Exodus through a volcanic location.

The Hebrew may have been an isolated people who gradually built up immunity to certain diseases. It is noteworthy that they were spared during a plague that decimated their Egyptian masters, and again when the Philistines and Assyrians in turn perished in other plagues, the first of which the Israelites attributed to the power of the Ark of the Covenant, a sacred chest, constructed at Mt. Sinai, containing stone tablets inscribed with the Ten Commandments. Lastly, most authorities agree that the Israelites were an Iron Age people who invaded Bronze Age Canaan. Today isolated groups in Africa claiming an ancient Hebraic origin - the Inadan (Niger), Beta Israel (Ethiopia), Yibir (Somalia), and Lemba (southern Africa) - are all associated with metalworking; and Islamic traditions hold that David and Solomon were both great armorers.

After 430 years in captivity, the Hebrew escaped under the leadership of Moses, who married the daughter of Jethro, a prominent prophet, and organized his followers (the Old Testament only gives the number of *men* who escaped – over 600,000) into a nomadic religious community under the Torah, thus fulfilling a divine mission as God's chosen people in search of the Promised Land. Moses left an indelible mark on his people forever through the Torah – the law. The Jewish philosopher Moses Maimonides (A.D. 1135-1204) later listed the laws as being 613 in number, dealing with all aspects of everyday life and justice. The powerful Hassidic Jewish sect in America, Europe, and modern Israel observes them all.

We do not know what language the original Hebrew spoke although a traditional belief has it as an early form of Aramaic. They may have lost it during their Egyptian captivity. But they also lost whatever language they spoke when they invaded the Promised Land under Joshua around 1200 B.C.E., adopting Canaanite instead. Biblical Hebrew contains words from Akkadian, Sumerian, and Indian languages but nothing from Egyptian. Moses' monotheism and lawgiving have been linked to the Egyptian pharaoh Akhenaton (ca. 1379 – 1362 B.C.E.). However, while they may have been contemporaries – one writer suggests they were the same man -

the Torah of Moses stands in sharp contrast to the sun worship of Akhenaton, which was totally lacking in commandments.

The story of Moses is associated with a volcanic region, and the dietary proscriptions in the Torah mention osprey, kite, coney (rabbit or hyrax), and some fish, suggesting that the original Hebrew homeland was located in mountain and desert areas near the sea. During the forty years of wandering between Egypt and the Promised Land, Moses faced a number of crises, not least the Hebrew's penchant for El, the Canaanite high god, symbolized by the golden calf; and Ba'al, a pagan deity of life and fertility popular not only among Semitic speaking peoples such as the Canaanites and Phoenicians but also among the Egyptians themselves during the New Kingdom period (ca. 1400 – 1082 B.C.E.), which covers the time of Moses' career, be it during Thumose III's reign or that of Ramses II. Canaanites believed that Ba'al was locked in perpetual combat with Mot, the god of death and sterility, and that seven-year cycles of plenty or famine reflected the state of the cosmic struggle. This is extremely significant given the nature of the story of Joseph, who gained his freedom and a powerful position in Egypt by interpreting pharaoh's dream about seven lean cattle devouring seven fat ones, correctly predicting that the Egyptians must prepare for a seven year famine. Given such a success and the prestige accorded Ba'al among the Hebrew themselves, it is extraordinary that Moses was successful in introducing a demanding legalistic cult whose deity, Yhwh, insisted on high-risk enterprises in exchange for rather nebulous future glory and divine blessing. Nevertheless the Yhwh cult survived Moses' unhappy fate. He incurred divine wrath for petty infringements of God's will and consequently was doomed never to reach the Promised Land.

The Old Testament states that even during the days of the Exodus there was a fratricidal struggle among the Hebrew as one group associated with a demanding xenophobic monotheism fought to eliminate the religious beliefs of another group that revered El and Ba'al. This struggle continued to polarize the twelve tribes of Israel thereafter and eventually transformed the Old Testament from a general historical account into an alleged divinely inspired constitution not only for Ezra's Zadokite ca. 400 B.C.E. Jerusalem theocracy but also for modern Judaism.

Moses' god, Yhwh, was associated with warfare and state building. Led by Joshua, the Hebrew, armed with iron weapons, conquered and united Bronze Age Canaan. Apart from Joshua and Caleb, the two remaining survivors of those who originally fled Egypt, the new conquerors had no experience of urban civilization, farming, or administration. As time went by the Hebrew increasingly became assimilated by the Canaanite tribes. It appears that the Israelite religion's detailed legal code was attractive to bureaucratic elites like the Canaanite priesthood. Political change followed. The old nomadic pastoralist patriarchal system was ill suited to the complexities of the new society with its urban centers, farming population, trade links, commercial enterprises, and rivalry from the Ammonites and Philistines. After a period of rule by judges (ca. 1200-1050 B.C.E.) the Israelites established a kingdom. With the assistance of the patriarch Samuel, Saul (ca. 1021-1000 B.C.E.) of the tribe of Benjamin became the first king. At his death he was succeeded by David of the tribe of Judah, and then by David's son Solomon. The new dynasty united the ten northern tribes of Israel and the two southern tribes of Judah to create a strong, centralized, and eventually extremely wealthy state.

An Arab tradition holds that the Israelites were the first to domesticate the camel. Whatever the truth of the matter, the advent of the Israelite kingdom coincided with the development of long-range camel-borne trading caravans. David and Solomon created a large centralized state with a cavalry force and archer infantry using iron weapons. They took control of the northern end of the Arabian trade from Yemen (Sheba) and the western end of the Mesopotamian trade through Taima. The priesthood, drawn from the family of Aaron, Moses' reputed brother and spokesman, as Moses had a speech impediment, [2] became more hierarchical as it became increasingly involved in court affairs and fought to maintain its authority against the new institution of the monarchy.

The new wealth enabled David and Solomon to undertake substantial public works. David established fortified garrisons, and Solomon built the First Temple, modeled on a Phoenician design. The temple, heavily decorated with gold and housing the Ark of the Covenant under a silk canopy, was oblong-shaped and not particularly large, but faced outwards to a huge courtyard that could accommodate thousands.

Solomon established trading and military colonies outside the kingdom. The association of the First Temple with the state of Judah gave rise to a new ethno-religious identity, *Israelite*, which was opened to everyone. Ruth, David's ancestor, was a convert as was Solomon's mother, Bathsheba, and his most famous associate, the Queen of Sheba. The conquered Canaanite population on the whole found their new masters' religion vengeful and demanding. Despite the tradition that the Israelite priests were strictly from the Hebrew tribe of Levi, Zadok, Solomon's high priest, appears to have been from a Jebusite (Canaanite tribe) priestly family (see DNA evidence pp. 180-181) and was awarded the post for helping Solomon defeat rivals for the kingship. If the House of Zadok were composed of converts, they certainly embraced the new faith with great fervor. Despite this, they seemingly disappeared during the later part of Solomon's reign. When they reappeared 300 years later the Zadokites were still fierce adherents of the uncompromising monotheist legalistic element in Israelite theology that would eventually marginalize other Israelite religious schools of thought.

However, the northern kingdom endured forced labor, and both kingdoms high taxation to pay for the public works program. The situation was partly ameliorated by Solomon's tolerance of some aspects of their former religions. Jebusite beliefs, such as the idea of God as the Creator of the world, were absorbed into the Israelite religion. The temple became the national symbol of the kingdom, consolidating the move from the worship of the Unknown God from a cult to a national religion. In addition, Solomon strengthened his influence through his famed wisdom as a judge and his numerous dynastic marriages (700 wives and 300 concubines, according to 1 Kings). However, the zenith of the Israelite state was very short lived, and the kingdom split after Solomon's death. It appears the Israelite religion, associated with Judaean military success and state building, had little appeal in the northern kingdom of Israel.

Solomon died around 920 B.C.E. The kingdom then split into its earlier original components: Israel in the north; and Judah in the south, based on Jerusalem. Israel contained ten of the twelve tribes and was the homeland of the Samaritans, who probably shared the Israelite historical experience until the occupation of Canaan; but they may have had a different ethnic origin. Some historians believe that some of the Promised Land's population were Hebrew before Joshua's arrival. The Hebrew word for Samaritan and black African is the same – *Kushi* - and the Samaritans' word for themselves – *Bet Israel* – is that used by remnant Black Jews in India and in Ethiopia. The kingdom of Judah to the south was the home of the tribe of the same name and part of the tribe of Benjamin. The people of Judah also referred to the Samaritans as "people of the land", which could have a class connotation. Racist attitudes may also have played a part. Did Solomon decree that the ten northern tribes (Bet Israel) be forced into labor because they were black and considered of low status? Recent genetic research has revealed that there was a large African influx into the eastern Mediterranean region in the years of Dynastic Egypt. This explains the high proportion of African DNA among Greeks, [3] and perhaps the African settlements in western Arabia.

The zenith of these kingdoms as a united state under Solomon appears to have been due to two major advantages. First, they were able to control major trade routes and thus accumulate great wealth. Second, they were able to do this at a time when the attention of more powerful states was diverted elsewhere. The pattern for establishing the Iron Age Israelite states had been repeated all over the Middle East. Three contending factions emerged - the Assyrians, the Arameans, and the Babylonians - all fighting for control of the same area. The Assyrians, originating in the area of northern modern Syria and Iraq, emerged as a power around 1208 B.C.E., competing with the migrating Arameans, another Semitic people from the same area. During the reigns of David and Solomon Egyptian attention on Arabia, which had earlier been distracted by combating the Iron Age Sea Peoples, was focused on Libyan attacks; while the Assyrians were still dealing with Aramean migration in the north.

Egypt had fought off the Sea Peoples but fell to Libyan invaders. Once the Libyans became entrenched, their leader Sheshonk (Shishak) led his new subjects in an attack on the Promised Land shortly after Solomon's death.

By that time the Israelite kingdom was already in crisis. In his final years Solomon had attempted to eliminate Jeroboam, an army commander responsible for organizing forced labor. Jeroboam appears to have been related to David, and a northern prophet foretold that he would become king of the northern ten tribes. Jeroboam fled to Egypt to Sheskonk's court. Rehoboam, Solomon's son, succeeded as king but exacerbated the hostility of the ten northern tribes by attempting to increase taxation and forced labor. The ten tribes broke away, leaving Rehoboam in control of Judah. Jeroboam became king of Israel, established a capital at Tirzah, and created temples at Bethel and Dan, where his subjects revered El and Ba'al, the Canaanite gods, along with Yhwh, to whom they later assigned a wife, Asherah, in Canaanite mythology the consort of both El and Ba'al. The year after Jeroboam and Rehoboam ascended their respective thrones, ca. 920 B.C.E., Sheskonk invaded Judah, and Rehoboam only saved Jerusalem by agreeing to pay tribute.

The decline in Judah's fortunes was only partially due to dynastic disputes, taxation demands, and court intrigue. The fortunes of many of the new Iron Age states depended on agriculture and control of trade routes. Some, like Aksum in the Ethiopian highlands, prospered on agriculture alone, control of trade routes being a bonus. Others, like Judah, had a disproportionate reliance on controlling trade routes. One highlight of Solomon's reign was the state visit of the Queen of Sheba, ruler of southern Arabia. The Old Testament interprets this visit as formalizing trade relations. Traditions say that Solomon annexed Taima in northern Arabia. If so, it would have brought control of trade from the Arabian Gulf.

Some commentators believe that after the division of the kingdom Israel prospered while Judah went into economic decline. The reason given is that, unlike Judah, Israel continued to control lucrative trade routes. Omri, king of Israel (885-874 B.C.E.), built a new capital at Samaria that eclipsed the splendor of Jerusalem.

Considering the political climate, the history of the trade routes, and the location of Samaria, none of this seems right. It is difficult to reconcile the changed circumstances with Israel's new prosperity. Prosperity under Solomon had most probably come from taxing the wealth of the Sheban and Taima trade routes. The people of the northern areas resented the tax and the enforced labor, and broke away. Yet after the split it was Israel in the north that prospered, although it is difficult to believe how Israel could do so with Judah standing between it and the Taima-Sheban trade routes. Moreover, Israel lacked a port, and the Egyptian trade from the Levant was seaborne from Phoenicia to the Nile Delta. A second point concerns the early period of the Hebrew's Egyptian captivity.

There was one important aberration to this pattern of establishing Iron Age states – Egypt. Pharaoh Ramses III (ca. 1187-66 B.C.E.) spent the first years of his reign dealing with the southern expansion into Syria of the Hittites, an Indo-European people whose empire was centered in modern-day Turkey. The Hittite empire then suddenly collapsed; the blame generally apportioned to massive attacks by the above mentioned Sea Peoples, aggressive groups from different parts of the eastern Mediterranean. These Sea People moved against Egypt itself but were defeated in two battles, one on land and the other at sea. They retreated and sailed westward, probably settling in Sardinia, Sicily, or Tuscany (Etruria). Ramses III's victory had an interesting consequence, for it spared Egypt the political upheaval of Iron Age conquest and massive technological change. But it also raises a serious concern. Egypt was not yet an Iron Age smelting country in 1166 B.C.E., yet biblical scholarship supports the notion that the Hebrew who fled Egypt in the Exodus, 100 to 300 years earlier, already practiced iron smelting, which provided them with weapons that enabled them to defeat the Bronze-Age Canaanites. These issues will be addressed in the next chapter.

Israel's prosperity soon attracted Assyrian interest. The Assyrians obliterated the kingdom of Israel in 721 B.C.E., deporting twenty-seven thousand citizens and replacing them with a more malleable population. The Assyrians were distracted from their attack on Judah, having first to deal with a relief army sent by Shabaka, the southern-based "Cushite" pharaoh of Egypt, who was allied with Hezekiah, king of Judah. The Assyrian leader Sennacherib decisively defeated the Cushites and then captured and looted forty-six walled cities in Judah. Jerusalem was saved apparently by the outbreak of the plague that struck the Assyrian army, causing its withdrawal. Despite this stroke of fortune, Judah's territory and influence had been severely curtailed.

In the three hundred years that the Zadokite priesthood was in the political wilderness, the twin Israelite kingdoms experienced varying degrees of syncretism, fostering the revival and occasional domination of Canaanite religious practices. Even so, there was a strong traditional belief that setbacks, political and otherwise, were punishment for forsaking the God who had led them to the Promised Land and given them an empire. King Hezekiah of Judah (ca. 716-687 B.C.E.) had been proclaimed Emmanuel, the Messiah, by the prophet Isaiah. Despite loss of territory to the Assyrians and deportation of many of Hezekiah's subjects, there were many who believed that the Assyrian withdrawal had been caused by divine intervention rather than a rodent-borne plague. If the Zadokite priesthood believed this was an opportunity for a return to strict observation of the Torah, they were disappointed, because Manasseh (ca. 687-642 B.C.E.) accommodated the pagan cults to the extent of permitting human sacrifice.

With the accession of Josiah (ca. 640-609 B.C.E.) to the throne, the House of Zadok at last, after a period of 300 years, [4] regained its ecclesiastical pre-eminence by capitalizing on the new king's wish to restore the temple to its former magnificence and through championing the widespread disdain of the excesses of paganism. The Zadokite high priest Hilkiah provided Josiah with divine encouragement in his task. A sacred book, almost certainly Deuteronomy, was "discovered" in the temple. Hilkiah read the text to Josiah, unnerving him with the revelation that it was not enough for a king merely to be of Davidic descent. The essential path to successful rule was strict observance of the Torah. Josiah took the reading to heart with a vengeance, conducting a murderous purge not only of the pagan shrines but also of the "deviant" Samaritans. Their holy places, including Jeroboam's rival temple at Bethel, were destroyed, and the remains of their deceased priests exhumed and burned.

In 626 B.C.E. an Aramean [5] general Nabopolassar, became ruler of Babylon, subsequently conquering and annexing the Assyrian empire. By that time Arameans, Assyrians, and Babylonians had merged together to such an extent that they could be considered a single people whose language was Aramaic.

King Josiah of Judah was killed in a battle against the Egyptians, who were themselves soon vanquished by the Babylonians.

In 597 B.C.E. the Babylonian leader Nebuchadnezzar II (605-562 B.C.E.) captured Jerusalem, looted the temple, and deported the late King Jehoiakim's son Jehoiachin, still a child, along with ten thousand members of the ruling class and all blacksmiths and metalworkers. Zedekiah, Jehoiachin's uncle, was installed as a puppet ruler, but eight years later rebelled. The Babylonians blinded him then systematically destroyed the temple, the royal palace, and every other substantial building in Jerusalem.

Nabodinus, Nebuchadnezzar's successor (556-539 B.C.E.), reputedly shifted the Babylonian capital to Taima, the Arabian commercial center, appointing his son Belshazzar as co-regent in Mesopotamia. The exile of the Judaeans lasted only forty-nine years before the Babylonians were conquered by the Persians. These Judaean exiles seem to have played a part in the downfall of the Babylonian ruling house, the prophet Daniel demoralizing the regime with his interpretation of the "Writing on the Wall" at Belshazzar's feast. The exiled community received preferential treatment from the new Persian king, Cyrus the Great, and they were permitted to establish a religious community under Persian authority in Palestine.

During the pre-Persian exile in Babylon the prophet Ezekiel, son of Buzi, one of the deported priests, had what can only be described as a very convenient revelation in which God told him that the Zadokites were the only true priests, and that they should control the spiritual destiny of His people along with a new temple, its surroundings, and (by implication) its revenues. The Levites, the traditional priesthood, were to be relegated to menial religious tasks. The book of Ezekiel, of which Ezekiel was probably a part author, was a plan for a new beginning of a theocratic community where the land would be divided between the twelve tribes (with a double portion allocated to the tribe of Joseph). It is not at all clear whether the book of Ezekiel refers to a return to the place from where the Israelites were deported or to another area where the Persians had agreed they could establish a new society. This is a matter of great importance given the archaeological evidence discussed in a later chapter. Ezekiel may well have believed he had received a celestial revelation but a a cybical view was that it was more probably blueprint designed in Mesopotamia to establish a theocracy in Persian-ruled Palestine. There are Old Testament passages that appear to be references to new settlements ("daughter of Jerusalem/Zion") rather than poetic allusions to the original cities. These passages point to a new beginning rather than to a return to a devastated land:

> She despises you [Sennacherib king of Assyria], she scorns you .... the Virgin daughter of Zion;
> *Isaiah 37:22b*

> she wags her head behind you .... The daughter of Jerusalem ...
> *Isaiah 31-32,*

> And the surviving remnant of the House of Judah shall again take root downward, and bear fruit upward;
> *2 Kings 19:21b*

> for out of Jerusalem shall go forth a remnant, and out of Mount Zion a band of survivors.
> *2 Kings 30-31*

> And you, O tower of the flock, hill of the daughter of Zion, to you shall it come, the former dominion shall come, the kingdom of the daughter of Jerusalem.
> *Micah 4:8*

> Rejoice greatly, O daughter of Zion; shout aloud, O daughter of Jerusalem. Lo, your king comes to you; triumphant and victorious is he, humble and riding on an ass, on a colt the foal of an ass.
> *Zechariah 9:9*

The man chosen to lead over forty thousand exiles to Jerusalem in 520 B.C.E. was Zerubbabel *(Seed of Babylon)*, the grandson of Jehoiachin, the deported son of Judah's last king. Zerubbabel, according to the First Book of Esdras 3:1 to 5:3, had been an imperial bodyguard and had won favor from the Persian monarch Cyrus for suggesting that the finest things in life were women and truth. This attitude most likely did not endear him to the priests, historically misogynist, who numbered one tenth of the new settlers.

Zerubbabel was appointed governor of Judah and began laying the foundations of the Second Temple, spurning offers of assistance from the Samaritans and the families of those Judaeans who had not been exiled.

This and subsequent decisions permanently alienated the Samaritan community. The Persians, however, perhaps with some prodding from the Zadokite priesthood, decided it was inadvisable to support a governor from the old royal house of Judah whom many people were already eager to proclaim the Messiah. The Zadokite priesthood seems to have decided that the Davidic monarchy was not conducive to theological rectitude and therefore espoused a theocracy that they themselves could direct. Zerubbabel was replaced by Persian administrators, and the Second Temple was completed in 515 B.C.E. under Zadokite direction. This had important repercussions, because Zerubbabel was Jesus Christ's direct paternal ancestor, and Christ viewed the political leadership of Jerusalem and control of the temple as his inherited birthright.

In 445 B.C.E. Nehemiah, an Israelite serving as cupbearer to the Persian monarch Artxerxes I, succeeded in persuading the king to allow him to go to Jerusalem to rebuild the rest of the city. On his arrival Nehemiah acted with extreme caution. The Persians had allocated building supplies, but Nehemiah faced opposition from officials governing areas hostile to the old Judah, such as Samaria. He gained the support of Jerusalem's residents and repaired the defensive walls in fifty-two days. A compulsory lottery system boosted the city's population, and Jerusalem eventually replaced neighboring Mizpah as the provincial capital. Nehemiah also began the policy, reinforced with vigor by the prophet Ezra, of forbidding the Israelites from marrying the *goyim*, people outside the religious community.

The Babylonian exiles had refrained from marrying foreign women or even converts of suspect sincerity. They saw themselves as racially purer than the Israelites left behind in the defeated kingdoms:

> All countries are dough (mixed) compared to the Land of Israel, and the land of Israel is dough compared to Babylon.
>
> Talmud (Kidduishin 71a)

Peter Marsden, writing in 1998 of the Taliban's draconian treatment of Afghan women explained:

> When groups feel threatened, attitudes within them tend to harden and they seek to define more clearly the aspects of their identity that differentiate them from other groups. Where nationalist or religious identity has been involved, women have often taken on a symbolic importance as the reproducers.[6]

It is likely Ezra's legislation was directed by a similar outlook. Ezra is credited with re-establishing the Jewish community as a distinct group forbidden to marry outsiders and as one adhering to strictures of the Torah. The terms *Judaism* and *Jew* date from his reforms. Ezra was not only a Zadokite priest but a scribe. He held high office under the Persians, probably as a sort of minister for Jewish affairs. He arrived under Persian orders in approximately 398 B.C.E. to bolster Jewish settlement, to provide subsidies, and to impose the Jewish legal code on the province of Judah. Armed with Persian imperial authority, Ezra created an uncompromising Zadokite state modeled on Ezekiel's vision. Salvation lay only through complete adherence to the Torah, administered by the Zadokite priesthood who controlled Aliyeh – the Place of Spiritual Ascension - which later became known as the *New Jerusalem*. Ezra also established a school of priestly scholarship that edited ancient sacred texts and produced new ones, including ones of his life and work, which were then canonized as Holy Writ. The *Book of Ezra* was the last book written for the Old Testament, and adherents of the reformed religious tradition now called *Judaism* regarded it as the last word on the subject.

Ezra decreed that (i) no "deviant" religious practices would be tolerated, (ii) "foreign" wives should be discarded, (iii) membership of the province should be confined solely to exiles and to their descendants, (iv) the temple should be the focus of the community, the Zadokites its guides and judges; and (v) all life would be determined by the Torah. Women were relegated below men to secondary status and were excluded from religious training and discussion. The population of this Persian imperial satrapy (province) of Azvar-nahara (Beyond the River Euphrates) would support the Zadokite priestly administration with a compulsory annual tax. This exclusive legalistic theocracy now set about determining the nature of the first draft of the Old Testament.

At this stage the story is no longer so much about the political legacies of Moses and Solomon. The days of a powerful Israelite kingdom seemed gone forever as long as the area was dominated by large empires. The Israelite state, despite conversions, was still very much associated with an ethnic group. The story, became at this stage the critical point for the Zadokite priesthood whose *raison d'être*, let alone its livelihood, had depended on the royal patronage of the kingdom of Judah. It is difficult not to be cynical when examining the events they themselves instigated and then canonized as Holy Writ in the Old Testament. The visions, the revelations and the rediscovery of ancient holy texts all came at amazingly appropriate times.

Ezra's fifth century B.C.E. administration collected all religious and other documentary materials and decided what was appropriate for canonization as Holy Writ. By this time Hebrew had been replaced by Aramaic. Ezra's circle drew from four or more different traditions, but the book they created represented the political legacy of the southern Kingdom of Judah, home to only two of the twelve tribes. Not unnaturally the Old Testament is the political statement of Judah. Consequently the Samaritans and other sects refused to recognize any but the first five books, and critics have accused Ezra's group of inventing material, particularly heavenly visions, that called for more wealth and power for the temple priesthood. Evidence supporting biblical textual manipulation includes poetry such as the *Blessings of Jacob*, *Song of Deborah*, *Song of Moses*, *Oracles of Baarlem*, and *Blessings of Moses*, written in archaic Hebrew, being intertwined with language from a much later date, rather like mixing Anglo-Saxon *Beowulf* with *Jane Eyre*. The language of the Old Testament, on the whole, dates from ca. 400 B.C.E., Ezra's period, and some sections were in fact written in Aramaic. The oldest surviving extracts of the Old Testament date from around 200 B.C.E. In about 250 B.C.E. the Old Testament was translated into Greek, which had by then become the language of education. The final version of the Old Testament, written at last with vowels, was completed in around A.D. 950 and will be discussed in detail later.

Ezra's New Jerusalem had depended on Persian goodwill, and the Jews were reluctant to shift support to the Greeks after Alexander III ("The Great") defeated the Persian leader Darius III in 333 B.C.E. Alexander died in 323 B.C.E. and six of his commanders then fought for control of his empire. In twenty years of fighting Jerusalem was captured six times by contending forces. Eventually, in 301 B.C.E., a new dynasty gained control, one ruled from Egypt under Ptolemy I Soter. The Greeks established a polis - a Greek model city with a gymnasium (intellectual center) throughout their new territories to consolidate their control and spread their culture. Although not chosen to be a polis, Jerusalem was nevertheless influenced by Hellenism (from the Greek word *Ellas*, meaning Greece), which challenged Jewish exclusiveness and racial purity with the concept of world citizenship and an open society. The first notable Hellenists in the Jewish camp were members of the Tobiah clan, but they were opposed by the Oniads, conservative Zadokite priests. These factions began a long process of allying themselves with external powers to advance their own cause. When a rival Greek dynasty, the Seleucids, invaded and eventually took control of Palestine, the Oniads were rewarded for their support and thereafter introduced a far harsher regime than Ezra's. Greeks were banned from entering the temple inner court and it was forbidden to utter the name of the Hebrew deity Yhwh. Jerusalem became an intensely spiritual place with a highly charged atmosphere that could overawe or even strike down the most powerful foreign intruders. Financial and political tensions arose when the Romans reduced the Seleucids to vassals, forcing them to pay tribute, a measure that exacerbated relations between the Seleucids and the temple treasury. The Seleucids deposed and backed high priests from both ideological camps in exchange for revenue. This caused civil strife, murder, and the advent in 172 B.C.E. of a non-Zadokite high priest, Menelaus. The Seleucids took advantage of the Hellenic party's attempted counter-coup by looting the temple. Then, weary of the chaos, they outlawed Judaism and reduced Jerusalem, which had briefly been raised to a polis, to the status of a garrison town.

The violation of the temple led to dispersal into the surrounding countryside and provoked the priest Mattathias with his five sons to revolt. Mattathias died in 166 B.C.E. and was succeeded by his son Judas Maccabeus. Capitalizing on the Seleucid preoccupation with Parthian aggression in Mesopotamia, Judas captured Jerusalem in 164 B.C.E. He followed this feat with an alliance with Rome, and in 142 B.C.E. he was recognized as an independent ruler. The new Hasmonean dynasty destroyed the Samaritan Temple at Mt. Gerezim in 125 B.C.E. John Hyrcanus (124-104 B.C.E.), expanded Hasmonean control, forcing the conquered population to accept Judaism. The priesthood remained beyond Zadokite control, and three main theological factions emerged: the Sadducees (tending towards Hellenism), the Pharisees (strict adherents to the Torah), and those acknowledging the authority of the Teacher of Righteousness (almost certainly Zadokites). Continued rivalry between the factions gave rise to civil war in 67 B.C.E. between the sons of Queen Salome, a supporter of the Pharisees. The Roman commander and politician Pompey terminated Seleucid rule in 64 B.C.E. and then sided with Salome's son Hyrcanus II against his brother Aristobulus II. Jerusalem fell in 63 B.C.E. and 12,000 of Aristobulus' supporters were killed.

The Romans permitted the Jews to govern four sections of Palestine, where they had a majority. This did not include Samaria, which separated Galilee from Judaea. In 49 B.C.E. Julius Caesar defeated Pompey and gave his support to Antipater, an Indumean general, whose House of Herod replaced the Hasmoneans. The last Hasmonean king, Antigonus, was executed by Mark Anthony, Caesar's initial political successor. In 37 B.C.E. Anthony assisted Herod, son of Antipater, capturing Jerusalem where another major massacre took place. Herod had the support of the Pharisees and managed to gain the confidence and support of Octavian (later the Emperor Augustus) when Octavian defeated Anthony.

The rise and fall of empires and factions, the founding of the New Jerusalem, and the establishment of the Hasmonean dynasty convinced many Jews that independence and a purified religion could be restored. Their desire gained support, for a growing section of the Jewish population began to consider independence as a means of ridding themselves of Roman-induced hardships, puppet rulers, and insulting demands. Palestine's inclusion as a partner in the Mediterranean world of the Roman Empire brought it a prosperity denied earlier, when it was merely on the periphery between the Egyptian and Assyrian/Babylonian Empires or an outpost of the Persian Empire. Unfortunately this new prosperity coincided with the Roman imperial policy of emperor worship and the practice of imperial officials attempting to enrich themselves during their brief service overseas. Although the Romans had initially been astonished by Jewish passive resistance when an attempt had been made to erect a statue of the emperor Caligula in the temple, they continued nevertheless to offend the Jews. The Roman officials' venal behavior threatened the temple treasury and incited a rebellion that became so egregious that the Romans eventually razed Jerusalem in A.D. 70, leaving only one wall of Herod's great temple standing. The Romans made no compromises. With Jewish military resistance crushed, the Roman emperor Hadrian (A.D. 117-138) ordered an end to circumcision and initiated a policy of national Hellenization. The Christians, in some ways Hellenized Jews, remained quiet, but the Jews, under Simeon Bar Kokhba, rebelled once again in A.D. 132. The Romans suffered severe setbacks, and Jerusalem fell. Hadrian himself took command, calling in an additional 35,000 Roman troops. Bar Kokhba was killed and his followers decimated in A.D. 135. Jewish losses were estimated at 580,000, excluding some deaths from disease and starvation. Jews were barred from Jerusalem, and the Romans ravaged the surrounding territory, slaughtering all those who had not fled.

In the years that followed, the *Diaspora* Jews made several attempts to create independent states, most notably in southern Arabia and in Mesopotamian Armenia. Paul (formerly Saul of Tarsus) realized however that Jewish racial exclusivity, dietary customs, circumcision, and other customs militated against widespread conversion to Christianity, and soon Judaism, which once seemed destined to become the principal religion of the Roman Empire, was peripheralized first by Christianity and then by Islam. Both of the two new faiths included beliefs hostile to Judaism, and thereafter life for Jews became increasingly difficult. As exclusion and massacres became an everyday occurrence, nostalgia grew for the world they had lost. Finally, after centuries of persecution and exclusion, many Jewish intellectuals in Europe embraced the concept of Zionism.

The term *Zionism*, coined in 1893, is defined as the national movement of the Jewish people to return to their original homeland, the Promised Land of the Hebrew Old Testament. The word derives from Mt. Zion, traditionally believed to be a powerful fortress offering sanctuary in King David's time. Theodor Herzl (1860 – 1904) was the visionary of Zionism. Born in the Austro-Hungarian Empire, he trained as a lawyer but worked as a writer, playwright, and journalist. He was fatalistic about anti-Semitism, believing it was too deeply ingrained in European culture to allow Jews to enjoy full participation in society. He concluded that Jewish salvation lay in establishing a Jewish state in Turkish-ruled Palestine. Herzl published his ideas in *Der Judenstaat* (The Jewish State) in 1896. He argued that it was fruitless for Jews to continue to appease those whom they lived amongst because it won them no favors. Jews would continue to be persecuted, excluded, ostracized, or discriminated against. They had endured 1800 years of such treatment, and the time had come to recognize the inevitable. They were better off elsewhere, that is, in a country of their own.

Herzl's vision extended beyond recreating an Old Testament scenario. He wanted to establish a modern Jewish socialist utopia, harnessing modern science and technology. In this new country the impoverished Jewish tenant peasant farmers of Eastern Europe would own their own land in prosperous cooperatives. Initially led, in Herzl's words, "by mediocre intellects which we produce so abundantly," they would then be joined by emigrants "of a higher grade." Herzl outlined practical guidelines for promoting Jewish emigration and for financing settlement through land acquisition and promoting trade and industry through investment. Disturbed by anti-Semitic pogroms in Russia, and the Dreyfus case in France, he considered temporary or permanent resettlement locations in Argentina and the Uganda-Kenya borderland. In chapter two of *Der Juderstaat* he rejected support for the promising Jewish settlement in Argentina and declared that Palestine was the only acceptable site for the new Zion. Herzl wrote:

> Palestine is our ever-memorable historic home. The very name of Palestine would attract our people with a force of marvelous potency. If His Majesty the Sultan were to give us Palestine, we could in return undertake to regulate the whole finances of Turkey. We should there form a portion of a rampart of Europe against Asia, an outpost of civilization as opposed to barbarism. We should as a neutral State remain in contact with all Europe, which would have to guarantee our existence. The sanctuaries of Christendom would be safeguarded by assigning to them an extra-territorial status such as is well-known to the law of nations. We should form a guard of honor about these sanctuaries, answering for the fulfillment of this duty with our existence. This guard of honor would be the great symbol of the solution of the Jewish question after eighteen centuries of Jewish suffering.

Herzl emphasized that this scheme required international backing otherwise the native population would become increasingly hostile as more settlers infiltrated their land. His views reflected his times. He believed in the moral and racial superiority of technically advanced peoples and accepted without question the right of imperial powers to create colonies and states wherever they wished. He totally failed to realize that the nationalism sweeping nineteenth century Europe would be matched by Arabs living under Turkish rule. Even if he had considered such a phenomenon, doubtless, he would have shared the mistaken belief of early Zionist settlers in Palestine: that the local inhabitants would welcome them for their technological superiority and social progress.

The First World War ended the Turkish Empire, but the victorious allies ignored and humiliated their Arab allies who had fought for independence. The French took control of Syria and crushed Arab resistance in Damascus. They agreed to let the British take control of Palestine as a mandate, partly because the British had captured it from the Turks and also because the British agreed to support French policy in the defeated German Rhineland. The rest of the former Turkish Arab territory also passed under British control. Faisal, the principal Arab leader in the revolt against Turkish rule, had hoped to establish an Arab state embracing Syria, Lebanon, Palestine, Trans-Jordan and Iraq. Driven from Syria by the French, he grudgingly accepted the British offer of kingship of Iraq. He led his new nation to independence in 1932, but died the following year.

During the First World War the chemical industrialist Chaim Weizmann (1874-1952), the Russian-born future president of Israel, won British gratitude for his process of extracting acetone, a vital component of cordite, from maize. Weizmann parlayed this good will into a British commitment in 1917, the *Balfour Declaration*, to establish a Jewish national home in Palestine. Many prominent British politicians had a strong belief, subsequently proven unjustified, in the unity and power of World Jewry and, having noted the role of Jews in revolutionary activities in Russia and Germany, hoped to use Zionism to divert Jews from supporting Communism.[7] Fifty-five thousand Jews in Palestine, many of them deeply religious people sustained by charity from Eastern Europe. The Balfour Declaration encouraged increased immigration intent on producing a viable economic community. In 1925, thirty-four thousand Poles arrived, fleeing anti-Semitism. By 1945 another three hundred and forty-five thousand Jews, mostly Central European survivors of the Nazi holocaust, had poured into Palestine. Relations between the settlers and British administration broke down, the area was partitioned, and in 1948 the United Nations recognized the independent state of Israel. Abba Eban, the Israeli United Nations representative, estimated that eighty per cent of the half million Palestinians living in Israel fled. Since then Israel has fought several major wars with its Arab neighbors, and what was initially interpreted as a conflict between Jewish settlers and Palestinians has become increasingly defined as the symbol of a global struggle between Western society and Islam, between the world's rich and poor, be they nations or classes.

In Herzl's day there was complete acceptance that Palestine was the Promised Land of the Old Testament. Site identification had been undertaken by the American biblical scholar Edward Robinson of the Union Theological Seminary in New York. Robinson visited Palestine in 1837-8 and 1852. He used the Hebrew text of the Old Testament and his knowledge of Arabic, which is closely related to Hebrew, to identify probable Old Testament sites. Robinson reasoned that since place names rarely change and Arabic was close to Hebrew, it was likely that if an Arabic name of a modern settlement was similar to a Hebrew biblical name, it marked the site of the location mentioned in the Old Testament. He never challenged the authority of the Old Testament references, and his unscientific haphazard conclusions formed the basis for much of what followed when professional archaeologists took over.

CHAPTER TWO

The Search for Evidence

> Israel is the very embodiment of Jewish continuity: It is the only nation on earth that inhabits the same land, bears the same name, speaks the same language, and worships the same God that it did 3,000 years ago. You dig the soil and you find pottery from Davidic times, coins from Bar Kokhba, and 2,000-year-old scrolls written in a script remarkably like the one that today advertises ice cream at the corner candy store.
>
> Charles Krauthammer
> (Columnist and former speechwriter to Vice President Walter Mondale)
>
> *The Weekly Standard* (U.S.A.), May 11, 1998

Islam had an understandable aversion to archaeology, seeing it as desecration of the dead, an attitude shared by many Jews. However, Jews who were prominent in the new sciences saw archaeology as supportive of the Zionist cause. This attitude was shared by Christian archaeologists and other professionals who perceived that if the Jews fulfilled their divine mission of reclaiming the Promised Land, then other related Holy Writ, namely, the New Testament, might also be fulfilled. With the departure of the Muslim Turks, archaeology under the British Mandate became possible. It was hardly coincidental that the first archaeologists into Palestine were committed Christians.

William Foxwell Albright (1891-1971) is the father of biblical archaeology. Born in Chile of Methodist missionaries, he took his doctorate in Semitic languages at Johns Hopkins University, in Baltimore, Maryland. In 1919, he became Fellow of the American School of Oriental Research in Jerusalem, and its director in the following year. When he finally retired in 1958 he had established himself as the leading authority on biblical archaeology, having undertaken excavations in Palestine, Jordan, and Saudi Arabia. Although he was a pioneer in the science of dating pottery, his greatest contribution was his emphasis on introducing biblical research to the allied disciplines of archaeology, linguistics, and topography. He uncritically used the Old Testament as his guide.

While Albright was a talented archaeologist and philologist, he was not a historian. As research into the origins and history of the Semitic-speaking peoples was still in its infancy, Albright was able to speculate without challenge on a level that would be completely unacceptable today. Prominent researchers of the early twentieth century such as the German Albrecht Alt and Albright himself professed deep respect for the authenticity of oral traditions. Nonetheless, this reverence extended only to Old Testament traditions associated with their own Christian background. Sir E. A. Wallis Budge, the translator of the Ge'ez (Ethiopic) *Kebra Nagast*, typified this class of highly educated Christian biblical researchers, dismissing anything seemingly at variance with the Old Testament record. Consequently, if archaeological evidence appeared to support the written text, it was interpreted as such. If it did not, the biblical account was still accepted as the chief authority, but allowances were given to the redactors who may have written some years after the event.

Albright was aware of criticism of over-enthusiastic amateurs and made some commentary on the archaeological methodology he had encountered:

> It is frequently said that the scientific quality of Palestinian archaeology has been seriously impaired by the religious preconceptions of scholars who have excavated in the Holy Land. It is true that some archaeologists have been drawn to Palestine by their interest in the Bible, and that some of them had received their previous training mainly as Biblical scholars. The writer has known many such scholars, but he recalls scarcely a single case where their religious views seriously influenced their results.

Yet Albright's own attitude towards his professional work is encapsulated in the title of his 1942 article: *Why the Near East Needs the Jews*. He saw archaeology as a means to strengthen the Jewish claim to Palestine.

After the Second World War, Palestine became the home to hundreds of thousands of Jews traumatized by the Holocaust. On May 14, 1948, they and earlier settlers proclaimed the state of Israel. All accepted that this land was the place given to them by God, their ancestral home, where they would no longer be persecuted and murdered because of their birth and beliefs. David Ben Gurion (1886-1973), Israel's first prime minister, read the proclamation of statehood:

> The Land of Israel was the birthplace of the Jewish people. Here their spiritual, religious and national identity was formed. Here they achieved independence and created a culture of national and universal significance. Here they wrote and gave the Bible to the world. Exiled from Palestine, the Jewish people remained, faithful to it in all countries of their dispersion, never ceasing to pray and hope for their return and the restoration of their national freedom. Accordingly we, the members of the National Council, representing the Jewish people in Palestine and the Zionist movement of the world, met together in solemn assemble today, the day of the termination of the British Mandate of Palestine, by virtue of the natural and historic right of the Jewish people and the Resolution of the General Assembly of the United Nations, hereby proclaim the establishment of the Jewish state in Palestine, to be called Israel. With trust in Almighty God, we set our hand to this declaration, at this session of the Provisional State Council, in the city of Tel Aviv, on this Sabbath eve, the fifth year of Iyar, 5708, the fourteenth day of May, 1948.

After the establishment of the state of Israel, Israeli archaeologists set to work in Albright's footsteps, searching for evidence from the remote past. Annually they were and are still joined by archaeologists and enthusiasts from all over the world. Their work is eagerly studied by millions of tourists, pilgrims, students, media personnel, and church members, most of whom will never visit the sites, but whose lives are very much governed by their history. Archaeologists are in general agreement on the evidence that would support the Old Testament record. The biblical narrative speaks of a violent invasion of Canaan by the Hebrew, an Iron Age people who established a strong, centralized, and eventually extremely wealthy state under David and Solomon. Archaeology would therefore show a clear break, as a Bronze Age culture - typified by small political groupings and a settled agricultural population - was dramatically overwhelmed and reconstituted into a centralized Iron Age state dominated by a huge alien pastoralist population undergoing urbanization, engaging in massive public works programs and in international trade. Archaeology would most certainly reveal widespread destruction and relocation.

From the very beginning archaeological investigations did not progress as hoped. Albright was disappointed with his excavations at At-Tall (identified as the biblical Ai) where he found no evidence of occupation in

Joshua's era. He suggested the biblical account had confused Ai with neighboring Beitin. Kathleen Kenyon excavated the ruins of Jericho for six years. Finding no evidence to support the biblical references, she refused to speculate, but concluded that Jericho had been deserted from the beginning of the fifteenth century to the eleventh century B.C.E. and had fallen long before Joshua. Later she gave her opinion on Old Testament archaeological evidence as a whole:

> The united Kingdom of Israel had a life span of only three quarters of a century. It was the only time in which the Jews were an important political power in western Asia. Its glories are triumphantly recorded in the Bible, and the recollections of this profoundly affected Jewish thoughts and aspirations. Yet the archaeological evidence for the period is meager in the extreme. [1]

The Old Testament states that King Solomon fortified Gezer, Hazor, and Megiddo. Israeli politician-archaeologist Yigael Yadin was not as cautious as Kenyon. When he discovered a gate at Hazor, constructed ca. tenth century B.C.E., and another at Megiddo, he linked both to a third discovered earlier at Gezer and claimed all three were the work of Solomon, although evidence showed they belonged to different periods. James Pritchard, writing in 1972, was forthright about Megiddo's links with Solomon: "No inscription names him and no specific find can be definitely related to any biblical reference." Later he stated:

> The so-called cities of Megiddo, Gezer, Hazor – all said to have been built by Solomon – Gibeon, the site of Solomon's holocausts, and Jerusalem itself, were in reality more like villages and surrounded by circumambulatory ramparts of roughly hewn stone. Within were relatively small public buildings and frequently poorly constructed dwellings with clay floors. ... compared with the culture ... of Phoenicia, Assyria and Egypt, the "magnificence" of the Age of Solomon is parochial and decidedly lackluster.

The Old Testament links the city of Hebron - thirty kilometers south of Jerusalem in Palestine - with the patriarch Abraham, and states David had chosen it as his first capital. In the 1980s Avi Ofer of the Institute of Archaeology of Tel Aviv carried out excavations in Hebron. Ofer concluded that Hebron was founded ca. 3300 B.C.E. and, that by ca. 1950 B.C.E., it had grown into a major urban center. It had a king, a central religious and political district, city walls, a literate bureaucracy, buildings several stories high, and a palace where large numbers of animals were sacrificed. By ca. 1500 B.C.E. Hebron was abandoned, almost certainly because of the climatic changes that had desiccated the land. Therefore when Joshua was supposed to have invaded the Promised Land, ca. 1200 B.C.E., he would have found only a handful of nomads roaming the ruins of Hebron, a Bronze Age city. The Old Testament account states that Joshua captured five royal cities, including Hebron; yet Ofer found that Hebron, like Jericho, had been abandoned for hundreds of years before Joshua's time.

The Old Testament states that Joshua destroyed Hazor, Mormah, Jericho and Ai. Archaeology has revealed that the latter three were unoccupied at that time. Evidence of destruction exists at Tell Abu Hawan, Tell Mor and Aphek, none of which is mentioned in the Old Testament; and at Lachish, Beth Shan, and Gezer, which, according to the Old Testament, were left undamaged.

The greatest disappointment is Jerusalem itself, and no number of excuses and explanations can suffice to detract from the archaeological indictment that it was an insignificant settlement until ca. 600 B.C.E., and was certainly never the terminus of a gold trade that gilded massive public buildings and supported a powerful, literate, temple bureaucracy during Solomon's reign.

Scientific developments have enabled archaeologists to gain a more accurate general demographic and climatic picture of Palestine than was available to Pritchard in the early 1970s. The evidence shows that ancient Palestine was a peripheral region, of little or no economic or strategic interest to the highly organized and powerful states of Egypt, Mesopotamia, or Syria. It did indeed have a mostly self-sufficient Bronze Age sedentary agricultural economy, but this was not replaced by any large powerful centralized political units. Society was based on small urban centers and hamlets with petty chiefs or headmen as rulers. Overpopulation and agricultural recession in the third millennium B.C.E. were followed by a hot and arid climatic change that lasted until ca. 1950 B.C.E. and also affected Egypt. Large sections of the population in the Levant migrated to Mesopotamia, leaving Palestine with a declining population. Between ca. 1950 and ca. 1700 B.C.E. the climate changed once again, and Palestine enjoyed a more humid period that resulted in the occupation of abandoned settlements, a return to sedentary farming, and a resurgent population. Some areas that had deteriorated into deserts (e.g. the Negev, Sinai, and the southern parts of Trans-Jordan) were abandoned, isolating the population in

Arabia. The Bronze Age gave way to the Iron Age between the thirteenth and the tenth centuries B.C.E., but the change was gradual and unconnected to any nomad invasion. Obviously states like Solomon's or Omri's did not exist in this area, even though the Assyrians and Moabites both mention Omri.

As for the investigation of individual sites, there is no archaeological evidence to support the "Golden Age" of David and Solomon. The "city-states" of the Old Testament proved to be little more than small market centers with populations numbering only a few thousand at most. It is clear that the whole area was never more than a marginal part of any regional political or economic power. The Egyptians occupied the area in the fifteenth century B.C.E. in an effort to create land communications with Mesopotamia and Syria, and undertake mining in Sinai. But the area had a fragile ecology, and the Egyptians, coming from a civilization having reliable water supplies, soon withdrew to the coastal strip. In the time when Joshua is supposed to have invaded and David and Solomon are supposed to have established a large, powerful, and wealthy kingdom, Palestine endured a lengthy period of drought that brought recurrent famine, a 20 per cent decrease in rainfall, and the decline of the neighboring Ugaritic and Mycenaean civilizations. The people of the purported Promised Land certainly did not enjoy a surfeit of milk and honey. Most of them abandoned the interior and moved to the coastal areas, where they established smaller and more sustainable agricultural communities. Pritchard, writing about the reputation of Solomon's kingdom, the zenith of Israelite political power, stated: "Solomon is mentioned in no Egyptian, Mesopotamian, or Phoenician document. Only from the Bible do we learn he lived." Pritchard drew attention to "the disparity between the cultural poverty of Palestine in this age and the impression of grandeur and wealth presented by the biblical account."

N. P. Lemche, discussing the lack of evidence to support Joshua's invasion, criticized

> ...some archaeologists (who) appear to find it more fascinating to hunt for 'proof' of the presence of Israel .... even the most minute changes in architecture, pottery, town lay-out, and so forth, have been taken to show the presence of new (foreign) elements among the existing population at this time. [2]

Keith Whitelam was equally damning:

> There has been an indecent haste to correlate archaeological findings with the biblical traditions, to identify a destruction level with some battle mentioned in the Bible, or to associate the fortification of a site with the building program of some Judaean or Israelite king who is given a few verses in the Deuteronomistic History.[3]

In contrast to the pre - 586 B.C.E. record, there is ample uncontroversial archaeological evidence to support the history of Jerusalem from the Greek conquest to the Roman destruction, the era in which the Jews re-established an independent state that had been destroyed and its population not only exiled but scattered. The archaeological evidence is corroborated by contemporary Greek, Roman, and Jewish written accounts. It is extremely odd that archaeologists, unable to correlate the pre – 586 B.C.E. Old Testament record with their findings, questioned neither how the written record was produced nor the motives of those who wrote it.

Good history is written from evidence. That evidence can come from a number of sources, including many made possible by recent scientific advances. There is archaeology, anthropology, oral traditions, demography, ethnomusicology, linguistics, satellite imaging, volcanology and DNA testing. Nevertheless, most important of all is the written record. Take, for example, the *Rosetta Stone*, the cipher to the history of dynastic Egypt, discovered during Napoleon's military expedition to Egypt. The Rosetta Stone is inscribed with the same passage in three languages - ancient Egyptian, Coptic, and Greek - and therefore provides a means of translating the myriad ancient Egyptian hieroglyphics that describe the exploits of Egypt's ruling class, their religion, their administrative methods, and other aspects of their existence that, but for the Rosetta stone, would remain a closed subject, perhaps forever. Other cultures, the Etruscans and people of Nilotic Meroe for example, have left behind inscriptions and other writings, but without a cipher very little can be read. Some insights may possibly be gained in Etruscan by investigating Albanian. In the case of Meroitic, all that scholars can surmise from comparing letter frequency is that it seems to be more closely related to languages to its west than to anywhere else; but that supposition has so far not made its meaning any clearer.

The case of biblical history is very special if not unique. A highly detailed record exists covering about 2000 years. The life of Joseph and Moses, the Exodus, Joshua's capture of the Promised Land, the story of Ruth, David's battle with Goliath, Solomon's building of the First Temple, the magnificence of the Queen of Sheba's visit, and the destruction of Judah by the Babylonian leader Nebuchadnezzar all seem highly believable events because they were written not merely to glorify past military and political successes but to come to terms with human failings and with the relationship between the known and unknown worlds and to try to make sense of extreme reverses of fortune. In this the Old Testament is very different from the Egyptian inscriptions that are forever in praise of the pharaoh.

Paul Bahn offers a cynical view of archaeology when there is no written text to support it:

> Archaeology is like a vast and fiendish jigsaw puzzle invented by the devil as an instrument of torment since:
>
> a) it will never be finished
> b) you don't know how many pieces are missing
> c) most of them are lost forever
> d) you cannot cheat by looking at the picture
>
> Much of the time, archaeological evidence is so patchy that anyone's guess is as valid as anyone else's. You cannot prove anything. Where the remote past is concerned, nobody knows what took place. The best that can be offered is an informed guess....Some eminent archaeologists have built their entire careers upon convincing bluff. [4]

A written text offers archaeologists a working "picture." That is why archaeologists working in Palestine are so frustrated. The world described in the historical narratives of the Old Testament seems so real. While the Hebrew text is highly detailed, the area described is quite small. Jewish and Christian traditions and the raison d'être of the state of Israel proclaim that this is the right place. But the failure to find a single trace of it is maddening.

The broad archaeological picture is clear. There is no evidence of the Exodus, the conquest of the Promised Land, the establishment of David's kingdom, the grandeur of Solomon's public works program, the First Temple, records from the highly organized court bureaucracy, the wealth gained from control of the trade routes, or Omri's impressive capital in Samaria.

In desperation some archaeologists have resorted to fantasy. There are some who vehemently insist that the evidence is there, even the chariot wheels of pharaoh's drowned pursuing forces. On a saner level supporters of the idea that ancient Judah and Israel were indeed in Palestine have fastened on to peripheral evidence to prove the major point.

One suggestion is that the First Temple and much more might still be uncovered; for instance, a long-lost volcano may exist under the Dead Sea and thus support the stories of the Burning Bush, the Exodus, and the destruction of Sodom and Gomorrah - all associated with volcanic activity. Exaggerated claims have been made of several discoveries. Ancient inscriptions were unvocalized and are therefore almost impossible to decipher accurately. The word *slm* can mean *'reward'*, *'spark'*, *'completeness'*, *'peace'*, *'good health,'* or it can be a greeting in Canaanite; but enthusiastic biblical researchers, eager to prove the city existed by that name in ancient times, have translated it from the Hebrew word for *Jerusalem*. In the case of the Jerusalem Siloam water tunnel (see below) an unvocalized inscription has been ambitiously translated as "this tunnel was dug in the reign of King Hezekiah" but an inspection of the inscription reveals no personal name, and the inscription on a hidden ledge is a piece of graffiti not a public announcement.

Popular writers often have a greater influence on public perceptions than academics. Werner Keller's *The Bible as History – Archaeology Confirms the Book of Books* has sold millions of copies worldwide, translated into many languages since its publication in 1956. The New York Times commented: "There is an atmosphere of excitement about this book that is contagious. It does not contain a single boring page." In chapter 20, Solomon the Copper King, Keller begins by quoting seven passages from the book of Kings; three of them refer to the immense gold trade, three to Solomon's cavalry force, and one to his oriental trading fleet. Keller, then, discusses the 1938-40 archaeological excavation of Tell el-Kheleifeh (Ezion-geber), a fortified port on the Gulf of Aqaba, active from about the tenth to the fourth centuries B.C.E., where substantial amounts of *copper,* not gold, were refined. Neighboring Sinai was the site of several copper mines. Gold came from Hijaz, Sheba, Ethiopia, and the Egyptian Red Sea coast. Although there is no evidence that links Tell el-Kheleifeh with Solomon, Keller, after enthusing about the thrill of finding the site, anoints Solomon as the *Copper King* when all traditions attest to his association with *gold.*

Jerusalem, as stated earlier, is Palestine's greatest archaeological disappointment. Solomon allegedly constructed a number of very large public buildings in a hilltop area. This arrangement was common in the ancient world, and the best known example is the Acropolis complex in

Athens. Solomon's buildings were the First Temple, the Royal Palace (which took twice as much time as the temple to build), the Treasury, and the Judgment Hall (where he placed his ivory throne), a palace for his most prestigious wife (pharaoh's daughter), and a large structure called the *House of the Forest of Lebanon*. No trace of any of these exists today. The archaeological record has revealed that during the time of Solomon's reign Jerusalem was one of about 100 small unfortified villages in a very poor agricultural area inhabited by a people indistinguishable from other Canaanites, who led a marginal existence herding goats, sheep, and oxen. Attempts to link small public works to the biblical record are unconvincing. The famed Siloam "water tunnel of Hezekiah" mentioned above owes its name to a passage in the Old Testament where Hezekiah is credited with building a pool and an "aqueduct" on the "west" side of the city. There are no remains of an aqueduct, and the tunnel (which could of course be described as a kind of aqueduct) is on the *eastern* edge of Jerusalem.

The most important piece of evidence is probably a stone fragment with inscriptions dealing with the misfortunes of the king of Moab at the hands of the Israelite monarch Omri, whom he had nevertheless successfully defied. This is known as the *Moabite Stone,* a basalt stele from about 850 B.C.E. inscribed with thirty-four lines of text in a script similar to later postexilic Hebrew. The stele was discovered at Dibon, east of the Dead Sea, in 1868. The Moabites were apparently closely related to the Israelites (Ruth was a Moabite), but the prophet Isaiah eventually condemned them as the enemies of God. The Moabite Stone is accepted as proof of the Israelite presence in Palestine, but the stone was most likely erected by Moabites who had fled Israelite aggression elsewhere, perhaps from the trade route hub of Jawf. No trace of Omri's capital has been found, but the Moabite Stone indicates that Israel, the northern kingdom, was in striking distance of the Trans-Jordan.

Beyond Palestine, the *Merneptah Stele*, dated 1207 B.C.E. and discovered in 1896 in Thebes (now Luxor), Egypt's ancient capital, has been used as proof of Israel's existence. The stele is named after the pharaoh who ruled Egypt from ca. 1212 to 1202 B.C.E. Its inscriptions include one line that has been interpreted as saying "Israel is laid waste, its seed is not." In 1990, Frank Yurco, a researcher at Chicago's Field Museum of Natural History, identified figures on the stele as ancient Israelites. Michael Hasel, a University of Arizona doctoral student researching the stele, concluded in 1994 that this indicated Israel was an important "socio-ethnic entity in the late 13th century B.C.E., one that is significant enough to be included in the military campaign against political powers in Canaan." It is far more likely that the places mentioned on the stele were in areas of strategic importance to Thebes so that if the reference to Israel really does mean the Hebrew or Israelites of the Old Testament it is a tantalizing hint that they were not in Palestine but either in Africa or in Arabia. Then again, why would the Egyptians have conducted a military campaign in Palestine, where, for economic and strategic purposes, such a venture would be totally unnecessary? The stele omits the names of significant political entities in Palestine. Other Egyptian references in a corrupted form of Akkadian in the *Amarna Letters*, discovered in 1887, speak of *pr* (vocalized as *'apiru* or *hapiru*) as being a problem in fourteenth century B.C.E. Canaan. Akkadian is too close to Canaanite/ Hebrew to confuse *pr* with *br*, the word for *Hebrew*. Historians and archaeologists generally concur that the *pr* seem to have been composed of isolated bands of outlaws expelled from city states; however they were not a separate people. Despite this, given the nomadic history of the Hebrew of Abraham and Moses, and the almost vagrant nature of modern Hebraic groups like the Somali Yibir, there might possibly be a link between the *pr* and *br*.

Sometimes archaeological finds have revealed biblical names. In 1986, a seal was identified as belonging to Neriah's son, Baruch, who wrote down Jeremiah's prophecies in 587 B.C.E, on the eve of the Babylonian conquest of Judah. The seal could have come from Palestine or been brought there from elsewhere. In 1993, archaeologists working at Tell Dan, in northern Israel, discovered an inscription on a piece of basalt that they vocalized to mean *House of David* and *King of Israel*. Unfortunately, because Semitic languages were unvocalized in the pre-Christian era, it is impossible to know the precise meaning of isolated inscriptions. Archaeological remains are also open to all sorts of interpretations. Baruch would have been written as *BRK*, a word that also means "blessing." Archaeological reconstruction depends on the researcher's imagination. One part of the ruins at Megiddo has been identified as stables for Solomon's numerous horses. An alternative view is that they are merely shop stalls. There are references other than the Old Testament that have been interpreted as referring to Judah and to Israel. They all belong to the period after Solomon, when the two kingdoms were divided.

The Egyptian ruler Sheskonk (Shishak) ruled from ca. 945 to ca. 924 B.C.E. and his depredations are noted in the Old Testament books of 1 Kings (14:25-26) and 2 Chronicles (12:2-9). Sheshonk's achievements are listed on the walls of the Temple of Ammon in Thebes. The record indicates that he invaded Judah and captured several cities but not Jerusalem, where he was bought off by Reheboam. This would indicate that Jerusalem was still a wealthy and powerful city. The Egyptians either did not feel confident enough to capture the city or believed that accepting tribute would establish a precedent for future relations. This implies that Jerusalem still controlled valuable trade routes to the south, and it was better to conclude a lucrative punitive expedition than to destroy the commercial and central administrative well-being of a state that could continue to provide Egypt with wealth. This certainly does not match the archaeological remains of Palestine's Jerusalem. Reheboam's Jerusalem must have been elsewhere. There is no unanimity about the consequences of finding no evidence to confirm that the events of Old Testament belong to Palestine. One theory is that the change from Bronze Age to Iron Age was as undramatic as the archaeological evidence testifies. In this scenario the Promised Land was already partially occupied by an earlier but peaceful Hebrew migration; and Joshua merely moved into Hebrew territory, achieving hegemony by a show of force rather than by force itself. Another theory is that Joshua led his Iron Age pastoralists to marginalized land away from the Canaanite peasantry and later took control of them, even though marginalized land would be of no use to Iron Age smelters. A third suggestion is that there was no invasion but merely an internal power struggle. All three hypotheses maintain that the Old Testament record is therefore exaggerated or inaccurate. An interesting re-assessment by J. M. Miller and J. Hayes accepts the Old Testament account as being accurate in terms of local standards:

> Solomon was probably an unusually wealthy and powerful ruler by the standards of Early Iron Age Palestine. Yet viewed in the broader context of the ancient Middle East, he is to be regarded more as a local ruler over an expanded city-state than as a world class emperor.[5]

A fourth suggestion is based purely on faith and maintains that, irrespective of evidence, the Old Testament not only took place in Palestine but Israelites left it to settle in northern Europe:

> The Jews are not the only descendants of the ancient 12-tribed nation of Israel, which includes the Anglo-Saxon-Celtic people and the British Commonwealth and certain countries in northwestern Europe. "British means "covenant man" being derived from two Hebrew words, "Brith", meaning covenant, and "ish", man.[6]

These beliefs, strong among small Christian cults associated with the British Israel movement, are echoed in unjustified historical certainty and ideological arrogance expressed by some modern Israeli researchers, apparently based on a sort of ethnic mysticism, as if faith and local experience not only gives them intellectual superiority but also an indivisible identity with people living thousands of years ago. Shoshana Ben-Dor, a researcher on Ethiopian Judaism and the present director of the North American Conference on Ethiopian Jewry, wrote to this writer on 20 October 1986:

> Anyone who has seen inscriptions in readable Biblical Hebrew, referring to places recorded in the Bible, pulled from the ground before their eyes is utterly convinced that Salibi [a critic] is wrong .... Finally, though I take it as a compliment the assumption that Jews influenced Africa in so many ways, I believe we cannot take all the credit you assign.

In 1986, the University Museum of the University of Pennsylvania published the findings of archaeological investigations undertaken between 1977 and 1981 on late Bronze age and early Iron age sites in the area of the central Trans-Jordan. The editor, Patrick McGovern, concluded that the evidence contradicted all three theories concerning Joshua's entry to the Promised Land. There had been no violent invasion, nor infiltration by nomads who then established settlements in unoccupied land. McGovern dismissed the idea of an internal revolt, stating that society in Joshua's era had been stable with an equitable distribution of wealth.

In 1992, Professor Thomas Thompson, one of the world's foremost biblical archaeologists, published his seminal *Early History of the Israelite People from the Written and Archaeological Sources*. Thompson's survey of Palestinian archaeology cannot be faulted. He emphasizes that excavations around Jerusalem had found no evidence of significant settlement during the time of David and Solomon's powerful and wealthy united kingdom. Conditions for such a state began to emerge a century later, but Jerusalem only became a relatively important urban center around 650 B.C.E. Thompson dismissed the notion that the area had any monarch on the scale of Saul, David and Solomon as "out of the question." Thompson concluded that the first ten books of the Old Testament had been the invention of priests in Jerusalem during Persian rule ca. 450 B.C.E. He suggests that the Assyrian and Babylonian conquests in the Middle East brought together in exiled captivity broken remnants of disparate peoples from former petty tribal groups and city-states united by the Aramaic language and eventually a relatively enlightened Persian administration. Thompson believes that Ezra's Jerusalem settlement was an administrative measure that created a well-organized urban theocracy in an imperial outpost. He envisages that the religion of the new settlement was originally Persian-based but then absorbed various traditions to create a mythical history with a fraudulent Holy Book for an invented people, the Jews, a process mirrored in the cynic view of the Mormons in nineteenth-century America.

One of Thompson's main points has a weak linguistic basis. He dismisses the notion that the *Song of Moses* (Exodus 15), the *Song of Deborah* (Judges 5), the *Blessings of Jacob* (Genesis 49), the *Blessings of Moses* (Deuteronomy 33), the *Oracles of Baarlam* (Numbers 23 - 4), the *Poem of Moses* (Deuteronomy 32), and *Psalm 68* are older than the other parts of the Old Testament; yet his dismissal was not founded on any analysis of the language concerned, which, as mentioned earlier, contains many archaic Hebrew words. Moreover, if Thompson is correct that the fifth century Jerusalem community "invented" Judaism, it is difficult to accept that they would also invent sacred texts in a dead language that contained several passages at variance with their own theology and political objectives

So long as only non-Israeli archaeologists questioned the veracity of the Old Testament account, Zionists could dismiss their findings as politically biased. However, the situation changed in 1999, when the Israeli archaeologist Ze'ev Hertzog lent support to Thompson's conclusions, doubting that there was ever an Egyptian captivity, an Exodus, or an invasion of Canaan. If David and Solomon had existed, they would have been little more than chiefs of a small tribal kingdom. These views were also supported by Israel Finkelstein, Hertzog's colleague at Tel Aviv University, and by Neil Silberman, an internationally acclaimed archaeologist, in their 2001 publication *The Bible Unearthed, Archaeology's New Vision of Ancient Israel and the Origin of Its Sacred Texts*. They argued that it really did not matter if Solomon's kingdom was "tiny" or that Jericho did not fall to trumpet blasts. "The power of the biblical saga," they wrote, "stems from its being a compelling and coherent narrative expression of the timeless themes of a people's liberation, continuing resistance to oppression, and the quest for social equality."

At the end of 2001 the American journal *Human Immunology* asked its subscribers to remove and destroy an article by nine Spanish-based academics entitled *The Origin of Palestinians and Their Genetic Relatedness with Other Mediterranean Populations* because of objections to a reference to "Jewish colonists" and a sentence that read: "Diaspora Palestinians (occurred after 1947), who have refugee status (about 40 per cent) and live either in concentration camps or are scattered in Jordan (38 per cent), Syria (12 per cent) and Lebanon (13 per cent)." The rest of the text supported the admission by the leader of the Spanish team, Antonio Arnaiz-Villena, that he had not realized that in English *colonist* and *concentration camp* are immensely emotive terms. A similar problem once arose when British Airways informed its German customers that they would be given *"special treatment,"* an innocuous phrase in English but in German, torture by the Hitler era Gestapo. Arnaiz-Villena's article is nevertheless of interest because of its genetic relationships. It concludes that Ashkenazi (European) Jews, Iranians, Cretans, Armenians, Turks, and non-Ashkenazi Jews are the populations genetically closest to the Palestinians, and that Jews and Palestinians have a common origin. The article also reveals that Greeks (but not Cretans) have such a high percentage of African genes that they are a genetic aberration among Mediterranean peoples, which supports Martin Bernal's *Black Athena.*

The Spanish team's findings appear to support the *fantasy* or *exaggeration* school (another term is *minimalist*) conclusions of Old Testament historians and archaeologists. As this book argues, however, it is more likely that the majority of Israelis are descendants of the population of Palestine who were forced to convert to Judaism during the time of the Hasmonean dynasty, from 124 to 49 B.C.E.

Finkelstein and Silberman's conclusions about Old Testament archaeology will doubtless be followed by similar explanations that the biblical message of striving for an ideal is greater than creating a prosperous powerful state. While unacceptable to fundamentalists who continue to assert that the evidence is literally waiting to be unearthed in Palestine, it eases the conscience of those Israelis who were inspired by the Zionist ideal of building a better world but have since been appalled at the consequences of the establishment of the State of Israel. Within the parameters of these new historical conclusions they believe there is still room to come to terms with the Palestinians whose land they occupy. Perhaps if more investigations support Finkelstein and Silberman, it will destroy the credibility of the extreme right and their West Bank settlement agenda.

This, however, is an illusion. Judaism has a long and respected intellectual history. Today, although Jews constitute only 2 per cent of the population of the USA, 19 per cent of the country's top university professors are Jews. In arts, sciences, literature, entertainment, finance, and music, Jews have made extraordinary achievements disproportionate to their numbers. It is ironic that Herzl believed that society would benefit more if Jews quit their homes and embraced Zionism in Palestine. Instead Zionism has become a huge unstable element in world politics. Despite the intellectual tradition, Zionism is still unable to consider unwelcome evidence let alone admit to making an appalling mistake.

Judaism deliberately demonized the Queen of Sheba, because the ancient and mediaeval tradition could not accept the idea of a woman challenging Solomon intellectually. In doing so, Judaism shut out the most important factor in developing the Zionist dream. In studying the life of the Queen of Sheba it becomes clear that the Old Testament is neither a fantasy nor an exaggerated account, but the events therein occurred in *western Arabia*, not in Palestine. Israel is in the wrong place.

CHAPTER THREE

Writing the Old Testament

The paradoxical idea that the Old Testament is an accurate document, but that modern Israel is in the wrong place requires lengthy explanation.

It is generally accepted that the Hebrew probably memorized an early form of the Law of Moses as verse in a language now lost, and that Israelite priests eventually wrote an expanded version in Canaanite hundreds of years after Moses' death.

Semitic writing was still in its infancy when Joshua reached the Promised Land, and it seems no Semitic-speaking people adopted the neighboring Egyptian hieroglyphic script. The first four books of the Old Testament may have only been written down for the first time during Solomon's reign in order to fortify the position of the clan of the new high priest, Zadok, and to imitate practices elsewhere in imperial Middle Eastern states, such as Assyria and Babylon, where sacred texts were housed in a temple. The Hebrew had already established a precedent by placing the written Ten Commandments in the Ark of the Covenant. Whatever they wrote would have omitted vowels, as these were believed to be the sounds of heaven. Hebrew scholars finally inserted vowels in the text of the Old Testament between A.D. 500 and 950, long after spoken Hebrew had died out around 400 B.C.E.

As mentioned earlier, Zadok was probably a Jebusite from Canaan, not a Hebrew. The subsequent success of the Zadokite priests was largely based on their possession and detailed knowledge of the Torah, and on Zadok's prestige as the incipient custodian of the Temple. As also mentioned earlier, when the Israelites entered the Promised Land or even by the time of Solomon's reign, the Torah was almost certainly not as fully developed as it is in its present form. The Zadokite priesthood must have undertaken some of the work, including additions, but the extent of it is unknown. Hilkiah most likely doctored Deuteronomy; and Ezra, in later years, was accused of altering original texts to denigrate the House of David, thereafter presenting the forgery as if it had been faithfully copied from very ancient and revered temple documents.

Such literary meddling matches the hypothesis put forward by the German scholar Julius Wellhausen (1844-1918). Wellhausen, writing at the close of the nineteenth century, concluded that the first six books of the Old Testament had been written by four different groups of people. The earliest group, called the *Yahwist*, wrote about the reigns of David and Solomon, the kingdom of Judah, and the House of David. The second group, known as the *Elohist*, recorded the period of the divided monarchy and the kingdom of Israel. The third group, called the *Deuteronomist*, wrote about Josiah's draconian activities on behalf of the Zadokites, the time of exile, and the work of Ezra. The last group, known as the *Priestly*, covered the exile and postexilic periods, and also propagated the interests of the Jerusalem priesthood. Biblical scholars have generally accepted Wellhausen's ideas.

Most authorities also agree with another German Biblical scholar, Martin Noth (1902-1968), who, in 1930, wrote that many different traditions and manuscripts existed separately until Ezra's time (ca. 400 B.C.E.) when the Jerusalem theocracy codified the Torah and added other books to produce the "standard" version of the Old Testament. Unfortunately nothing survives from that period. The oldest fragments of Old Testament manuscripts, which date from ca. 200 B.C.E., were discovered in the early 1950s among the *Dead Sea Scrolls*.

The contents of the Old Testament, as canonized by Ezra and his successors, consist of twenty-four sacred books originally written on twenty-four scrolls. The Old Testament of the King James Bible divides the books of Samuel, Kings, and Chronicles each into two parts and lists the twelve books of the so-called minor prophets separately, making 39 books in all. The Old Testament of the Ethiopian and Eritrean Orthodox churches contains eighty-one books; some texts - such as *Jubilees* and *Enoch* - were lost to the Jews in earlier times and are now only available in Ge'ez, the ancient liturgical language of Ethiopia and Eritrea. There are also references in the Old Testament to other books, now lost, such as the *Book of Jashar*, and the *Acts of Solomon*. The Bible of the Roman Catholic Church contains other writings later than the last book of the Hebrew Old Testament. These are known as the *Apocrypha*.

The contents of the Old Testament cover approximately 2000 years or more and were produced at different stages. The Torah - Genesis, Exodus,

Leviticus, Numbers, and Deuteronomy - is the oldest, and much of it must have been composed in the language spoken before Hebrew was adopted from the Canaanites. Next came the twenty-one books associated with the prophets. Four of these - Joshua, Judges, Samuel and Kings 1 and 2 - deal very much with military and political history. Three books - Isaiah, Jeremiah and Ezekiel - are credited to major prophets; and twelve to minor ones - Hosea, Joel, Amos, Obadiah, Jonah, Micah, Nahum, Habakkuk, Zephaniah, Haggai, Zechariah and Malachi. Then there are the thirteen books of Writings - Psalms, Proverbs, Job, Song of Solomon, Ruth, Lamentations, Ecclesiastes, Ester, Daniel, Ezra, and Nehemiah - dealing with religious and erotic poetry and miscellany; and the two books of Chronicles that contain the Zadokites' own account of the national past.

By the time Hebrew had died out as a living language, ca. 400 B.C.E., religious leaders had decided that the five books of the Torah – from Genesis to Deuteronomy - were divinely inspired. By ca. 200 B.C.E. the works of the prophets received the same status, although not among certain groups, including the Sadducees, Samaritans, and Israelite communities in Arabia who may have been Nazarenes. Then, between ca. 130 and ca. 100 B.C.E., came staggered recognition for the Writings, most of the texts written in Hebrew except for parts of Daniel and Ezra, which are in Aramaic.

The account of the Hebrew's origins, their early history, their captivity in Egypt, the Exodus, the creation of a religious community governed by the Torah, and the death of Moses at the gateway to the Promised Land are recorded in the first five books of the Old Testament. The Torah is enumerated throughout from the second to fifth books - Exodus, Numbers, Leviticus, and Deuteronomy. The Torah is ostensibly the legal code for a *future* state in Canaan that would be ruled by a monarch but answerable to a priesthood. The 613 regulations would govern religious beliefs, daily religious observances, conduct in holy places, the priesthood, sacrifices, vows, ritual purity, temple donations, diet, festivals, administration, judicial matters, idolatry, war, social relations, foreign relations, blasphemy, agriculture, business dealings, sexual prohibitions, and the conduct of the king. In addition, there were eight laws dedicated to the conduct of the Nazirites, an ecstatic warrior group forbidden to cut their hair, or to eat any part of a grape, which extended to drinking wine. Nazirites today are only found among the Ethiopian Beta Israel.

Whether or not the Torah was divinely ordained, its provisions neither reflect a society influenced by Egypt nor a nomadic host wandering through the desert. Moses' rule was dictatorial. A man gathering firewood on the Sabbath was stoned to death, and 250 advocates of a more democratic system of decision-making met a horrible end. The Torah, however, deals with a different sort of society, one with a long-established bureaucracy, army, and administration. Disregarding the notion that it was divinely ordained, the Torah seems very much the Zadokite priesthood elaboration on the legal code that Moses introduced, with insertions of additional laws arising from their experiences with the monarchy and rival cults as well as their experiences adopting agriculture and their involvement in commerce. Solomon's numerous marriages were blamed for the rise of syncretism, thus the Torah had a provision stating that it was God's will that kings should not take many wives. The Torah was almost certainly compiled in its present version by the Zadokites after the establishment of the First Temple. Although the Torah does not mention the temple by name, its frequent references to idolatry and to a standardized priesthood tied to a single recognized religious center reflect all too clearly the Zadokite power struggle for their own personal control of a single temple during and after Solomon's reign. The Zadokites then declared the expanded edition of Moses' work as the Torah, thus canonizing their own decisions as Holy Writ, a process they were to repeat hundreds of years later. The book of Deuteronomy, almost certainly the sacred work "discovered" in King Josiah's day, the reading of which so unnerved him, looks very much like a careful rendering of ancient traditions mingled with more recent insights to produce an ideal vehicle for Zadokite resurgence.

Until their captivity in Babylon, the Zadokite priesthood relied upon Israelite royal patronage. When Zerubbabel led the exiles to Aliyeh, the New Jerusalem, it appeared likely that a state similar to Solomon's would develop albeit subservient to Persia. Most exiles remained in Babylon, and what happened next in New Jerusalem became a pattern there in later years. The Zadokite priests were no longer content to rely on patronage from the House of David. Instead they chose to become rulers themselves. Zerubbabel was ousted and a theocracy took over. The sacred books were gathered, edited, and embellished. The result was certainly not acceptable in many sectors of the Israelite community and became a major source of friction between contending sects when the area came under new rulers.

The history of Palestine from the removal of the Zadodite high priest in 172 B.C.E. until the destruction of Jerusalem in A.D. 70 is now under intense scholastic scrutiny. It was a time of vicious political and theological rivalry. Authorities dispute whether the Zadokites were a dynasty or school of thought. Much discussion has been evoked by the Dead Sea Scrolls, the ancient leather and papyrus manuscripts discovered in five desolate areas near the Dead Sea between 1947 and the 1960s, which contain many references to the Zadokite priesthood. One interpretation of some of these texts is that the writers supported the House of Zadok, which had been ousted from its long control of the temple. The scrolls have been linked to the town of Qumran, which many researchers believe was a monastic settlement for the Essene sect. Others say Qumran was nothing of the sort, arguing that it was just a town next to a major highway. Their argument is that the scrolls were collections of documents gathered from different parts of the region for safe keeping and for their ultimate delivery elsewhere. Fascinating as this subject is, unfortunately the present text cannot digress too far in that direction and will therefore use the term *Zadokite* to mean both a dynastic priesthood and adherents to their school of thought. It was also in this highly charged period of political ferment that Zerubbabel's descendant, Jesus, son of Joseph, made a peaceful attempt to seize Jerusalem and be proclaimed king. One analysis of his actions is that he miscalculated Roman tolerance and, having seen his cousin John the Baptist executed, realized his only credible path lay in martyrdom and the promise to his believers of a heavenly kingdom.

It is likely that Christ's followers would have remained a small Judaic sect had it not been for the work of the apostle Paul (Saul). Paul argued that Christ would soon return to judge the world and create a new society – heaven on earth. Salvation would be open to all (Jews would no longer be regarded as the Chosen People), and achieved through faith, not adherence to the Mosaic Law, which would be replaced by the guiding power of the Holy Spirit. Since the early Christians ate communally, Paul faced strong opposition from Christians from Jewish backgrounds who regarded Gentiles (non-Jews) unclean. Paul persevered, attracting adherents from the hellenized Jews of the Mediterranean who opposed Jewish dietary laws and other laws such as circumcision. Former pagans, disillusioned with the Roman imperial pantheon, also joined the Church in increasing numbers. Paul's work ensured that Christianity developed into a separate world religion with sacred texts in Greek instead of Hebrew.

Nevertheless, when the Jews were dispersed and exiled from Palestine after A.D. 143 it seemed unlikely that Christianity would emerge as a major force. The exiled Jews were extremely successful in Babylon, establishing centers of learning and being largely responsible for the administration of their own areas. As early as A.D. 30, Helena, queen of Adiabene on the northern side of the Tigris River, converted to Judaism and supported the Jews in their rebellion in Judaea against Roman rule A.D. 66-73. In A.D. 116, Jews in Mesopotamia briefly ousted the Romans before being reconquered. However, the main Jewish uprising in the early 500s in this area was not against the Romans but the Persians. From around the end of the second century A.D. the Jews of Persian-controlled Babylon were represented by members of the House of David, the *Exilarchs*. These traced their ancestry to Jehoiakim, King of Judah (634-598 B.C.E.), his exiled son Jehoiachin, released by the Persians, being the first Exilarch. In A.D. 513, one of the Exilarchs, Mar Zutra II (reportedly the twenty-fourth direct descendant of Jehoiachin), established an independent Jewish state at Mahoza on the Tigris River. The Persians retaliated, defeating and crucifying him in A.D. 520.

Militant Judaism had already experienced a serious setback when the Emperor Constantine (A.D. 312–337) made Christianity the Roman Empire's official religion. Constantine had become a covert to Christianity in A.D. 312, following a Christian vision before the Battle of the Milvian Bridge, where he had defeated the emperor Maxentius and seized the throne himself. He had ordered his soldiers to paint the Christian *Chi-Rho* symbol on their shields. Constantine's victory determined his choice of Christianity as the official religion of the empire. Being of a practical administrative bent, he wanted to ensure there was unanimity in dogma and therefore convened the Council of Nicaea, one of the most important events in the history of Christianity.

The Council of Nicaea met in A.D. 325 under Constantine's direction, to standardize the faith throughout the Roman Empire. In this he was almost completely successful. All major Christian denominations today (the Jehovah's Witnesses, of Arian origin, being an exception) adhere to the Nicaean Creed hammered out at the council as the basis of Christian belief: "I believe in God the Father Almighty, maker of heaven and earth ....". Some dissension followed and other councils convened, but Constantine's success in blending Christ's teachings with Paul's interpretations and popular pagan festivals and rituals transformed the faith into a world religion. The New Testament was then canonized as Holy Writ, including *Matthew 27:25*, a fabricated account stating that the Jews fervently accepted responsibility for Christ's martyrdom, thus ensuring eternal damnation.

Whatever hopes Judaism had when the Roman Empire of the West fell in A.D. 478 were dashed when the victorious Germanic tribes adopted

Christianity, partly because the church's structure, education system, and legal expertise assisted central government. Nevertheless, militant Messianic elements still continued to agitate for an independent Jewish state.

In the 520s, the Jews in Mahoza and in Himyar (southern Arabia) respectively challenged the imperial authority of Persia and of Aksum (Ethiopia) and, although both were crushed, their defeats were viewed as temporary setbacks. The situation dramatically changed with the astonishing success of Islam after A.D. 632. Jewish intellectual centers in Babylon, the Holy Land, North Africa, and Spain came under Islamic rule, whose relative tolerance posed a greater threat than Christianity to the survival of Judaism. Muslims permitted freedom of religion to Christians and Jews so long as they paid a special tax. If they chose to embrace Islam the tax was lifted. The Muslims supra-tribal outlook offered opportunities to all sectors of society - irrespective of race, class or background - once they became Muslims, and this produced a brilliant flowering of culture as the Muslims absorbed Greek, Persian, Jewish, and other traditions.

The Jewish reaction to this political and religious setback followed past precedents. Jews had no wish to become assimilated and thus to disappear as separate entities like the ten "lost" tribes of the northern kingdom of Israel. Bernhard Berenson (1865-1959), a convert to Catholicism, criticized this attitude, implying the Rabbinical Judaism that dominated the exilic communities was self seeking, for without a following the scholar-priests, *rabbis*, would have no support or purpose:

> From Ezra down, this Jewish exclusiveness was due less and less to a feeling of superiority, certainly not in the ways of this world, but rather to a fear of contamination. Rabbinical Judaism is first and foremost an organization for keeping a small minority, scattered among the nations, from dissolving and disappearing. It was thus based on fear.[1]

The priesthood demanded stricter control of their communities and to this end worked to produce uniformity of doctrine and scripture to combat fragmentation of their faith. At the end of the eighth century A.D. the authority of Rabbinical Judaism was challenged in Babylon by the Karaites. Rabbinical Judaism should be seen as the ideological successor of the Zadokites, although tradition tells us that it was developed by the scribe class of Pharisees. The Karaites rejected the Talmud, the Zadokite commentaries on the Torah, upholding the principle that the Torah was open to everyone without intercession of the priesthood. A similar challenge to the priesthood had taken place within Christendom, when the Gnostics, drawing much support from financially independent Roman women, had been brutally crushed by the established church and their sacred texts proscribed.

One major task facing the Rabbinical school of thought was to standardize the Old Testament using old Hebrew texts. As mentioned earlier, we have no idea which language Moses spoke when he gave the Hebrews the Torah. The Old Testament hints that it may have been an early form of Aramaic. But it is pertinent to note that the Beta Israel, the so-called Black Jews of Ethiopia, as late as the nineteenth century A.D. retained ancient Judaic liturgy in Qwarenya, [2] their Cushitic Agaw language, which they uttered but no longer understood, [3] because most had adopted Amharic, a Semitic language. When Joshua led the Hebrew into the Promised Land (ca. 1400 B.C.E.) they adopted Canaanite and developed a dialect that they called Ibrit *(brt)* after themselves *('br)*. Modern Hebrew is called *Ivrit*.

Only Joshua and Caleb survived the entire Exodus from Egyptian captivity until the conquest of the Promised Land. If the Torah had been memorized or written down, it would have been lost when the language changed to Canaanite. Hardly anything is known about the way Hebrew/Canaanite was spoken or written around 1000 B.C.E. when King Solomon established his Israelite kingdom as a major power in the Middle East; but within three hundred years it was being challenged by Aramaic and was fatally wounded when Judah fell in 586 B.C.E. The Samaritans from the northern kingdom of Israel retained a different writing system from those in Judah. The kingdom of Judah adopted a squarish version of the Aramaic alphabet very similar to that used by the Moabites. Hebrew died out around 400 B.C.E. Jews in the Middle East spoke Aramaic until it was replaced by Arabic after the seventh century. In Europe they developed dialects based on Hebraic-Aramaic mixes with local languages, most notably Yiddish from German and Ladino from Spanish.

The Jewish scholars who undertook the definitive editing of the Old Testament were known as the Masoretes and were based in academies in Tiberias (Galilee), Sura, and Nehardea (Babylon). Their mother tongues were Aramaic and Arabic. By the time they completed their work, ca. A.D. 900, Hebrew had been dead for 1300 years, and most of their writings discussing their editorial work was in Arabic.

There is no doubting the sincerity of the Masoretes. They gathered the most prestigious texts of the Old Testament and set out to determine which were authentic. Naturally there had been some deviations over the years as scribes occasionally miscopied from older texts. Despite this the deviations were not serious, and the texts available to the Masoretes were fairly uniform. Recently texts dating back to ca. 200 B.C.E. have been discovered, and they are very close to those the Masoretes must have used to produce the definitive version of the Old Testament.

Nevertheless, the major problem facing the Masoretes was that none of the texts they consulted contained any vowels. The Hebrew originally wrote their sacred texts using only consonants. Vowels were omitted as vowel sounds were considered to be heavenly and therefore, like the image of God, too sacred to portray with the human hand. The sacred texts were written on leather scrolls, and the priests were trained to memorize the absent vowels as they read the texts. This might have proven an effective method if language never changed. This, of course, was not the case. By the time Masoretic scholars finally inserted what they believed to be the correct vowels the Hebrew language had not only changed considerably, it was also long dead.

Different languages use consonants and vowels in different proportions, but the ratio is usually two consonants to a vowel. English, like Hebrew, uses more consonants than vowels. This means that if you spell a word in English omitting the vowels it will be easier to understand than a word that omits the consonants. For example if you take a place name in America and spell it only with the vowels, *AIO*, it would be extremely difficult to identify the full word; but if you spell it only with consonants, *WSHNGTN*, most would recognize it as *Washington*. That does not look difficult, but it is an example taken from modern English. If we go back in time, most English speakers would find Chaucer's spoken English of 600 years ago almost unintelligible and Bede's written Anglo-Saxon of nearly 1300 years ago a complete mystery, especially so if it were written only in consonants. Here is an example from unvocalized Anglo-Saxon: *fdr r Þ rt n hfnm*. Even if you were told that *Þ* should be transcribed like *th,* few English speakers would recognize this phrase as the ancient way of saying "Our Father who is in heaven" although *hfnm* does look like *heaven* and *rt* as *art*, the archaic way of saying *is*.

It is generally acknowledged that the Old Testament text without vowels was drawn up from other texts, some of which have been lost, ca. 500 B.C.E. during exile in Babylon. The historical events described in the

Old Testament cover the period ca. 1400 to ca. 500 B.C.E., from Moses to Queen Esther of Persia. There is not much difference between the language of the earliest books and that of the latest ones. This indicates that most of the original form of the Old Testament is lost to us. The Song of Solomon, for instance, contains vocabulary dating it to the Babylonian captivity five hundred years after Solomon's reign. The oldest Hebrew is found in the *Song of Moses* (Exodus 15), the *Song of Deborah* (Judges 5), the *Blessings of Jacob* (Genesis 49), the *Blessings of Moses* (Deuteronomy 33), the *Oracles of Baarlam* (Numbers 23-4), the *Poem of Moses* (Deuteronomy 32), and *Psalm 68*. They include different terms from later Hebrew, for example words for *prince, gold, listen, know, be, man, judge, see, do/make, wine, strike,* and *become angry*. All these older passages constitute poems and songs and are easier to memorize than prose. [4]

One major problem facing the Jews after Ezra produced the Old Testament was that Hebrew had given way to Aramaic, but the language of education was Greek. Ca. 250 B.C.E. the first books of the Old Testament were translated into Greek, followed by the remaining books over the next century. This Greek Old Testament text was known as the Septuagint from the Latin word for seventy, a reference to the alleged number of translators who prepared it for Greek-speaking Jewish communities, particularly those in Egypt. When the Christian church made translations into Ge'ez, Latin, Armenian, and other languages for their Bible, they worked from the Greek Septuagint because the Hebrew text still remained without vowels.

Flavius Josephus, writing ca. A.D. 93, stated that the Jerusalem Jews maintained a standard reference copy of the Hebrew Old Testament. Unfortunately it has not survived. As mentioned earlier, some Hebrew texts were discovered among the Dead Sea Scrolls dating from ca. 200 B.C.E. but nothing else has survived between then and A.D. 600 when the Masoretes were engaged in their final redaction of the definitive Old Testament text. The Galilean and Babylonian Masoretes kept notes of their work. When there was a dispute they would write: "We in Babylon think this but those in Galilee think that." Although they had been trained to memorize the missing vowel sounds, they did not always understand what they read. In the final version of the Old Testament there are about 350 places where they admitted they could come to no agreement about the meaning of the text.

The Masoretes faced many problems in vocalizing the texts. They had been trained for hundreds of years to memorize the missing vowel sounds but this did not mean they always understood what they recited. Take for example passages in the Old Testament concerning the prophet Elijah. The Masoretes decided that Elijah was fed in the desert by ravens, not a very convincing scenario in a location where a raven would be hard pressed to care for itself and its own, let alone some peripatetic ecclesiastical eccentric. The word *ravens* is a translation of *orbm*. The original Hebrew text actually stated *rbm* and the Masoretes decided to place an *o* in front of it. However, it is more probable that they should have placed an *a* instead, so that the word would have read *arbm*, meaning that Elijah was sustained by *Arabs* not ravens.

Perhaps the Masoretes could not accept that the Old Testament may have taken place in Arabia not Palestine, hence their refusal to write *Arabs*. Theology also influenced the vocalization. The original unvocalized Hebrew text seems to have stated that the *gods*, not *God*, ordered Abraham to sacrifice Isaac. When Isaac asked the whereabouts of the sacrificial ram, Abraham told him the One True God would provide. Since the Masoretes refused to accept the idea of more than one God they changed their vocalization accordingly, making it seem that God ordered human sacrifice but then provided a ram.

Hebrew, like other Semitic languages, is typified by a stem modified verbal system based on a single root word, for example *DBR* and *ŠBR*. In Biblical Hebrew the letters *DBR* can take different meanings, depending on the vowels. *DiBeR* means *he spoke,* while *DeBaR* means *the word of.* In the case of *ŠBR*, *ŠaBaR* means *he broke*, *ŠiBBeR*-he broke to pieces, *niŠBaR* - *he was stranded.* This modified verbal system, which spaces the root letters in different places to change meaning, is difficult enough for non-native speakers to interpret with a living language; it is even more so when dealing with an extinct tongue that lacks vowels.

The Masoretes may have claimed a traditional knowledge of the correct vowels, but modern research has concluded that they relied more on Aramaic pronunciation than on ancient knowledge of the true values. Similar vowel sounds could be interpreted different ways. One sound could mean either *to him* or *not*. Vocabulary also changes. For example, in English the word *treacle* once meant "a wild animal," and *villain* referred to a farm worker, while the Biblical Hebrew word for *destroy* means *repair* in modern Hebrew. Semitic languages like Hebrew experience a process called *metathesis* whereby two sounds or letters in a word change places. [5] An English example would be the change from the Old English *ðridda* to Modern English *third*. In the Old Testament Book of Psalms an example of metathesis occurs where *qrbm* (their inward thoughts) has come to mean *qbrm* (their grave). Other errors can occur when a copyist sees two sentences ending with the same word and neglects to copy one of them. Sometimes a copyist can see a rare word and can decide to put in a more commonly used one, and in other places can fail to copy a letter when it occurs twice in a word. Lastly, several Hebrew letters are similar in appearance, and it is obvious when comparing recently discovered Qumran texts with the Masoretes' work that there has been some confusion.

Despite all these problems, it is most likely that the content of the Masoretic vocalized version of the Old Testament was very close in meaning to the original Old Testament compiled between 500 B.C.E and 100 B.C.E. The two most controversial aspects of the work were the language and the place names.

Biblical Hebrew is an artificial language that was never spoken. It is in essence a mixture of sixth to fifth century B.C.E. Hebrew consonants and A.D. eighth to ninth century Aramaic vowels. Its vocabulary is small, representing maybe a fifth of the original spoken language. The vocabulary has limited functions inevitably concerned with migration, religion, government, warfare, and law. The lack of material makes it difficult to ascertain certain points of grammar. When Eliezer ben Yehuda (aka Eliezer Yitzhak Perelman) and others developed Modern Hebrew towards the end of the nineteenth century they adapted words from Arabic, Aramaic, and other Semitic languages to create an adequate Modern Hebrew vocabulary. Modern Hebrew (Ivrit) is therefore even more of an artificial language than Biblical Hebrew, having a similar history to L. L. Zamenhof's Esperanto, an artificial language developed in the same era, with vocabulary adapted from several Indo-European languages; and Ivar Aasen's Nynorsk (New Norwegian), a composite of "pure" Norwegian dialects free of the Danish modifications that characterize Norway's other official Norwegian language.

The question of place names is far more serious. The vocalization of the Old Testament was dominated by the Tiberian school of the Ben Asher priestly house. The Masoretes scholars as a whole had a very powerful political agenda. They were God's Chosen People, they had a Promised Land, they expected the coming of a military Messiah, and they wished to re-establish a theocracy in Jerusalem. Their insistence that Jews adhere to the Torah was meaningless unless they had a vision for the future, irrespective of any success or happiness they achieved in another country. To obey the Torah was not enough; Jews must restore what had been lost, because without doing so, their existence would be pointless. To them the return to the Promised Land was divinely ordained.

There is no question that the Jews established a theocracy in Jerusalem ca. 400 B.C.E. and later ruled their own independent kingdom. It is not at all certain that this Jerusalem was one and the same place as Solomon's Jerusalem.

Professor Thomas Thompson, whose archaeological work was discussed in the last chapter, commented on 21 August 2000 on this writer's belief that Old and New Jerusalem were not the same place:

> We need a scenario to explain how the misunderstanding of the tradition's geography came about. Conspiracy theories are difficult at best.

This is a very difficult problem to resolve and the answer probably lies in unrecorded discussions in Babylon. There had been two promised lands; one for Abraham, the other for Moses. Jewish tradition identifies both in modern Israel/Palestine although, as shown later, western Arabia is a far more likely candidate. The resolution to Thompson's proposal lies somewhere in the continuum between *agenda* and *conspiracy*. Ezra's group was later severely criticized for doctoring the Old Testament but at the same time the final books of the Old Testament appear to suffer from an enormous lack of editing.

In ninth-century A.D. Babylon and Galilee such an issue was probably of no consequence. Palestinian Jerusalem had been Ezekiel's dream. It was the child of Ezra, the site of Herod's great temple, and the capital of the great rebellion against Roman rule. But were the Old Testament texts deliberately vocalized accordingly to fit the scenario that Palestinian Jerusalem had been the Solomon's Jerusalem and Palestine the Promised Land? Certainly the Masoretes made Old Testament locations match their own worldview. The original text said Abraham came from *R*, Noah's Ark rested on dry land at *rrt*, and that Joshua crossed the *h-yrdn* to reach the Promised Land. The Masoretes placed vowels in these words to match place names they knew. They decided that Abraham came from *Ur* in Mesopotamia and the Ark of Noah came down on *Ararat*. The original text for Abraham's first home is *R*, which is vocalized elsewhere as *'Ir* meaning *city* as in the City of David. As for Ararat being the Ark's resting place, *rrt* more likely means a high place (as in the Arabic word *herrat*) than a mountain in Turkey near the place where they were editing the final version of the Old Testament. *H-yrdn*, which the Masoretes vocalized to mean *the Jordan*, is never referred to as a river in the Old Testament. Most likely it meant a ridge or escarpment, while the words *Msrm* and *Kws*, which were taken to mean Egypt and Ethiopia/Sudan, probably refer to ancient cities near Yemen, an idea to be examined later.

Despite Ezra's codification of the Old Testament, the Jewish community of New Jerusalem as a whole was neither a literate nor well-informed one. The Muslims were later shocked to find that the Jews had no well-defined method of transmitting sacred texts from the earliest times down through the ages. A copy of the Old Testament was kept in the temple but rarely consulted. Other materials were rare and have long disappeared. Both Josephus and Paul owned prestigious texts, now lost, that held different information from that found in the Old Testament. How well any fifth-century B.C.E. Jerusalem priest or citizen knew Middle Eastern geography is difficult to ascertain. Ezra's community was originally known as *Aliyeh*, the name the Romans themselves later called it. Only later did it become Jerusalem. For a people so acutely aware of their history it is odd that the whereabouts of the ten "lost" tribes was never discovered, and also that the loss the Ark of the Covenant went unreported. While these two anomalies are nowhere near clinching arguments, they do convey a feeling of vagueness. As later Muslim commentators discovered, the Jewish priesthood, let alone the ordinary people, seemed to know very little about the origin and transmission of their most sacred texts through the ages. Perhaps Zerubbabel's followers were initially aware that the Palestinian *Aliyeh* was not Solomon's ancient capital, and that only later did the priesthood begin to blur the two, a process accelerated when the Maccabees created an independent state centered on the new Jerusalem and Herod built a magnificent new temple.

The nature of the Zadokite tradition indicates the generations after Ezra sincerely believed that Palestine was the Promised Land. Much of the Old Testament's appeal comes from faith, the belief that an inflexible will in pursuit of a clear objective, however difficult, will be ultimately rewarded. If they believed Palestine was not the Promised Land, they would have made every effort to regain the true location. Perhaps Zerubbabel and Ezra saw the Aliyeh settlement as the first step to an empire that would eventually regain the true Promised Land. Certainly the militant Judaic rulers of sixth-century A.D. Mahoza and Himyar saw their struggle in global terms. Whatever their attitudes, by A.D. 143, when the Palestine Jews were dispersed, all Jews firmly believed that Palestine was the

Promised Land. In addition, the concept of invading and taking land away from a long-established native population was not seriously challenged until the second half of the twentieth century A.D. It was within this mental framework that the definitive version of the Old Testament was written. In conclusion it seems that although the exilic Jews of Babylon had a relatively privileged position, they wanted their own state. The offer of Aliyeh in Palestine presented an opportunity to begin again like Moses in Sinai. Most likely in Solomon's day a small Israelite community had indeed lived in Aliyeh and the city had been considered either a staging post for later expansion to the real Promised Land or an ancient temporary outpost of the old Solomonid Empire, an idea supported by the presence there of a sizeable Samaritan community when Zerubbabel led the Judaean exiles to Palestine to build the New Jerusalem. None could foresee the future, where a new science called archaeology would uncover the past. Even if Aliyeh had never been part of the Promised Land, it seemed to matter little because it became the center of the Hasmonean state, the Second Temple, and the ferocious resistance to the Romans - reasons enough to respect it as the location of a major part of Jewish history. However, claiming it to be the site of the Old Testament has not only brought tragedy to the Palestinians but also insult and ridicule to the history, traditions, and religions of Arabia and Ethiopia, in particular to the memory of the Queen of Sheba. This is extremely ironic, because the Queen of Sheba is the key to discovering the true location of the Promised Land.

CHAPTER FOUR

The Queen of Sheba

> Fundamentalism provides security. For the fundamentalist, as for all reactionaries, everything has been decided. Truth has been agreed and nothing must change. For serene liberals, on the other hand, the consolations of knowing seem less satisfying than the pleasures of puzzlement, and of wanting to discover for oneself.
>
> Hanif Kureishi. *Independent*, UK, Saturday, 9 August 1997

The landscape of the northern Ethiopian highlands, which also cross into southern Eritrea, is rocky, barren, and frequently dry. Nevertheless, it is still a beautiful place, and its high altitude allows for a pleasant climate. Once, however, it must have seemed a paradise. In the past there were great forests and permanent rivers. Elephant, rhino, crocodile, and other game were abundant, and rainfall so reliable that crops could be harvested twice a year without the need for irrigation. Remains of some of the world's earliest hominids dating back millions of years have been uncovered in the southeast, where erosion has enabled excavation on the lower slopes towards Djibouti. The first known examples of *Homo sapiens*, modern people, also had their home here. They were slightly built hunter-gatherers, identical to the San (Bushmen) of the Kalahari. Ancient Egyptian records speak also of pygmies. Much later, but still thousands of years ago, farmers inhabited the coastal plains of Sudan in the northwest and traded with the ancient Egyptians. Several locations have been put forward as the possible location of the legendary land of Punt, but this area, ranging from the Red Sea coast around Suakin to the Gash Delta around Kassala in Sudan, is the most convincing candidate. Punt provided exotic luxuries for the Egyptian ruling elite – ivory, ebony, frankincense, gold, and slaves, especially pygmies. In about 1100 B.C.E., the Egyptian trade with Punt ceased after the pharaohs moved their capital to the Nile Delta. The climate was also changing and the plains below the Ethiopian plateau were becoming increasingly inhospitable. The farmers made their way up to the Ethiopian plateau from the river valleys of Punt in the north and the flood plain of the Awash in the south. On the plateau they developed market centers and trading links not only with the Nile valley but also with Arabia, Persia, and the Greek city states. Legend has it that eventually they traded with and settled in Madagascar and in East Africa.

Ethiopia may very well be the cradle of human beings. Many theories exist as to why millions of years ago slight monkey-like creatures evolved into bipeds that made stone tools and weapons. Human beings have two fewer chromosomes than bonobos and chimpanzees, animals so closely related to people that some zoologists say they, along with gorillas and orangutans, should be classified as such. The reason for evolution may rest with a changing environment. Another theory is that the loss of two chromosomes was caused by radon gas produced by the Rift valley's shifting tectonic plates, vaporizing ancient radium deposits. According to this theory radon gas caused a sustained genetic mutation generation after generation until the ancestors of modern people emerged. Whatever the cause, Ethiopia will remain a principal area for investigating the origins of human beings.

Approximately 3,000 years ago farmers entered the Ethiopian plateau and developed small markets. New archaeological evidence suggests that these plateau market centers evolved into states probably before 1000 B.C.E. Remains at Gobedra near Aksum, generally considered the birthplace of the Ethiopian state and its Christian culture, have revealed iron smelting dating back ca.1000 B.C.E. Red-orange pottery mixed with iron slag at Gobedra is linked to Shurab el Gash, 35 kilometers south of Kassala in Sudan. Possibly, this was the route along which iron smelting was introduced from southwest Arabia. The iron workers herded cattle, and it is likely they also grew crops. Certainly iron implements would have made land clearance and cultivation easier.

Aksumite traditions state that the first capital was established by Ithiopis, son of Kush. Its name was Mazber and lay on a hill north east of May Qoho, near modern Aksum. The second city, Asba (or Asfa) was founded by the Queen of Sheba on the slopes or even the summit of Beta Giyorgis hill overlooking the site of modern Aksum, which was, until the fourth century A.D., a large swamp. Asba was also known as Dabra

Makeda (the place of the Queen of Sheba). The present city of Aksum was established in the fourth century A.D. on former swampland below Beta Giyorgis.

The most recent major archaeological report on the western and southern slopes of Beta Giyorgis reveals that, in the Pre-Aksumite Phase I archaeological stratum (ca. late 2nd – early 1st millennium B.C.E.), a more sophisticated culture was emerging that included foot washing basins and large high necked jars.[1]

The early Semitic-speaking Ethiopians left inscriptions. Semitic speakers include Hebrew, Sabaeans, Arabs, Akkadians, and Arameans, none of whom wrote with vowels until the Christian era. The Ge'ez speakers of Ethiopia were the first Semitic people to write with vowels, but the surviving inscriptions of this era (ca. 1000 - 500 B.C.E.) were written only with consonants. The first major state is therefore known to us only as D'mt, its capital most likely Yeha. The inscriptions are from that area.

Archaeology at Yeha (Level II) has uncovered the same red-orange pottery found at Gobedra (Level II) and Shurab el Gash. Today Yeha is a scrubby little village next to a wide well-watered plain where cattle graze. It is a respected center of the Ethiopian Orthodox Church and the priests there will show visitors illuminated Bibles as well as crowns worn by the late emperor Haile Selaisse (1930-1974). Dotted through the village among the cacti, where parrots flutter, are the remains of substantial ancient buildings; and although some of the huge building blocks have been removed for other purposes, a very large edifice remains, accepted by most as a temple dating back to ca. 500 B.C.E. The temple at Yeha is composed of large, smooth stone blocks, most likely built without mortar. The stones are put together in such a way as to channel rain away from the seams. The temple is twenty meters long, fifteen meters wide and twelve meters high. A later Christian ruler increased the height of the walls with inferior brickwork and left a frame outside marking his own great height. Christians, however, were not responsible for the temple's large baptistery, which Christian churches later imitated. The Orthodox churches of the Horn of Africa are noteworthy for their prominent baptisteries, which are set aside from the main part of the church and consist, as at the Yeha temple, of steps descending to an oval pool. It is interesting to see that the Yeha temple, with links to the Sabaeans of southern Arabia, represents a pagan culture that inspired later Christian ecclesiastical architecture.

The Sabaeans are better known outside Arabia and Ethiopia by their other name – *Shebans*. The southern Arabians shared close ethnic and linguistic traits with the peoples of the Ethiopian plateau. Sabaeans were found on both sides of the Red Sea in the first millennium B.C.E. but eventually lost their separate identity in Ethiopia.

Across the northern Ethiopian border lies the state of Eritrea, which shares much of Ethiopia's culture and history. From 1890 until the Second World War, Eritrea was an Italian colony with a large socially diverse Italian population. Eritrea in the 1940s was Africa's second most industrialized country and was hopeful of attaining freedom under a democratic parliamentary system. In 1952, it became, under controversial circumstances, a federation with feudal, autocratic Ethiopia. The Ethiopians abolished the Eritrean assembly, turned the country into a province in 1962, and incited a vicious thirty-year war of independence. Since 1993, Eritrea has been an independent country but deeply scarred by the war's destruction, and subsequent conflict. Its capital is Asmara, one of the most beautiful and well-organized cities in Africa. Asmara has boulevards, villas, houses, a magnificent opera house, parks, squares, government buildings, a university, a cafe society, and an Italian style Catholic cathedral. Most Asmarans over fifty still understand and speak Italian.

In Asmara, there is a fertile strip of land that begins below the Italian-built University of Asmara. This strip follows an ancient watercourse, *Mai Bela*. Even in the recent past the area was forested and well watered, but during the late 1980s the Ethiopian army stripped the area bare of trees for cooking fuel. Consequently, the Mai Bela stream of today is rarely a river, remaining for most of the year a series of pools that merge only when there is a downpour. The old riverbed winds northeast, away from the city, across a wide often wind-swept plain. Twelve kilometers from the city it passes two kilometers below the ancient settlement of Tsa'edakristyan, which means *White Christian* in Tigrinya, the local language. Here the stream contains more water than elsewhere, and it seems that in the past, where the stream curves, there must have been a wide pool. The water at this point is still relatively deep, and there are thick reeds on the far bank where weaverbirds have made their nests. On the riverbank facing the distant village there is a rocky outcrop, and here you will find a vandalized memorial. A single obelisk in the ancient Aksumite style stands about six meters tall in the middle of a small semicircular wall. There used to be a plaque at its base, but this has been wrenched off and destroyed. As an added indignity, a bicycle tire has been tossed over the top of the obelisk, becoming wedged a meter from its pinnacle. Unless you look around this lonely spot to ask (and few people pass this way), there is no way of knowing what the ruined monument commemorates.

Tradition claims that this is the place where the biblical Queen of Sheba gave birth to her only child, Bayna Lekhem, better known as Menelik, after returning from her state visit to the court of King Solomon, ruler of Judah and Israel. During Ethiopian rule, the local Eritrean population regularly vandalized the monument, which commemorated Menelik's birth, because it was associated with the Ethiopian emperor Haile Selaisse, whose authority over Eritrea was based on his claim as the descendant of Menelik. Local tradition says that the words "Mai Bela," were uttered by the queen after giving birth and mean either "Give me water," or "Give me a razor [to cut the umbilical cord]."

The Eritrean and Ethiopian plateau is full of unexplored archaeological sites. Most of the remains belong to the time when Aksum had become a large trading empire, i.e., from ca. 200 B.C.E. onwards. There are substantial ruins dating back from hundreds of years earlier than this, but it is probable that nothing can specifically be linked to the time of the Queen of Sheba (ca. 970 B.C.E.). At Cohaito, overlooking the coastal plain, there are ruins of an ancient city extending twelve by six kilometers. It was here that the Aksumites of the Red Sea port of Adulis took refuge from the summer heat. From Cohaito inland to Aksum and Yeha are a large number of ancient towns dating from this period, all of them having prospered on trade and agriculture. Many are associated with the Queen of Sheba. At Cohaito there is a large oval area marked by green grass that is nurtured by underground water and edged with stones. It is known as the Queen of Sheba's bath. In Aksum there is a large reservoir with the same name. Hinzat and Gulo Makeda near Aksum are respectively believed to have been her capital and birthplace. Moreover, at Cohaito there is a cave that tradition says is the entrance to a labyrinth that the queen followed during her journey to Aksum. A similar story comes from nearby Metera and from Aksum itself, where, in fact, many man-made tunnels exist. Other buildings are erroneously associated with the Queen of Sheba but date long after her time, among them the palace outside Aksum and the massive Marib dam in Yemen as well as Marib itself. It is therefore interesting to see that the Mai Bela memorial is far from away from any modern settlement or discernable ancient ruin and rather far away to the north of the other sites associated with the queen.

The Old Testament mentions several historical figures from other Middle Eastern states prior to the Babylonian captivity such as Sheshonk,

Shabaka, and Sennacherib. The most important figure to support the Old Testament's veracity is, however, the Queen of Sheba, who paid a state visit to Solomon's court and is mentioned in the book of Kings, the book of Chronicles, in the New Testament by Christ in Matthew and in Luke, by Flavius Josephus, in the Islamic Qur'an, and in the Ge'ez *Kebra Nagast*.

If the story of the Queen of Sheba is true, it can therefore prove that the Old Testament is also true. But this presents a paradox. Jewish tradition and even modern scholarship not only denigrate the Queen of Sheba but often dismiss her as a myth.

Of all the figures in the Old Testament, the Queen of Sheba was the only one with a truly questioning mind, the one person who wanted to find the truth, and not have it dictated to her. Her story deals with more than a meeting with Solomon. It also covers the founding of a new Zion in Africa, but most of all it tells the story of her life, which is the key to understanding the history of the Old Testament, the minds of the priests that created Judaism, and the world that women lost. The story of the Queen of Sheba is very much about the human spirit, freedom of thought, intellectual inquiry, and confidence in the essential goodness of people.

Sheba's realm is usually referred to by archaeologists as *Sabaea*. Today people in the area she once ruled in Africa will look blankly if asked about "Sheba" but respond enthusiastically to "Saba." All authorities agree that Sabaea was located at the southern end of the Red Sea in Arabia but also extended to substantial settlements in Africa.

Strong monsoons brought increased rainfall to southern Arabia between 7000 and 3000 B.C.E. producing thick vegetation, which in turn produced highly fertile soils. The era from 3000 to 1000 B.C.E. was southern Arabia's Bronze Age. Early in this period terraced cultivation was introduced that sustained a large population. Even today Yemen has one of the highest population densities in the Middle East (100-150 per square kilometer). Arab traditions say that the Arabs are descended from two groups of people: the first from north-central Arabia associated with Ishmael, Abraham's son by Hagar; and the second from the southwest corner of Yemen. The origins of the Bronze Age Yemenis are unknown, but it is possible they were African Semitic or even Cushitic speakers.

By the time the first written inscriptions began appearing in southern Arabia around 1000 B.C.E. it is clear that one population group identified itself as Sabaeans (Shebans) and had achieved some influence or control over other peoples in the same area. From this evidence it seems that the

Sabaeans were Iron Age Ishmaelite Semites who immigrated to the Yemen, initially to dominate, but eventually mixing with the local population.

The Queen of Sheba is associated with the town of Marib in the southern part of Yemen. This is where the Sabaeans, a Semitic speaking people, eventually established hegemony over other Semitic and perhaps Cushitic speakers. Although recent excavations at Marib indicate it was an important center during the queen's era, it is probable that she had her capital more to the north. There are indications that the Sabaeans in the past were in the Hijaz area of modern Saudi Arabia. A number of Lihyanic (Old South Semitic) inscriptions have been discovered in the region between Khaybar and Taima dating from at least the sixth century B.C.E. Some researchers have identified this area with biblical Dedan, and it later became the northernmost frontier of traders from Yemen in the early Christian era. H. St John Philby, in his book on the Queen of Sheba, believed that her realm was located in northern Arabia during Solomon's time and that the Sabaeans, or more likely their ruling house, did not move south until the seventh century B.C.E., probably as a result of Assyrian expansion. This is in line with recent suggestions that, while the queen did control Marib, her political capital was in the area of Khamis Mushait in Saudi Arabia. Linguistic evidence and Arab traditions testify that western Arabia's population as a whole appears to have migrated from the south northwards, but the ruling houses and the populations they ruled often were of separate origin and could also make some quite dramatic relocations, for example the Hebrew Exodus, the seventh-century A.D. Islamic expansion from Arabia, and the eleventh century A.D. migration of the Banu Hillal and Banu Salaim Bedouin from Egypt westwards across northern Africa. The Queen of Sheba herself seems to have ruled in Arabia at the beginning of her career and in Ethiopia at its end. Onomastic (study of names) evidence links Sabaean to the language of the Amorites, rulers of Mesopotamia ca. 1900-1600 B.C.E.

Most of what we know about the Sabaeans comes centuries after the time of the Queen of Sheba, when Marib was indeed the center of the Sabaean state. The northern parts of Sabaea, in the Yemeni provinces of Asir and Jizan, were forcibly annexed by Saudi Arabia in the 1930s. Unfortunately the Saudis have what can only be politely called a different intellectual outlook from the Yemenis, so there has been no significant research undertaken there on the Sabaean past. Impressive research has been accomplished in depth on some aspects of Sabaean civilization in Yemen, Ethiopia, and Eritrea but hardly anything on the vital Saudi Arabia section linking the two areas. This area of Saudi Arabia almost certainly contains answers not only to Sabaean, but, as will be shown later, to early Old Testament history.

Looking at the evidence solely from the Yemen, archaeologists have concluded that Sabaean civilization should be divided into three main periods: the *ancient*, being the 1,000 years before Christ; the *middle* from the time of Christ till the fourth century A.D.; and the *late*, from the end of fourth century until the sixth century A.D. After that, the area came under Islamic rule, and the Sabaean language was superseded by Classical Arabic. The ancient period, which most concerns this study, was divided into two sub periods, the first lasting until about 500 B.C.E. and the second until the time of Christ.

The Sabaean alphabet possessed twenty-nine consonants, which exceeded those of any other Semitic language. Three different kinds of the letter *s* are transcribed in Roman script as s^1, s^2, and s^3 while the sound represented by ^{C} is identical to the pharyngeal Arabic *'ayn*. In the first part of the ancient period, the time of the Queen of Sheba, the population of Yemen was organized in small social and political units called *'s^2 ^Cb* (singular *s^2 ^Cb*). These *'s^2 ^Cb* were small autonomous or independent political entities with a center where Yemenis took communal decisions, for instance, on maintenance and control of the irrigation system, and where the local religious cult leader organized ceremonies. The ruler's title was either *mlk* (king or queen) or *bkr* (first born) and he or she exercised authority over a village serving not only as the local market but also as the administrative and religious cult center. It appears that around the time of the Queen of Sheba, the Sabaeans created a large confederation of the *'s^2 ^Cb*, whose leader was known as the *mkrb SB*. The title of *mkrb* referred to a priest-king or priestess-queen.[2] The Queen of Sheba was most probably the leader of the Sabaean religious cult. The *Kebra Nagast* (chapter 27) records her description of the state religion:

> We worship the sun like our ancestors also did. We revere the sun as the most important of the gods. There are some amongst us who acknowledge other deities from nature such as rocks and trees, while others have carved figures representing divine forces. We worship the sun because...she lightens the darkness and banishes fear. We call her "Our Queen" and "Our Creator."

South Arabian inscriptions also speak of a single deity, *the* God, named *Rahman* (the Merciful One). The Prophet Muhammad, tried to make his followers refer to the One True God as *Rahman*, but eventually abandoned the attempt as they were too used to *Allah*. Charles Cutler Torrey, describing inscriptions from a southern Arabian monument associated with Rahman, noted:

> Here we find clearly indicated the doctrines of the divine forgiveness of sins, the acceptance of sacrifice, the contrast between this world and the next, and the evil of "associating" other deities with the Rahman.[3]

The political confederation in the early Yemenite confederation consisted of a core of Sabaeans ruling non-Sabaean $`s^{2C}b$ who were referred to as *w-gwm*, meaning other non-Sabaean communities. The Sabaeans/Shebans were known as $s^{2C}b$ *Saba'* and referred to on inscriptions as *SB* or *'SB'N*.

By 500 B.C.E. this Sabaean confederation had contracted, and the leaders of the core Sabaean element no longer styled themselves *mkrb*. After that date communities associated with the concept of Sabaea were often not Sabaeans themselves but drawn from non-Sabaean $`s^{2C}b$. The Sabaeans established a center in Marib, but political control over the rest of Yemen and respect for the Sabaean deity *Almaqah*, a moon god whose prestige must have eclipsed the queen's sun god *Shams*, fluctuated to such an extent that it would be a misnomer to term this arrangement a state; rather an area sharing a common culture and association with a long established political institution of local origin whose earlier power had considerably waned. It is reasonable to conclude that the long-standing respect accorded to the Sabaean ruling dynasty stemmed from the early Ancient period when it was at its most powerful and prosperous. This matches the biblical account of the Queen of Sheba's visit to Jerusalem, when it was clear that her realm controlled considerable wealth.

The Sabaeans developed an extensive irrigation system that later included the massive earthen dam at Marib and supported what in Arabia was a relatively prosperous agricultural economy. Much of their society was based on cooperation in controlling and allocating water supplies, a system that became more complex as the Arabian interior began to dry up around 2000 B.C.E. Trade routes realigned themselves to the more fertile highland escarpments that also sustained cash crops exported to Egypt and to the Mediterranean region. Domestication of the camel in about 1300 B.C.E. enabled the Sabaeans to engage in long-distance overland trade, while their geographic position also encouraged sea trade with East Africa and India.

The inhabitants of the rapidly encroaching deserts adopted a nomadic existence, while the settled agricultural areas of the southern Arabian highlands developed prosperous urban areas. Trade commodities were highly varied. Sabaea produced gold, frankincense, and myrrh. The Red Sea area (Somalia and South Arabia) were home to many different kinds of aromatic plants. Chief among them were the oleo gum resins frankincense and myrrh, as valuable as gold, from the botanical family *Burseraceae*. Frankincense (genus *Boswelli*) varied from yellowish-brown to an almost colorless state and was burned throughout the ancient world for religious ceremonies and funerals. Myrrh (genus *Commiphora*), a reddish gum resin, was equally in demand for a vast range of medicinal purposes and embalming the dead. Myrrh was and is still used as a local anesthetic, an aphrodisiac paste, and to treat snakebite, gum disease, stomach and chest ailments, scurvy, internal parasites, malaria, and wounds. It has proven anti bacterial and fungal properties and is reputed to strengthen teeth. [4] Today the most prized frankincense comes from Dhofar on the Yemen-Oman border and it is likely the case was the same in the remote past. Myrrh is found in the same area but today the bulk is harvested in Somalia, Kenya, and Ethiopia. The marks of ancient but now abandoned camel caravan routes can still be seen throughout southern Arabia. The use of camels provided a safer transport alternative for traders who had lost so many cargoes at sea because of piracy or the northern winds that blew across the Arabian Gulf and Red Sea for most of the year. Spices, perfumes, and precious stones passed through from India, and their volume was such that the Hebrew of Solomon's time adopted several Indian words including, according to Chaim Rabin, what seems to be ancient Tamil [5] for trade goods in this period. From Dhofar the routes stretched west to Shibam, Shabwa, Tumna, and Marib and then north through Najran to Medina, Taima and Petra; and north across the Rub al Khali to the Arabian Gulf and Mesopotamia. Large caravan cities developed at strategic centers such as Najran and Taima, where traders could obtain fresh water supplies, food, fodder, and stable government.

Royal houses were often associated with different religions. In the southern Saudi city of Najran there are a number of unexcavated archaeological sites significantly predating Islam. Among them is a wall exhibiting a giant snake. Although visitors are forbidden to inspect this area, where a major pagan pilgrim shrine once existed as well as a Christian cathedral of later importance, the snake motive is probably a relic of an ancient but widespread religion linked to ruling houses. Across the Red Sea in Ethiopian Aksum, the city that launched Caleb's sixth century A.D. Christian crusade to Najran after its Christian inhabitants had been slaughtered by Yusuf, the Jewish king of Himyar, there are a number of large stelae marking the graves of ancient rulers. Several of them have toppled over. One has an engraved outline of a house or box, which some people believe depicts the Ark of the Covenant. This stele has fallen on uneven ground, so it is possible to look under it and see the engraved outline of a giant serpent. No one knows with any certainty the origin of giant snake cults there. It is possible the Egyptians were influential in their proliferation, because in dynastic Egypt large snakes symbolized royal power and wisdom, and this belief was echoed in other parts of Africa and Arabia. An ancient story tells of a shipwrecked sailor washed up on an island, probably Socotra (whose name, incidentally, is Sanskrit in origin), where he encounters the ruler, a giant serpent covered in gold, that helps him find his way home and declines offers of gifts because it is too rich to need any.

If the snake god cult was inspired by Bronze Age Egypt, it is significant that replacing it with the Sabaean sun god in southern Arabia occurred at the beginning of the Iron Age, for the Sabaeans, like the Hebrew, were an Iron Age people. This change also took place across the Red Sea in Aksum, a city centered in an area with Sabaean links. Aksumite traditions say that their city was once ruled by a dynasty of the snake-god king of foreign origin named Arwe. Around 1370 B.C.E. under Za Besi Angabo this dynasty was replaced by a local ruling house. This new dynasty ruled for about 350 years and it is from that Makeda, Queen of Sheba, descended.

Makeda may not have been the queen's original name. Josephus referred to her as Nikaule, which in Greek means *conqueror*. Arab traditions say her name was Bilqis (Bilkis/Belkis/Balkis), perhaps a corruption of the Hebrew word *pilgesh* (concubine). However Bilqis was probably a Himyarite princess of the fourth century A.D., not the Queen of Sheba. Professor Bill Glanzman, a Canadian archaeologist specializing on Sheba, reports that Bilqis may be a contraction of *Bi al-Qos*, meaning a woman connected to *al-Qos (or Qosh)*, a north Arabian deity. The earliest record of this name is the ninth century A.D. Azariah, the Zadokite high priest, is reported to have given the queen the name Makeda after his arrival in her capital explaining its meaning as *"not this way"*. Conversely, the queen's name may have been Bilqis, which was then adopted into Hebrew deliberately as a word to mean concubine in order to insult and denigrate her.

According to Ethiopian traditions a ruler named Za Sebado (ca. 1070-1026 B.C.E.) had a daughter named Ismenie who married the kingdom's chief minister. This minister then ruled jointly as king with his royally born wife from about 1026 –1005 B.C.E. They had two children, Makeda and Noural Rouz, a boy who died in childhood after being accidentally burned. Interestingly, the word *rouz* occurs in earliest known Hebrew and means "prince". Makeda was born ca. 1020 B.C.E. and became queen when she was fifteen, ruling until about 955 B.C.E. when she surrendered the throne to her son Menelik. Her supposed birthplace is Gulo Makeda, a short instance to the northwest of Yeha on the Ethiopian-Eritrean border, and her capital was Hinzat, a town east of Adwa. Gulo Makeda and Hinzat were two of many prosperous settlements on the route from the Red Sea port Adulis to Aksum. Hinzat has visible ancient ruins, but no archaeological work has been carried out there.

This tradition concerning Makeda's background resembles others from southern Arabia. A tenth century A.D. Muslim writer named Hamdani, who died in Sana'a in Yemen, wrote that the Queen of Sheba was born in Arabia, the daughter of Ekeye Azeb, an Aksumite princess, and Shar Habil, ruler of Yemen. Hamdani said that the Queen of Sheba's name was Bilqis and that she spent part of her youth in Aksum, returning to Arabia just before her father's death. A second Yemeni tradition, recorded by Saadiah Ben Joseph in about A.D. 1702, said that the Queen of Sheba's father was a chief minister to the king of Sheba, but that her mother was a *jinn* (genie). It is not known if the word *jinn* has always meant a fantasy being. In other cultures references to fairies, "little people," and others of the kind have occasionally had an historical basis. It is likely that in ancient times farming and pastoral societies encountered small hunter-gatherer peoples credited with magical powers - the San of the Kalahari desert and Namibia are modern examples; and perhaps the Grendel story of the Anglo-Saxon epic *Beowulf* refers to a remnant Neanderthal or hominid population now long extinct. DNA testing in Wales, in mountainous western Britain, has revealed the existence of a pre-Celtic population remnant related to highland peoples in Papua New Guinea,[6] giving strength to the belief that thousands of years ago there was a worldwide population of small hunter-gatherers who were obliterated or absorbed by later migrations of farmers and pastoralists. Their remnants still exist today in Tanzania, southern

Africa, Socotra, India, the Andaman Islands, Malaysia, Philippines, and Papua New Guinea. In modern Yemen there is a caste of menial laborers called *akhdam*, whose social rank is lower than former slaves. Marriage into the higher *qaba'il* social levels are rare, the reason often being given that the Akhdam are jinn. The Akhdam have African ancestry but discrimination against them seems based more on caste connotations. Perhaps the reference to the Queen of Sheba's mother as a jinn meant she was not a mischievous spirit but either a foreigner with unusual powers (perhaps a knowledge of medicine, divination, even rainmaking) or a member of an unrelated ethnic group famed for magical practices or skills such as metalworking. This aspect is worth emphasizing because it could explain the success the Queen of Sheba had in the next part of her career.

When the future queen was twelve, i.e. marriageable, the King of Sheba, deeply impressed by her intelligence, successfully approached her father to take her as his wife to make her joint ruler as Queen of Sheba. This tradition is supported by Sabaean inscriptions at Abuna Garima near Mekele in northern Ethiopia that testify to the joint rule of Sabaean kings and queens, a practice imitated in Aksum even as late as the mid-sixth century A.D. when two kings ruled jointly. The young woman remained queen after her husband's death and was assisted by the jinn, her mother's people. Perhaps the seeming fantasy of this story is in fact an account of two different groups in Arabia that the queen united as her parents came from each side. From the other traditions it would appear that one community would be Sabaeans moving south; the other, a Semitic people from or closely related to the people of Aksum with whom the Sabaeans intermarried.

A third tradition, from Arabia, again maintains that the Queen of Sheba was the daughter of the *chief minister* of Shar Habil, ruler of Yemen, and a jinn. When ordered to marry the king she got him drunk and beheaded him, after which she was proclaimed queen. Another Muslim writer, al-Kisa`i, speaks of Dhu Sharkh ibn Hudad, an extremely good-looking *wazir* (minister) of the ruler of Sheba. This young man was smitten by the beauty of 'Umarah, daughter of the king of the jinn. He obtained permission to marry 'Umarah and she bore Bilqis, the future Queen of Sheba who ascended to the monarchy, according to al-Kisa`i's account, by beheading Sharakh ibn Sharahil, the tyrannical ruler of Sheba. Nashwan ibn Sa'id al-Himyari, writing in the twelfth century A.D. and claiming to be descended from the Queen of Sheba's family, said her father's name was al-Hadhad ibn Sharah ibn Dhu Sahar. The similarities of the traditions - the minister father, a foreign or magical mother, links with both Africa and Arabia, her intelligence and beauty, and her youth when she became ruler - strongly indicate a common origin. The Persians, who later ruled Yemen, believe the Queen of Sheba was the daughter of a Chinese king and a *peri*, in Persian tradition a beautiful supernatural being. It has also been suggested that the early Zhou dynasty (ca. 1000 B.C.E.) beliefs about Xi Wang Mu, a Chinese Daoist deity known as the Queen of the West with jurisdiction over female jinn, evolved from stories of the Queen of Sheba.

As a child, according to Wahb ibn Munabbihi, the Queen of Sheba was as "radiant as the brightest sun" and grew up to be the greatest beauty in the land. The traditions of the Yemeni Jews confirm this but testified also to her intelligence for "she was more able at solving riddles [than her talented mother]."

Very little is known about everyday life during the time of the Queen of Sheba, i.e. 3000 years ago. Commentators suggest that society was probably very much the same a thousand years after her death, partly because southern Arabia's geographical isolation and control of lucrative trade routes enabled the people to maintain a prosperous, peaceful, and relatively egalitarian society. Women had far more influence than their contemporaries in Judah, and this was evidently conducive to a more balanced society. This is not to say Sabaea was some sort of utopia, for traditions speak of power struggles and court intrigues involving the queen herself. However, the relationship between men and women were not thrown seriously out of balance until the sixth and seventh centuries A.D., when male-dominated religions, e.g. Jewish, Christian, and Persian Zoroastrianism (in which Primal Woman is a prostitute), brought their theological and political disputes to the region and were then overwhelmed by Islam. The reason that women retained an equitable position in societies after the introduction of a centralized Iron Age state may be linked to the nature of the Sabaean economy. Perhaps large numbers of both male and female workers were needed for cultivating and harvesting frankincense, and for maintaining terraced agriculture, irrigation works, long-range camel caravan trading, and other activities. If women were vital to the state's prosperity it is logical that they would have been given far more freedom than in societies where profitable activities such as trade and the priesthood were controlled exclusively by men. Recent experience shows that in a traditional male-dominated society - South Korea's for example - economic prosperity at first enables women to attain more freedom, but during a recession women are the first to lose their jobs. The strictures enumerated in the Hebrew Torah reflect a nomad society where close control of womenfolk was considered a vital part of survival. Such a social structure would not have served the Sabaeans very well.

From the queen's own statements in chapter 27 of the *Kebra Nagast*, her deities were remote, and people's minds were not fettered by an ever-present, demanding, perhaps even suffocating all-powerful god. This is not a fanciful picture, because it is clear from modern-day study of religions developing in this period that free will and women were collectively regarded as evils to be curbed, and the Queen of Sheba became a symbol of both. The Queen of Sheba revered the sun god, in her mind a benign reliable force that did not impede the development of intellectual potential. Her words stand in sharp contrast to the Old Testament tradition that straitjacketed and discouraged intellectual development:

> Listen to me, my people, and take note of what I say. I desire wisdom and my heart yearns for understanding. I am in love with wisdom, and I am led by the leash of understanding, for wisdom is greater than any wealth, and nothing you will find in this world can compete with it. So what can you compare it to? It is sweeter than honey, and more enjoyable than wine. It dims the sun and devalues the most precious gem. It sustains you more than oil, it's more delicious than the choicest food, and a wealthy man without it is nobody...No realm can survive without wisdom, nor can prosperity continue without it.
>
> *Kebra Nagast*, chapter 24

There are differing accounts that explain why the queen came to Solomon's court. The first written Israelite account of the story of Solomon and Sheba may have been in *The Book of the Acts of Solomon*, which *1 Kings 11:41* refers to but no longer exists, although it is possible that accounts of the queen's dealings with Solomon by Flavius Josephus (ca. A.D. 37/38 – 100) and in the *Sheba-Menelik Cycle* of the *Kebra Nagast* are based on it. This is the account in 1 Kings, Chapter 10:1-13:

> The Queen of Sheba heard of Solomon's fame through the name of Yhwh and she came to test him with riddles.(2) She arrived in Jerusalem with a very large retinue and with camels bearing spices, a great quantity of gold, and precious stones. When she came to Solomon, she asked him all that was on her mind. (3) Solomon had answers for all of her questions; there was nothing that he did not know, anything to which he could not give an answer. (4) When the Queen of Sheba observed all of Solomon's wisdom and the palace that he had built (5)

and the fare of his table, the seating of his retainers, the service and attire of his attendants, his wine service, and the burnt offerings that he offered at the House of Yhwh, it broke her spirit. (6) She said to the king, "The report that I heard in my own land about you and your wisdom was true. (7) But I did not believe the reports until I came and saw with my own eyes that what had been told me was not even the half of it. Your wisdom and wealth surpass the reports that I heard. (8) How fortunate are your people and servants, those who stand always before you and listen to your wisdom. (9) Blessed be Yhwh your God who delighted in you and set you on the throne of Israel. It is because of Yhwh's eternal love for Israel that he made you king to administer justice and rule with righteousness." (10) She then presented the king with 120 bars of gold and an enormous quantity of spices and precious stones. Never again did so vast a quantity of spices arrive as that which the Queen of Sheba gave Solomon. (13) King Solomon [reciprocated] satisfying all the Queen of Sheba's desires in addition to what he gave her in his official capacity as king. Then she and her retainers left and returned to her own land.

Flavius Josephus published his work in Greek at the end of the first century A.D. He drew information from his own collection of unnamed ancient documents. His account of the Queen of Sheba's visit to Solomon's court is related in his *Antiquities of the Jews* and resembles a summary of the second half of chapter 21 through to chapter 26 of the *Kebra Nagast*. The second half of chapter 21 marks the beginning of the *Sheba-Menelik Cycle*, that part of the *Kebra Nagast* translated into Ge'ez from Arabic. Here is Josephus's account.

There was then a woman, queen of Egypt and Ethiopia; she was inquisitive into philosophy, and one that on other accounts also was to be admired. When this queen heard of the virtue and prudence of Solomon, she had a great mind to see him, and the reports that went everyday abroad induced her to come to him, she being desirous to be satisfied by her own experience, and not by a bare hearing, (for reports thus heard, are likely enough to comply with a false opinion, while they wholly depend on the credit of the relaters;) so she resolved to come to him, and that especially, in order to have a trial of his wisdom, while she proposed questions of very great difficulty, and entreated that he would solve their hidden meaning. Accordingly, she came to Jerusalem with great splendor and rich furniture; for she brought with her camels laden with gold, with several sorts of sweet spices, and with precious stones. Now, upon the king's kind reception of her, he both showed a great desire to please her; and easily comprehending in his mind the meaning of the curious questions she propounded to him, he resolved them sooner than anybody could have expected. So she was amazed at the wisdom of Solomon, and discovered that it was more excellent upon trial than what she had heard by report beforehand; and especially she was surprised at the fineness and largeness of his royal palace, and not less so at the good order of the apartments, for she observed that the king had therein shown great wisdom; but she was beyond measure astonished at the house which was called The Forest of Lebanon, and also at the magnificence of his daily table, and the circumstances of its preparation and ministration, with the apparel of his servants that waited, and the skilful and decent management of their attendance: nor was she less affected with those daily sacrifices which were offered to God, and the careful management which the priests and Levites used about them. When she saw this done every day, she was in the greatest admiration imaginable, insomuch that she was not able to contain the surprise she was in, but openly confessed how wonderfully she was affected; for she proceeded to discourse with the king, and thereby owned that she was overcome with admiration at the things before related; and said, "All things, indeed, O king, that came to our knowledge by report came with uncertainty as to our belief of them, but as to those good things that to thee appertain, both such as thou thyself possesses, I mean wisdom and prudence, and the happiness thou hast from thy kingdom, certainly the same that came to us was no falsity; it was not only a true report, but it related thy happiness after a much lower manner than I now see it to be before my eyes. For as for the report, it only attempted to persuade our hearing, but did not so make known the dignity of the things themselves as does the sight of them, and being present among them. I, indeed, who did not believe what was reported, by reason of the multitude and grandeur of the things I inquired about, do see them to be much more numerous than they were reported to be. Accordingly, I esteem the Hebrew people, as well as thy servants and friends, to be happy, who enjoy thy presence and hear thy wisdom every day continually. One should therefore bless God, who hath so loved this country, and those that inhabit therein, as to make thee king over them." Now when the queen had thus demonstrated in words how deeply the king had affected her, her disposition was known by certain presents, for she gave him twenty talents of gold, and an immense quantity of spices and precious stones. (They say also that we possess the root of that balsam which our country still bears by this woman's gift.) Solomon also repaid her with many good things, and principally by bestowing upon her what she chose of her own inclination, for there was nothing that she desired which he denied her; and as he was very generous and liberal in his own temper, so did he show the greatness of his soul by bestowing on her what she herself desired of him. So when this queen of Ethiopia had obtained what we have already given an account of, and had again communicated to the king what she brought with her, she returned to her own kingdom.

In the ruins of modern Aksum this writer noticed a rather unusual looking bird picking its way around the fallen stele that has an engraved serpent on its underside. The bird was a hoopoe, which is linked in several stories to Solomon and the Queen of Sheba. The accounts of Solomon and Sheba in the Old Testament, Josephus, and the *Kebra Nagast* do not engage in magical fantasies. In contrast, Jewish and Islamic traditions link Solomon to supernatural powers, stating that he had the power to control spirits and animals. The hoopoe is given prominence in these stories. It reports to Solomon about the Queen of Sheba and carries his letter to her.

A *Targum* is a Jewish adaptation in Aramaic of a sacred text. The Old Testament book of Esther concerns events during the Israelites' exile in Babylon, but the Targum Sheni (second Aramaic translation) of the book of Esther has additional material that deals with the Queen of Sheba's visit to Solomon. Bluntly stated, Solomon threatened her with war unless she acknowledged him as overlord:

> All the kings of the East and West, and the North and South, come to pay me homage. If you would come to do likewise, I will honor you more than any kingly guest of mine, but if you refuse and do not appear before me to pay homage, I shall send out against you generals, contingents, and riders.

The Yemenite account (ca. A.D. 1702) of the Queen of Sheba mentioned earlier appears to be taken from long-established folklore. According to that tradition Solomon had recently conquered an island kingdom, hanged its ruler, and abducted his daughter:

> When the Queen of Sheba's court heard all that and all the stories of [Solomon's] power and bravery as well as the full account of Solomon's greatness, they were overcome with awe of him and their hearts were filled with utter dismay. It were as though those hearts melted and turned to water. And so, she said, "I shall go to him and hear directly his wisdom and see the wonderful and awesome things that he alone among humans can accomplish."

The Islamic Qur'an of the seventh century A.D. also tells of a threat. Solomon gives the order:

> Take this writing of mine and deliver it to them (Shebans); then withdraw, and see what they reply. [The Queen of Sheba] said, "O peers, there has been delivered to me a noble writing. It is from Solomon; it runs, "In the name of God, the Merciful, the Compassionate; do not act proudly against me, but come to me in humble submission."

The queen then tries to buy Solomon off with tribute, but this angers him, for Solomon insists that wealth is not his purpose; only her and her subjects' abandonment of sun-worship and submission to the One True God. The queen then obeys him by coming in person to pay homage.

The Targum Sheni to the book of Esther, the Qur'an, and Muslim traditions all speak of Solomon's gift of conversing with and controlling animals, birds, insects, reptiles, jinn, and the winds; they state that it was the hoopoe that first brought the Queen of Sheba to Solomon's attention and later acted as a messenger between them.

It is possible that an ancient oral tradition spoke not of a bird but of a scout or water diviner. As the meaning of words changed over the years however, the word became associated with the hoopoe in the same way as the Old Testament prescription that the prophet Elijah was fed in the desert by ravens *(rbm)* when *Arabs* (also *rbm*) would seem to make more sense. As already mentioned, the Queen of Sheba has been linked with Dhu Sharkh ibn *Hudad* and al-*Hadhad* ibn Sharah ibn Dhu Sahar so maybe the Arabic word for hoopoe, *hudhud*, has been confused with earlier partially comprehended oral or unvocalized written traditions. Of course, it may just be that there was no confusion at all, and that the hoopoe story was advanced as an example of Solomon's magical powers. Whatever the basis of the hoopoe story, in all Islamic traditions Solomon was attracted to Sheba because of its wealth, the beauty of its queen, and its ignorance of the One True God.

According to the Targum Sheni Solomon was hosting visiting rulers and decided to entertain them with a parade of the zoological and supernatural elements of his army. The hoopoe was missing and Solomon, in anger, promised severe retribution for the bird. The hoopoe eventually reappeared and begged for mercy, saying that in the east it had found a fabulous realm ruled by a queen whose inhabitants did not possess bows and arrows, let alone understand or practice warfare. Solomon sent the hoopoe back to the queen's capital of Kitor with a letter demanding she submit to his authority. The queen, a sun-worshipper, became confused and tore her clothes in despair when the hoopoe and an accompanying host of other birds blocked the sun's rays. In the confusion the hoopoe landed in her room, and when the queen noticed the letter attached to its wing, she removed it and read its contents:

> From me, Solomon the King, who sends greetings. Peace to you and your leaders, Queen of Sheba! You are aware that the Lord of the Universe has made me ruler of all animals, the birds in the air, and the demons, spirits and hellish night creatures [Liliths]. All the kings of the East and West, and the North and South kneel before me in homage. If you come to do likewise, I will honor you more than any other ruler, but if you decline, I will make war against you. You ask with what? My generals are the beasts of the field, my cavalry the birds of the air, and my troops the demons, spirits and night creatures [Liliths] who will strangle you in your beds. The animals will kill you on the battlefield and the birds will devour your remains.

The Qur'anic account is similar. Solomon's air force is summoned but the hoopoe is missing. Solomon threatens the miscreant with severe punishment, even death. The hoopoe returns, is contrite, and tells of its journey to Sheba, a country of sun-worshippers ruled by a queen. Solomon sends the bird back to the queen and her subjects with a letter demanding:

> In the name of God, the Merciful and Compassionate: Do not be proud! Come to me submitting as Muslims.

Other Islamic written accounts concerning the hoopoe were recorded in the eleventh century A.D. by two writers: Ahmad b. Muhammad b. Ibrahim al-Nisaburi (who wrote under the name of al-Tha'labi), and al-Kisa'i. Both state that Solomon, along with his extraordinary army, left Jerusalem on a giant magic carpet for the *sacred land*, a reference to the area in Hijaz surrounding Mecca. There he foretold the coming of the Prophet Muhammad and then advanced southwards towards Yemen, which he reached in a few hours. Camping in a beautiful lush valley, the king and his retinue were unable to find surface water; so the hoopoe, whose name was Ya'fur, was summoned, for it possessed the skill of seeing water beneath the ground. The hoopoe was missing, for it had gone exploring, discovering the realm of Sheba. There Ya'fur encountered a hoopoe from Yemen named 'Afir. The birds exchanged information, and Ya'fur set off on its return flight and met an eagle that Solomon had sent to bring it home. The hoopoe persuaded Solomon to curb his anger and told him about Sheba, its wealth, and its queen. The hoopoe was sent back to Sheba with a letter. There are varying accounts of what happened next. One story follows the Targum Sheni, relating that the hoopoe blocked the sunlight, causing the queen to oversleep and receive the letter when she eventually awoke. Another says the bird dropped the letter on the queen's neck as she lay asleep on her back. A third story says it fluttered above her while she was in conference, only dropping the letter on her as she looked up. The message was the same as quoted in the Qur'an: become Muslims and submit to Solomon's authority!

The establishment of the First Temple and its concomitant grandeur as the religious center of Solomon's powerful and wealthy empire prompted a call for incense from Sheba's realm. The Torah decreed that incense should be burned twice a day on the temple Golden Altar (Exodus 30:7), but there was also demand for other luxuries from India and Africa that Sheba controlled. Besides the magnificent temple and palace, al-Kisa'i stated that Solomon had twelve thousand chairs made from ivory and aloe wood and a throne made of gold and ivory and encrusted with precious stones.

We, therefore, have two major differing traditions concerning the queen's visit to Solomon's court. The Old Testament, Josephus, and the *Kebra Nagast* say that it was trade relations and a love of wisdom that brought the queen north. The Jewish Targums and the Islamic record disagree; stating the queen had no choice, for a refusal would have brought annihilation. The aftermath of the visit indicates that both traditions are correct. Even if Solomon's threat had not been explicit, it was understood. And if even if the queen had ostensibly come for love of wisdom and to escape invasion, she intended to best Solomon. The contest was unexpectedly inconclusive and still, as Christ observed, awaits resolution.

If the traditions are correct, Solomon wanted to reduce Sabaea to a client state or colony ruled by a child he would father by the queen. The queen wanted to create good relations with Solomon, to learn from his experience, and to probe the extent of his wisdom. As part of her strategy she employed riddles. Yemeni traditions say that riddles helped the queen gain her throne. During her father's time there was a Sabaean king who used riddles to extort wealth from his subjects. Notables were asked riddles. If they failed to give the correct answer, they were given a chance to redeem themselves by undertaking a journey within a prescribed time. Before she was born the queen's father failed to answer a riddle and set out on the journey allotted him. During his travels he encountered two snakes - one white, one black - fighting to the death. The white snake was exhausted and begged him for water. Revived after drinking the water, the white snake turned on the black snake and killed it. Later on the journey Sheba's father met a jinn who introduced himself as the former white snake. The jinn, in gratitude for the help he had received in killing the black snake (a rebellious slave), offered his beautiful and brilliant jinn sister in marriage. The new bride quickly made her mark solving riddles for the king's beleaguered subjects to their great happiness and the king's consternation. Their daughter became Queen of Sheba. The association of snakes with jinn is perhaps a reference to the presence of a snake-worshipping people, perhaps one and the same as those who revered the snake god Arwe.

The Queen of Sheba's reputation for her skill in solving riddles surpassed even her mother's, and she utilized this skill to test Solomon's intellectual powers. Solomon's success in answering them has been interpreted by commentators as proof that he had a mind superior to the queen's, an odd conclusion since he was the one being tested and asked her nothing in return. The Old Testament, Josephus, and the *Kebra Nagast* do not elaborate on the riddles or other tests she set the king. These belong to much later texts. Four are listed in the Midrash Mishle. The same four appear in the Midrash ha-Hefez along with fifteen more. Three appear in the Targum Sheni to the book of Esther.

We know very little of Hebrew court etiquette ca. 1000 B.C.E., but it seems likely that state visits commenced with foreign dignitaries being put to the test and reciprocating likewise. One common ploy was to see if the visitor recognized the true king. The queen is alleged to have been greeted by Benaiah, the handsome son of Jehoiada. The queen asked Benaiah if he were Solomon. When she learned otherwise, she observed that you could tell the nature of a lion by its den, meaning perhaps that not only did this lion have confidence in the wonder of its surroundings but also had no fear of male rivals. Perhaps the magnificence of her entourage and the value of her gifts or tribute spared the queen from having to guess which notable was Solomon, a test that would confront her son two decades later.

Below are the riddles and tests the Queen of Sheba allegedly used to gauge Solomon's wisdom.

Riddles and Tests in the Midrash ha-Hefez. Riddles and Tests in the Midrash Mishle are marked with an asterisk*.

	Riddles	*Answers*
1.*	Seven go out and nine go in, two offer drink but only one accepts	*The menstrual cycle, pregnancy, breasts, and a baby.*
2.*	Who was the mother that told her son that his father is her father, that she is also his sister and the	*One of Lot's daughters.*

	daughter of his grandfather?	
3.	Who has neither been born nor died?	*God*
4.	Which place has only seen the sun once?	*The ocean bed*
5.	Which enclosure has ten entrances but when one is open, nine close and when nine open one is shut?	*The uterus*
6.	What only moves after you've killed it?	*A boat*
7.	Which three had neither life nor sustenance yet saved three others?	*The seal, a thread, and a staff.*
8.	Which three went into a cave and came out as five?	*Lot, his two daughters and their two sons.*
9.	Who was the dead person who lived and prayed in a moving grave?	*Jonah in the whale.*
10.	Which three ate and drank in this world but had no gender?	*Three angels who visited Abraham.*
11.	Which four entered a place of the dead but emerged alive and which two entered a place of life but lost their lives?	*Daniel, Hananiah, Mishael and Azariah; Nadab and Abihu.*
12.	Who was born but won't die?	*Elijah and the Messiah.*
13.	What was never born but was given life?	*The Golden Calf.*

14.	What is produced in the ground but humans produce it; its food is from what the ground produces?	*A wick*
15.	Who married two men and had two sons but all four of these men had one father.	*Tamar*
16.	There was a house that was a graveyard but no dead were brought there and nobody left it alive. What am I talking about?	*Samson and the Philistines.*

	Tests	*Answers*
1.*	The queen gave Solomon a sawn section of a cedar log was asked him to identify which end had grown nearer the sky	*When the log was put in water, the end that had grown nearer the root sank down.*
2.*	The queen presented a number of youngsters in identical clothes and asked Solomon to distinguish the boys from the girls.	*The children were offered food. The boys accepted them with open hands. The girls demurely extended their hands beneath their clothes so that their uncovered hands would not be seen.*
3.	The queen asked Solomon to distinguish between circumcised and uncircumcised boys.	*Solomon ordered the Ark to be revealed. The circumcised knelt on one knee; the others prostrated themselves.*

Riddles in the Targum Sheni to the Book of Esther

	Riddles	Answers
1.	What is it? A wooden basin and an iron bucket; it draws out stones but pours out water.	*A cosmetic box*
2.	What is it? It comes from the soil and feeds on it too. It flows like water but lights the house	*Naphtha*
3.	It goes in front of everything. It laments and cries. It is flexible as a reed. It enhances the nobility but burdens the poor. It uplifts the dead but brings sorrow to the living. Birds love it but fish fear it.	*Flax*

Solutions to eleven of the nineteen riddles and tests in the Midrash ha-Hefez and in the Midrash Mishle require knowledge of the Old Testament, but riddles 9, 11, and 12 refer to people who lived long after the Queen of Sheba's era. Two riddles concern female biology, and the remaining six riddles and tests were probably taken from traditional Middle East wisdom. None of the riddles or tests specifically reflects Sabaean origin. The stories of Abraham and Lot may also be part of Sabaean tradition, but those of the Golden Calf, Tamar, Samson, as well as the customs linked to the Ark of the Covenant were strictly Israelite. One might have expected Sheba to have asked more universal riddles rather than quiz Solomon on his own heritage. Since we know that three riddles were fabrications, the *nature* of the riddles becomes our concern because the Jewish historians used them to prove a point.

The Jewish writers abhorred women entering what they believed to be the exclusively male preserves of religion and statecraft. The queen was an immensely proud and confident young woman who, some traditions state, rejected every offer of marriage as beneath her. The queen may very well have come to challenge what most of Solomon's court believed was the natural order of things. What the queen thought as the natural order and what the Zadokite tradition *thought* she thought were two different things.

The queen represented a more peaceful and tolerant realm, a result perhaps of more equitable relations between men and women, which supports the notion that women are influential in promoting compassion, a heightened sense of community, and a willingness to arbitrate rather than to assert. This was not the way the Zadokite priesthood interpreted affairs. Blind to female opinion, their collective psyche was obsessed with blurring gender roles, fearing that the presence of an articulate, beautiful, and intelligent ruler meant that women wanted to become like men, even physically. Moreover, the Zadokites were opposed to any form of democratization, be it class or gender, which would undermine their dominance of society. This theme is echoed in the Gnostic St. Thomas Gospel, where Christ states that if women want to enter the kingdom of heaven they must first become men [since the Gnostic gospels indicate most of Christ's followers were women, the remark may have been a critical observation on priestly attitudes]; and in Zen Buddhist tradition, where So Chieluo, the intellectually brilliant Dragon Princess, is only able to reach enlightenment by changing gender. [7]

Prominent among the riddles ascribed to Sheba are those concerned with gender blurring, and with scandalous family relationships. Lot had incestuous relationships with his daughters, and Tamar was raped by her half-brother Amnon. Lest the lesson be lost that Sheba was associated with attempting to become a man, later Jewish traditions elaborated on this theme in the Targum Sheni to the book of Esther. The Targum Sheni to the book of Esther belongs to the period during the fourth to the fifth centuries A.D. and was written in Aramaic in Babylon. It includes an account whereby Solomon tricked the Queen of Sheba into lifting her robe to reveal legs covered in thick hair. This report was utilized then and thereafter by those who wanted to denigrate or lampoon the queen and denounce her as a threat to the natural order, the legs symbolizing her attempt to challenge and assume a man's role. A similar account appears in *Surah xxxviii:30-36* of the Qur'an, compiled in the seventh century A.D. This states that Solomon tricked the queen into revealing her ankles but makes no mention of hair. It therefore appears that the Targum Sheni and the Qur'an drew from an earlier common tradition but the Targum Sheni contorted the image of the queen by adding information relating to Znwbya Bat Zabbai (Zenobia), the Aramaic-speaking queen of Palmyra (Syria) who ruled ca. A.D. 267-272. Zenobia defied Roman rule, overrunning Egypt as well as parts of Asia Minor before being defeated and taken to Rome. Part of her name, *Zabbai* (her father's name), is the same as the Arabic word *al-Zabba*, meaning a hairy person. This seems to have been taken by the writers of the

Targum Sheni as a fortuitous means of not only undermining the Queen of Sheba's indubitably deserved reputation as a great beauty but also as presenting her as a woman wanting to cross gender boundaries. Zenobia had briefly been queen of Egypt; so too, according to Josephus, had Sheba. In their cynical logic the queen of Egypt had a name meaning *hairy*, and since the Queen of Sheba was queen of Egypt she must have had hairy legs and was evolving into a man.

The fullest account of events during the remainder of the queen's visit to Solomon is covered in the *Kebra Nagast*. The queen spent several months at Solomon's court observing the construction of the temple and the way he conducted his administration. Solomon was more liberal than his priesthood, and it is probably his tolerance of other creeds that persuaded the queen that adoption of the Israelite faith might be advantageous to her realm. Archaeology has revealed that she ruled diverse peoples. Like the Israelites the Sabaeans had entered a land inhabited by Bronze Age settlers. One advantage of the Israelite cult was its legal system, which brought uniformity in administration, dispensation of justice, land and property rights, and inheritance. The priesthood was a sort of sacred public service, and if its theological and social excesses could be balanced by a worldly monarchy, the result might be viewed as attractive. Other written systems had existed in the Middle East, for example, the *Code of Hammurabi* in Babylon, which had 282 laws. The Torah provided guidance for many situations, for example, in England in A.D. 1659, providing a legal justification to execute King Charles I. A legal system was essential for central administration and uniform government, and the Torah was essentially a national constitution, albeit divinely directed. The Queen of Sheba would have regarded the Torah in the same way as the leaders of modern-day newly independent former subject territories (e.g., India, Jamaica, Lesotho) or as leaders of an established state that had undergone dramatic political change (e.g., Japan, Haiti, post Soviet Hungary) would look to laws and constitutions of other states for a model. The Queen of Sheba highly valued the concept of law and maintained strict adherence to it. Solomon's realization of her integrity in keeping her word and her respect for the law formed the basis of his sordid plot to bed her.

It is also not clear whether the Torah at the time of Sheba's visit was as fully developed as we now know it. The *Kebra Nagast* indicates that it was not. The oldest section of the *Kebra Nagast* is the *Sheba-Menelik Cycle*, translated from an Arabic source and entirely pre-Christian Israelite in its content. Chapters 41, 42, 89, 90, and 91 deal with the Torah *(Appendix B)*.

Chapter 41 deals with social and religious behavior. Chapter 42 lists and elaborates on the Ten Commandments, then details which sexual relationships are forbidden. In the Old Testament, these laws belong to Leviticus 17-26, and are known as the Holiness Code. They are acknowledged as being older material than other parts of the Torah, supporting the theory that the *Sheba-Menelik Cycle* has an origin predating Ezra's fifth-century B.C.E editing of the Old Testament. Chapter 90 deals with idolatry and unclean foods. Chapter 91 is the most wide-ranging. The Torah demands that people use peaceful means to resolve disputes and to abstain from violence and plunder. If people found stray livestock or other lost possessions, they should endeavor to return them to their rightful owners. People should help each other and share work. Bribery and all other forms of corruption were forbidden. Poor people, orphans, and those with disabilities should be helped and protected from exploitation. Animals and birds should be protected and treated with kindness. Part of each harvest should be set aside for visitors. People should acknowledge and revere only the One True God and honor wisdom. There is nothing about maintaining a priesthood and paying taxes for their upkeep. If this was the Torah in existence in Sheba's time, she would have found far it more attractive than the final edition. Most of the Torah's legislation on women is in Deuteronomy, probably compiled after Sheba's time although written to include the *Song of Moses*, whose ancient language places it earlier than Sheba. Deuteronomy neglects all mention of rituals concerning the Ark of the Covenant, a clue that its disappearance could be dated to Sheba's era. The worst remarks in the Old Testament about women, such as Ecclesiastes 25:24, "Woman is the origin of sin, and it is through her that we all die," belonged to the future.

The *Sheba-Menelik Cycle* states that the queen stayed six months at Solomon's court, and when the time came for her to leave, with her honor intact, he became quite distressed. A final celebration was prepared, which the queen observed from an elevated pavilion, where she was privately served food doctored with powerful spices. She prepared for bed. Other Ethiopian traditions say with her handmaiden slept by her side. Solomon then appeared, announcing that he intended to sleep on the other side of the pavilion. This displeased the queen, and she would not allow it until he gave his word that he would not attempt anything in the night. He agreed but only on the condition that she in turn agreed not to take any of his property. The queen was highly contemptuous of such a suggestion but agreed. In the night, plagued by a colossal thirst from the spiced food, she crossed the floor to help herself to some water by Solomon's bed. Before she could drink, Solomon grabbed her arm and reminded her that if she drank the water, she would break her word. At last encountering the sordid dimensions of Solomon's ruthless character and with no hope of slaking her raging thirst in the room or in any part of the kingdom without breaking her word, the queen had to endure Solomon's triumph. Next, according to the Ethiopians, Solomon bedded the handmaiden as well.

The queen then left for the south, taking with her a ring Solomon insisted on presenting to her as a gift for their future child. The Queen of Sheba had warned Solomon that only virgins could rule in Sabaea and a pregnancy could cost her the throne. Traditions exist that state Solomon married the queen or arranged for her to be married to another ruler from southern Arabia. There are other stories that both Solomon and his successor and son Rehoboam ruled Yemen for a total of forty years after which it reverted to a local ruler. Control of Yemen's gold or other Arabian minerals may be the source of the stories concerning King Solomon's mines. The *Kebra Nagast* implies that at the beginning of her reign, the queen was based in Arabia but spent her last days in Africa. The general impression is that her visit to Solomon weakened her political power. Professor Bill Glanzman and other academics suggest that Marib may have been a thriving Sheban city in the queen's day, but it still seems too distant from Asir, let alone Palestine, to warrant the incredible trading mission recorded in the Old Testament or for the queen's court to be troubled by any threats from Solomon. It is more likely that the queen had her capital in or near Asir, and the Israelites and Shebans were vying for control of the area during the temporary Assyrian and Egyptian withdrawals.

The next part the Queen of Sheba's story is so controversial that many authorities simply ignore it, for acceptance means declaring null and void what must be one of the largest and definitely one of the oldest and most respected bodies of academic research in the world – Old Testament scholarship. Those who have challenged it can expect vilification, marginalization, censorship, unemployment, and even, like the late Al Glock, assassination.[8] Cautious academics find it safer not to follow where the evidence leads, even if this means the queen will never be accorded her true historical and theological status.

The aim of this book is to show that the life of the Queen of Sheba is the key to proving the Old Testament is neither fantasy nor exaggeration but indeed an accurate account. The most convincing argument comes from an Arabic text translated into Ge'ez (Ethiopic), the contents of which are not only supported by ancient inscriptions at Abuna Garima near Mekele in Ethiopia but also by the presence of remnant Hebraic groups in Eritrea and Somalia, one of which is named on the inscriptions. The Arabic text translated into Ge'ez was the *Sheba-Menelik Cycle* of the *Kebra Nagast*.

CHAPTER FIVE

The *Kebra Nagast*

The principal evidence concerning the life and legacy of the Queen of Sheba remains the *Kebra Nagast* (The Glory of the Kings), an Ethiopic (Ge'ez) document most probably compiled in Aksum in northern Ethiopia ca. A.D. 520 and then slightly enlarged in the first part of the fourteenth century A.D.

The *Kebra Nagast* does not make easy reading, for it is a composite document drawn from three separate eras. It attempts to unify three divergent political objectives into a single divinely ordained destiny. Its redactors used documents from two languages, one of them a language they did not always understand. They were claiming the heritage of Solomon's kingdom while hating the Jews. In addition, the geography of the *Kebra Nagast* appears not only inaccurate but also ludicrous, and to compound all these problems the final redactors tried to pass off their own interpolations as part of the original text.

The *Kebra Nagast* has 117 sections, usually referred to as chapters, and is composed of more than 64,000 words. It is usually considered the document that legitimized the rule of the kings of Aksum and later the emperors of Ethiopia. For this reason some later copies of the *Kebra Nagast* included details of land grants, because the *Kebra Nagast* was regarded as the country's divinely inspired constitution. The *Kebra Nagast* was utilized in 1952 in the constitutional arrangements that united democratic Eritrea and feudal Ethiopia into a federation and existed as Ethiopia's constitutional centerpiece until 1974 when the monarchy was overthrown and Haile Selaisse imprisoned, tortured, and murdered.

If textual analysis relied solely on literary sources, the *Kebra Nagast* would erroneously appear to be merely a rag-tag collection of random borrowings from ancient documents. There are 364 references, allusions or possible influences linked to passages in 32 books of the Old Testament – e.g., 62 references to the Book of Genesis, 37 to Exodus, 49 to Deuteronomy and 1 to Ruth. There are 176 links to quotations from 20 books of the New Testament, 41 to Matthew alone. Jewish sources such as the Targum, Talmud, Midrashim, the Zohar, rabbinical commentaries, Josephus, and Ben Sira account for 77 references, while the Qur'an accounts for 28; Islamic commentators 5; Old Testament Apocryphal writings, 105 (in 21 books), mostly references from the Cave of Treasures (in 16 books) and Enoch (18); and New Testament Apocryphal writings 25, (in 20 books). Text in the *Kebra Nagast* is also linked to works of 28 early church fathers, e.g., Origen and Gregory of Nyssa; while other parts are connected with the Nicaean Creed and with miscellaneous works such as Ethiopian liturgical texts. [1]

However, these references are overwhelmingly confined to the Christian era chapters of the *Kebra Nagast*. If those chapters were removed, what would remain is a single story free of any Christian content, about 30,000 words in length - almost half the content of the entire *Kebra Nagast*. This section is known as the *Sheba-Menelik Cycle*, the story of Solomon and Sheba and the consequences of their relationship. In the *Sheba-Menelik Cycle* there have been several interpolations by Christians in what is clearly a pre-Christian account, but these are so obvious that the original text can easily be recognized. The *Sheba-Menelik Cycle* is also important, as it contains text that has evidently been mistranslated from Arabic, confirming that this was indeed a separate Arabic text before becoming part of the Ge'ez *Kebra Nagast*. When the *Kebra Nagast* came to the attention of Western scholars in the late nineteenth and early twentieth centuries, all major researchers - Bezold, Nöldeke, Praetorius, Zoltenberg, Guidi, Dillmann, and Cerulli - noted that the *Sheba-Menelik Cycle* contained so many Arabic influences that it must have been translated from that language into Ge'ez. Praetorius, writing in Latin, stated *"...dicti libri vocabulis arabicis valde repleta"* (the said texts are exceedingly replete with Arabic words) while Zoltenberg found that some Arabic proper names had been transcribed directly into Ge'ez. Bezold and Guidi made a list of Arabic loan words and passages to enable researchers to understand some sections of the *Sheba-Menelik Cycle*. Examples included food and utensils for Solomon's feast for the Queen of Sheba, place names, the queen's name *Makeda/not thus/ not this way*, and strange grammatical constructions.

There is general agreement that the *Sheba-Menelik Cycle* consists of chapters 22 to 28A, 29B - 34A, 35-43, 45-63A, 84-93A, and 94 of the *Kebra Nagast*. However, this writer maintains the description of the Queen of Sheba, chapter 21B, should also belong to the *Sheba-Menelik Cycle* to form the opening paragraph.

The first part of the *Sheba-Menelik Cycle* resembles Josephus's account to such an extent that he almost certainly summarized a very similar text. However, Josephus's account concerning Sheba ends with her departure from Jerusalem, and it is highly unlikely that he would have omitted summarizing any additional text at his disposal, particularly text as dramatic as the theft of the Ark of the Covenant. This is the vital part of the *Kebra Nagast* and an issue that Zadokite compilers of the Old Testament totally ignored. Scrutiny of the *Sheba-Menelik Cycle* not only reveals a plausible explanation for the Ark's disappearance but also sheds considerable light on a variety of subjects, including the origins of Solomon's name, the illogical dispersal pattern of Jewish settlements in Arabia, the origins of Hebraic/Israelite groups in Eritrea, Ethiopia, and Somalia; the linguistic riddle of the name for the Ark, Sabaean inscriptions mentioning Hebrew in Ethiopia and a solution to the problems of Old Testament archaeology.

The *Sheba-Menelik Cycle* begins with a description of the Queen of Sheba as a beautiful and brilliant young woman whose country was enjoying unprecedented prosperity from trade (chapter 21B). The queen learned about Solomon from Tamrin, her chief trader, who was supplying materials for the new temple in Jerusalem. Desirous of experiencing Solomon's wisdom first hand, the queen set out with a 797-strong camel caravan to visit him (chapters 22-24). This journey reportedly occurred in the sixth year of her reign (chapter 30) and in the seventh of Solomon's (chapter 37).

The queen stayed in Jerusalem for six months. She was deeply impressed by what she saw in Jerusalem, studying Solomon's administrative methods, and witnessing his benevolent treatment of ordinary people (chapters 25-27), a practice that, according to the Old Testament, degenerated into harshness in later years. The queen decided to convert to the Israelite religion, while on his part Solomon grew increasingly anxious to bed her (chapter 28). He succeeded in his quest, and she left bearing a ring he had given her (chapters 29B-31).

The next part of the *Sheba-Menelik Cycle* deals with the real life consequences of a vision Solomon had on the night he slept with the queen. He dreamed that the sun moved from Israel and shone on the queen's realm (chapter 30):

> A brilliant sun rose up before King Solomon. It swept down from heaven and shone with a brilliant light over his kingdom. And as he watched it hang over his realm he saw it suddenly soar away moving across the sky until it settled over the Queen's country where it shone even brighter than before as if it wished to remain there for all eternity.

The remainder of the *Sheba-Menelik Cycle* is concerned with this theme. Meanwhile the story continues. The queen gives birth to Menelik at Bala Zadisareya. It is not known if this name is associated with the Mai Bela River bend, the traditional site for Menelik's birthplace. The *Sheba-Menelik Cycle* states that the queen gave birth before reaching her own country (chapter 32), and no mention is made of the huge caravan that accompanied her to Jerusalem. It seems unlikely that it could take nine months and five days (chapter 32) to travel south and still fail to reach the queen's Arabian home. The Sabaean inscriptions near Mekele on the Ethiopian plateau state that three queens of Sheba ruled there not long after Solomon's era, and the legends of Makeda's early life indicate her mother was not from southern Arabia, but from Africa. It seems therefore reasonable to suggest she gave birth to her son as she was returning from the Aksum area (which the tenth-century Yemeni historian Hamdani states was "her mother's country") on her way to Arabia.

The name of the Queen of Sheba's son is usually given as Menelik. The *Kebra Nagast* refers to him as Bayna Lekhem, which means *son of the wise man* (Solomon). He was also known as David or Daud, in honor of Solomon's father, his own grandfather. The name Menelik is usually taken to be a corruption of Bayna Lekhem, its Arabic equivalent *Ibn Hakim* or a title *Ibn Malik* (son of the king). When Menelik reached the age of twelve his companions asked him who his father was. He approached his mother:

> The Queen spoke to him angrily, intending to discourage him from discovering the truth and visiting Solomon, "Why do you ask me about your father? I am your father and mother, so do not mention the subject again." (Chapter 32)

This failed to have the desired effect and the boy persisted. At last the queen relented:

> "His country is a long way away and it's a difficult journey. Don't you want to stay here?"
> The young man was good-looking. His eyes, legs, his way of walking, indeed his whole appearance resembled his father. At the age of twenty-two he excelled as a soldier, horseman and hunter and in everything else expected of a young man. He told the Queen: "I am now going to see my father but I will return here by the grace of God, the Lord of Israel."
> (Chapter 32)

The Queen of Sheba arranged his passage with Tamrin to Gaza on the Israelite frontier, a city ceded by Solomon to the queen. Before he left the queen handed Menelik the ring Solomon gave her (chapter 33).

Chapter 34 infers that Menelik was probably in Ethiopia at the start of his journey, for the text states his next destination was "his mother's country" – Arabia. In Gaza the local population noticed his close resemblance to Solomon, and his presence was reported to Jerusalem. Benaiah, who had met the queen years earlier, was sent to bring the young man to Jerusalem (chapters 34-35).

Solomon, amazed at the young man's appearance, told him that he did not so much resemble him but his own father King David and arranged for Menelik to be given royal robes. When they were alone Menelik handed his father the ring given years before to the Queen of Sheba and requested that Solomon give him a part of the fringe of one of the three silk covers that shrouded the Ark of the Covenant. Tamrin explained Menelik's instructions to Solomon:

> "Listen Your Majesty, this is what the Queen asks of you. Take this young man, anoint, consecrate and bless him so he can become king over our country."
> (Chapter 36)

The *Sheba-Menelik Cycle* seems to have been translated and incorporated into the *Kebra Nagast* by Christian priests in about A.D. 520, then copied in the first years of the fourteenth century A.D. Chapter 36 states the Queen of Sheba agreed in accordance with Israelite practice that thereafter only men would be rulers. Knowing her character and experience, it is very difficult to accept that she agreed to such a measure, especially when we know that queens later ruled in Ethiopia, Arabia, Syria, and even in Judah itself. The tradition of the Queen of Sheba is strongest in Ethiopia, but the evidence suggests her first realm was in southern Arabia. It is possible that the increase in trade reflected in the prosperity of Sabaea and the need for close relations with Solomon also had implications for northeastern Africa, where the Sabaeans had some political control, as attested by the plateau Sabaean inscriptions. If it is true that the queen lost control of Yemen to Solomon, she still held royal rank in Ethiopia. In order to consolidate her rule there, however, she may have agreed to concessions, including Solomon's designation of Menelik as future Israelite ruler in order to be accepted by a Hebrew or Israelite population on the Ethiopian plateau. Conversely, the sections of the *Sheba-Menelik Cycle* stating that only men should rule thereafter may be politically motivated interpolations of the fourteenth-century tradition for reasons that will be explained when discussing the third part of the *Kebra Nagast*.

Solomon, in fact, did not want this son to return to Ethiopia. At that time he only had one son, Rehoboam, still a child. Menelik's parentage gave him indubitable dynastic advantages. Solomon entreated his son to stay on in Jerusalem, but the young man insisted on returning to his mother, respecting to an oath he had given her. Reluctantly Solomon acceded to his request but decided to strengthen his ties with the queen's realm. Menelik had told him:

> "My mother the Queen has kept her word to you and has already done away with the worship of idols. She has brought our people to Zion [the Israelite religion] and the Torah."
>
> (Chapter 37)

Solomon gave some thought to the matter and then came to a decision, which he announced to the kingdom's leaders:

> "I have not been able to convince this young man to stay here so this is what I've decided to do. We will make him the king of Ethiopia along with your own first born children serving him in the same capacity as you serve me."
>
> (Chapter 38)

Menelik's coronation followed. Zadok, the temple high priest, lectured him on the need to follow the God of Israel and to obey the Torah, listing the terrors and misfortunes that would strike if he erred (chapters 39 - 42).

The twenty-one first-born males of the kingdom were extremely fearful of the dismal prospects. Their leader was Azariah, son of Zadok. The

Sheba-Menelik Cycle records his advice, having first made them swear to secrecy:

> "What shall we do? ... let us take the Ark of the Covenant. You think it is not possible? Well, I will show you. If you do as I say and God is with us we will succeed. If we are discovered and are put to death, we will have died for Zion [the Ark]."
>
> (Chapter 45)

Benaiah's son Zechariah was supportive but pessimistic:

> "None of the priests may enter where they keep the Ark, except your father once a year when he offers a sacrifice in the Holy of Holies."
>
> (Chapter 45)

Azariah told him to keep faith and asked each first-born male to hand over ten double drachmas for the scheme he had in mind. His idea was to commission a carpenter ostensibly to build parts for an emergency raft, the sort used by ancient mariners to serve as a life raft when a ship foundered. He would then take the pieces into the temple, where he would assemble them as a box. Next he would remove the Ark and replace it with the box beneath the silk covers. The Ark would be hidden in a hole and removed when the time came for Menelik to leave (chapter 45).

Zechariah spoke of Azariah's knowledge of the temple and its "hidden openings" as well as his frequent custodianship of the keys, but chapter 46 of the *Sheba-Menelik Cycle* says an angel revealed a plan to Azariah that was far superior to mere burglary.

Azariah, complying with the angel's advice, persuaded Menelik, who was ignorant of the plan, to approach Solomon for permission to make a sacrifice with Azariah and three others before the Ark. Permission was granted; the king and other notables attended the ceremony. What happened next was ascribed to the angel, but it looks very much as if Azariah drugged the celebrants. There had been a considerable feast. Chapter 47 says cryptically that Azariah "mingled his offerings with those of the king, and he did likewise with the drinks, just as the Angel of the Lord had commanded him in the night."

In the night Azariah, Elmeyas (son of the temple archdeacon), 'Abesa (son of the tax assessor), and Makari (son of the palace judge) brought the unassembled sections of the wooden box to the temple, which they found unguarded and all its doors open. They quickly constructed the box and substituted it for the Ark, which they hid for the week prior to their departure (chapter 47). The time came for them to leave. Solomon blessed his son and told him to have faith in what had made Israel great: God, the Israelite divine destiny as the Chosen People, the Torah, and the Ark of the Covenant, which contained the tablets of the Ten Commandments. Solomon and his people felt desolate, experiencing a terrible sense of loss. Solomon then recalled Tamrin's message requesting a piece of the cover of the Ark and dispatched Zadok to deal with it. The high priest complied without checking whether the Ark was still in place. The piece of silk was handed over to Menelik, still ignorant of the theft of the Ark (chapters 48-51). At last Menelik's party left for the south.

We now come to the most important part of the story, chapters 52 - 59 of the *Sheba-Menelik Cycle*, looking first at what that section covers. Azariah waited until they had reached the Egyptian border before telling Menelik of the theft of the Ark.

> "Can you keep a secret?" he asked. "Yes, I can," replied the king [Menelik], "and if you tell one to me I will keep it so until the day I die."

Then Azariah motioned to Elmeyas, one of those who had helped him remove the Ark from the temple and told him to get the Ark ready for Menelik to see. Menelik was shocked but then recovered and danced before the Ark as his grandfather David had done, accepting that divine grace had delivered it to him. Finally he ordered the Ark to be carried openly and the party set out again for Ethiopia (chapters 52-55).

Meanwhile in Jerusalem King Solomon was sorrowfully reminiscing to Zadok about times past and confided to him the vision he had experienced the night he bedded the Queen of Sheba. Zadok was horrified, interpreting the vision correctly as a prediction that the Ark would be stolen and taken to Ethiopia. He rushed to the temple, found Azariah's box and fainted. On recovering he sped to Solomon to tell him the disastrous news. Solomon dispatched a cavalry force and then he himself joined the pursuit, vowing the culprits would be butchered. It was all in vain and Solomon returned in sorrow to Jerusalem, blaming his deviation from the Torah for this dreadful misfortune (chapters 56-60).

As mentioned, the *Sheba-Menelik Cycle* was translated into Ge'ez from Arabic. The original text has no reference to anything Christian so, taken with Josephus's text, which seems to be a summary of the *Sheba-*

Menelik Cycle text from chapter 21b of the *Kebra Nagast* until the queen's departure in chapter 31, it would appear that the *Sheba-Menelik Cycle* was written before the Christian era. The *Sheba-Menelik Cycle* pays a lot of attention to details, for example, the number of camels the queen brought, the security of the temple, the nature of the queen's religion, the way that Solomon forced the queen into bed, Azariah's ruse to steal the Ark. It is also interesting to note what the *Sheba-Menelik Cycle* does *not* mention: Jewish records stating that the high priesthood disappeared from Jerusalem during the ministry of Azariah, and re-emerging 300 years later. The *Sheba-Menelik Cycle* says Azariah stole the Ark but does not press the point that the high priesthood disappeared. The *Sheba-Menelik Cycle* explains how the Ark was stolen but makes no reference to the subsequent silence about the matter in Jewish literature, sacred or otherwise. The *Sheba-Menelik Cycle* does not list the Torah in full, which indicates it probably was not fully developed when the *Sheba-Menelik Cycle* was written. Aforementioned, the parts it quotes are considered the most ancient. Lastly, the *Sheba-Menelik Cycle* makes no mention of the disasters that befell Israel and Judah at the hands of the Assyrians and Babylonians. Had it been written at a later date, the authors would certainly have used these catastrophes to elaborate on the points raised in the vision of Solomon, that divine grace deserted the king and his realm on the night he bedded the queen. Taking all that into consideration it is therefore extraordinary that the *Sheba-Menelik Cycle*'s account of Menelik's escape with the Ark and Solomon's pursuit seems to make absolute nonsense.

Arab and Ethiopian scribes would have a basic knowledge of Middle East geography. If they did not, later editors would correct their work. This is in fact what happened. The redactors of the *Kebra Nagast* took the *Sheba-Menelik Cycle* text and, realizing its geography was skewed, they inserted helpful points that unfortunately only made things much worse. For a start they inserted the Archangel Michael into the text and said the whole party flew. Let us examine the text, ignoring references to Michael and flying. In chapter 52 Menelik's party leaves Jerusalem for Gaza. Then they pass to the border of Mesrin (Egypt), where they reach "the river of Ethiopia," a journey of a single day instead of the usual thirteen. There Menelik is told about the theft of the Ark of the Covenant. Next they come to the Sea of Eritrea (the Red Sea), crossing it, arriving opposite Mt. Sinai and traveling on from there to Ethiopia. If we take this account seriously, Menelik's party would have gone from Jerusalem to Gaza and then down to the Nile to the Takezze River junction, where they then crossed the Red

MAP 7

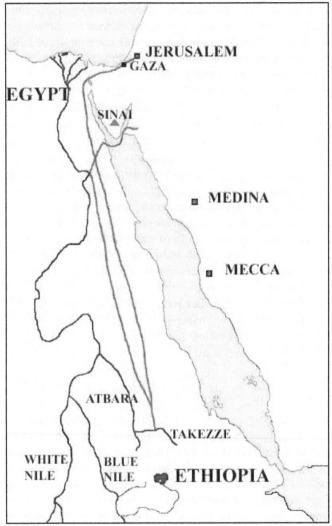

**The geography of Menelik's route according to the *Kebra Nagast*
with Jerusalem in Palestine and *Msr/Msrm* translated to mean *Egypt***
Jerusalem – Gaza – border of Egypt – Waters of Ethiopia – Brook of
Egypt – Sea of Eritrea – arrival in Ethiopia opposite Mt Sinai

Sea over to Arabia, where they arrived in Ethiopia (sic). This makes no sense; and neither does the account of Solomon's pursuit. On discovering the theft of the Ark, Solomon's troops ride out for Mesr (Egypt), where they are informed that Menelik's party had left nine days earlier. Some of the troops, returning to Solomon, report that Menelik had taken three days to travel from Jerusalem to the Takezze.

Meanwhile the remaining force continues the pursuit to the Red Sea. Solomon himself then joins the chase and reaches Gaza (*see Map 7*). After that, thwarted, he returns in sorrow to Jerusalem. Chapter 59 of the *Kebra Nagast* is an interpolation. It states that Solomon met a messenger sent from Alexandria by the Egyptian pharaoh, who informed him that he had seen Menelik's party pass through Cairo, which they had reached after three days from "the river of Egypt." This section can be disregarded because Alexandria and Cairo were respectively founded 600 and 900 years after Solomon. Martin Gilbert's *Atlas of Jewish History* places "the river of Egypt" at Wadi al-Arish just south of modern Gaza.

Chapters 61 - 62 deal with memories of the Ark, its role in Israelite history and the agreement Solomon made with his notables never to reveal its loss. Chapter 63A records that Solomon's marriage to pharaoh's daughter led him to tolerate her pagan religious practices. The last part of the *Sheba-Menelik Cycle*, (chapters 84-93A) concerns Menelik's return to Ethiopia with the Ark. It states that the queen abdicated in favor of her son and created an Israelite state under the Torah with a priesthood under Azariah as high priest and Elmeyas as chief deacon.

The *Sheba-Menelik Cycle* is the earliest part of the *Kebra Nagast*. Its message reveals that Ethiopia was the successor state to Solomon's kingdom, and its king was the descendant of King Solomon and the Queen of Sheba, who ruled over a mixed population of Israelites and Sabaeans.

Southwest Arabian, Old Testament and northeast African studies are specialized fields. Sometimes, though not frequently enough, scholars take an interest in all three areas. This lack of cross specialization results in researchers working in separate fields, finding puzzling information that would make more sense if they worked together. Second, monolingual English researchers can miss vital information published in another language.

In 1973, Roger Schneider, an archaeologist from Luxembourg, published a work in French in the Dutch journal *Bibliotheca Orientalis* entitled *Deux inscriptions Sudarabiques du Tigré* ("Two South Arabian Inscriptions from Tigre"). Other researchers quoted his work, especially

Italian archaeologist Rodolfo Fattovich. [2] None, including Schneider, realized the importance of the inscriptions for Old Testament archaeology and for verifying the narrative of the *Sheba-Menelik Cycle*. Unfortunately Schneider never responded to this writer's many attempts to discuss his article and died only a few months before this manuscript was completed.

The Sabaean inscriptions are on two stone incense burners at Adde Kawerh, Abuna Garima, on the Genfel River south-southwest of Wuqro near Mekele in Ethiopia and date from ca. 800 B.C.E. They give the names of four Sheban kings of D'mt: W'm Hywt, Rd'm, Rbh, and Lmn, who bore the titles, *mlk sr'n, syrt, mkrb d'mt, mlk sr'n yg'dyn*, and *mkrb d'mt wsb*. The offices of Mlk (king) and Mkrb (mukarrib) may have possessed the same regal and priestly authority as in Sabaea. These inscriptions are the earliest non-biblical references to queens of Sheba for they state that the first three rulers governed with queens, ruling together over the *sb* and the *br*, the *Reds* and the *Blacks*.[3]

Modern Ethiopians and Eritreans still maintain such a division. Reds refer to Semitic speakers (Tigrinya, Amhara, Gurage, and Tigré) and Blacks to Cushitic speakers (Agaw, Oromo, and Somali). Reds and Blacks in the Queen of Sheba's day may have had the same connotation. Archaeological evidence shows that two different groups entered the plateau from the north and from the southeast around 1100 B.C.E. as the climate in the plains became hotter and drier. The northern group were probably Semitic-speaking peoples descended from a group that never left Africa. These were supplemented by small groups of Semites from Arabia such as the Sabaeans. The traditional idea that the Semitic speakers of Ethiopia and Eritrea have an Arabian origin is currently being challenged and will be discussed later. The southeast group would have been Cushitic speakers whose descendants, such as the Saho, have lived for so long beside the Semitic speakers that they share a common culture. This leads to a very interesting problem.

All authorities accept that the name *sb* on the inscriptions means Shebans/Sabaeans, although (as discussed earlier) it was used in the time of the Queen of Sheba to describe small political units in Sheba itself, most likely called *Sab*. Schneider did not however translate *br*; he merely noted that "*La signification du mot est obscure ici. Mis en opposition avec sb'. Il semble designer un groupe de population.*" ("The significance of this word is not clear here. It is contrasted with sb. It seems to denote a population group.") Had the word *br* been discovered near Palestine, the biblical archaeological world would have been ecstatic because this word means *Hebrew*.

Schneider and others who have quoted his findings left the word *br* untranslated although the Ethiopian Orthodox Church asserts that in the past the areas around Yeha, Adwa and Adigrat were heavily Israelite. There is, however, a strong reason why many academics find the idea of Hebrew living in Ethiopia around 800 B.C.E. unacceptable, even though Jacqueline Pirenne had already speculated that some may have moved there after the 721 B.C.E. Assyrian destruction of the northern kingdom of Israel.

Racism has plagued Africa and the study of its history as much as religious faith has bedeviled biblical scholarship. The nineteenth to mid twentieth centuries were the zenith of European racist attitudes, and many European historians believed that all or most African technological and state building innovations must have been introduced by outside "superior" civilizations. Even though knowledge of Africa's history has advanced, European popular attitudes lag far behind. A travel book or novel about Africa will usually sell far more copies if its author is European or speaks of European experiences in Africa. Graham Hancock's book on the Ark of the Covenant, although entertaining, is far better known than Roderick Grierson and Stuart Munro Hay's superior work because it associates (albeit erroneously) the European Knights Templar with the Ark in Ethiopia. Whereas popular works on Africa sell better if European readers can relate to its characters, academics would either display extreme caution or derision if any work dared to suggest African history owed much to direct Israelite involvement.

It is also interesting, given that *kushi* in Hebrew means both *Samaritan* and *black person*, to read that the Hebrew of ninth century B.C.E. Adde Kawerh were regarded as blacks. Elaboration will come in the chapter below.

The *sb* and *br* inscriptions are not the only evidence supporting the *Sheba-Menelik Cycle*'s account that a Queen of Sheba ruled a mixed population of Shebans and Hebrew in Ethiopia. In north and central Somalia there are a number of "occupational castes" living like serfs to "noble" Somali clans, traditionally their protectors. They are collectively called *sab*, ("low caste") and constitute less than 1 per cent of the population. There are three groups belonging to the *sab*: the Yibir (or Ibro), Midgan, and Tumal. The Somalis believe the Yibir (*br*) to be ethnic Hebrew, and share anthropologists' beliefs that the Yibir are the original inhabitants of the area. The Yibir are associated with "unclean tasks" such as leatherworking, blacksmithing and circumcision. In the past they were landless and their testimony of no account in court procedures. They were forbidden to marry into the gentry (gob), but their women could be taken as concubines by their masters. The Somalis despise and fear their witchcraft and regard the Yibir as Hebrew converted to Islam. Nevertheless, their existence was tolerated until the Israeli-Palestinian conflict made them suspect. Their situation deteriorated further because of their association with Somali dictator Siad Barre, who had given them more rights. Many Yibir fled from Somalia after Barre's fall. The Yibir have their own dialect (some think it is just a code), examples from which are *dalanga* (any animal or bird), *iftin* (any shining object such as the moon, silver, white), and *lawo* (water, rain, river, year). Some Yibir are hunters but, according to one researcher, do not appear to have clearly defined words for animals. For example, *dalangihi walakumo ku dashiya* (Orynx) means "an animal with spears". Somalis state that the Yibir earned most of their income from a toll they collected on marriages and the birth of a child. This was always willingly paid to the first Yibir to arrive and in return the Yibir would present *makharam*, a charm bracelet of leather containing piece of his sacred tree.[4]

Critics of this interpretation state that the BR inscription refers to the presence of the Nilotic Kunama people, now resident in the north-west of modern Eritrea. Inscriptions exist stating that the Aksumite ruler Ezana (ca. A.D. 330) campaigned on their behalf against the Noba. The vocalization fo the BR mentioned on his victory inscription is however *Barya* or *Baria*, names still associated with the Kunama. The Marxist regime in Addis Ababa once proscribed use of the word because it also means *slave*.

The presence of and nature of *sb* (Sab) and *br* (Yibir/ Hebrew) in Somalia in an area a few days foot journey from the ancient Sabaean inscriptions bearing the same names supports the *Sheba-Menelik Cycle* narrative. Other support comes from the disappearance of the Zadokite high priesthood of Jerusalem under Azariah during Solomon's reign. In addition, Ethiopia, Eritrea, and Somalia possess Hebraic populations so old that they are ethnically indistinguishable from their neighbors. Lastly, Ethiopian culture is heavily dependent on the Ark. Reproductions are present in every church, and the original is believed to be held in an underground chamber in Aksum with a special priest assigned to guard it until his dying day. As will be discussed in a later chapter, the Ark in Ethiopia does not fit the Old Testament description. The reason is probably that the Old Testament description was added much later, maybe in Ezra's time. Furthermore, as chapter 7 of this text explains, the Ge'ez word for the Ark, *tabot*, is of ancient origin and was adopted from Hebrew *before* Ezra's time.

Paradoxically, the clinching argument that the *Sheba-Menelik Cycle* account is genuine rests with the seemingly ridiculous geographical references mentioned above. These references are ludicrous when applied to Palestine and Egypt but, as will be discussed later, make sense if placed in western Arabia.

The *Sheba-Menelik Cycle* may never have survived had it not been used to bolster the *Caleb Cycle*, a text whose contents have been verified by the *Book of the Himyarites*, discovered in the early twentieth century. The *Caleb Cycle* forms the other half of the *Kebra Nagast*. The subject matter of its contents requires elaboration, for although it was dependent on the *Sheba-Menelik Cycle*, its theological and political environment were far removed from that of Solomon and Sheba. Its main character is King Caleb (ca. A.D. 520-40), who most likely came to the throne as a pagan but in his time was one of the world's two most important Christian monarchs and Christianity's leading crusader. He ruled from Aksum and saw himself as the political heir of Solomon and the Queen of Sheba, respectively, as the king of true Israelites and the rightful ruler of southern Arabia. Moreover, he was proclaimed as the world's most senior Christian leader and a blood relative of Christ.

The Queen of Sheba, who lived around 1000 B.C.E., is associated more with the Aksum region than elsewhere. Recent archaeology in Aksum has revealed that, although it was probably not known by the name of Aksum until much later, the site was occupied by an Iron Age people during the Queen of Sheba's time. It is estimated that about 5 per cent of Aksum's archaeological sites have so far been investigated. Whether or not the queen herself ruled there, Israelite religion or Ethiopian customs resembling Israelite practices may have been influential in the area from her time onwards. Nevertheless, the rulers reverted to syncretism and paganism soon after her reign. Why should a newly founded Israelite state revert to paganism?

Although the Israelite religion and Judaism are certainly not the same thing, it is usual in academic circles to take the example of the post-Ezra Zadokite religious tradition as "normative Judaism," because eventually it led to modern Judaism. It is probable that without Persian backing Ezra's faith and its association with Palestine would never have developed into modern Judaism and the state of Israel. Most Israelites did not go down Ezra's path but instead followed the example of the ten tribes of the kingdom of Israel by assimilating with their neighbors or maintaining pre-exilic faith and customs. Jewish exclusiveness stems mostly from Ezra's time and was a phenomenon associated with the political aspirations of the Zadokite priesthood but not the population of Palestine as a whole. As mentioned earlier, the full text of the Torah was probably compiled after the destruction of the kingdom of Israel, so there would have been several Israelite communities whose Torah was confined to dietary and social issues but, as in the *Sheba-Menelik Cycle*, lacked the clauses dealing with the upkeep of a temple-oriented priesthood. Examples include the Bene Israel and Cochin Jews of India, and the Lemba of southern Africa. The Zadokite cause declined when the kingdom split following Solomon's death. The temple cult, linked to the monarchy, therefore lost considerable prestige and influence, and while Aksum/Ethiopia may have considered itself the successor state – no other state claimed a Davidic royal line – it does not follow that it possessed let alone adhered to Ezra's 5th century B.C.E. version of the Torah. While Azariah may have been a Zadokite high priest, it was the low-profile Levite priesthood that survived in Ethiopia and Eritrea. Ethiopian "Judaism" is a controversial subject, discussed here later under the more appropriate title of Ethiopian Israelite religion, but if the traditions of an ancient presence are true, the Ethiopian Israelites appear to have been either ignorant of or reluctant to imitate the Judaic society developed under Ezra. To them it must have seemed a very unsuccessful example of state building.

The Queen of Sheba's realm in southern Arabia never regained the central control it enjoyed during her time. In contrast, the D'mt kingdom of the Ethiopian plateau that developed from about 1000 B.C.E. grew into a large centralized state eventually based on Aksum. Aksum lay in good agricultural land with regular rainfall and ground water near the surface, so irrigation works on the scale known in Arabian Sabaea were unnecessary. The city lay astride important trade routes. One led from Adulis on the Red Sea up to Aswan on the Nile, while others connected with the Sasu gold fields and Barbaria (Somalia). The Aksumite kings permitted groups under their control to retain their traditional rulers, so long as they paid annual tribute. They often defaulted and were punished by military expeditions. Some Aksumite garrisons were stationed among subject peoples but the kingdom was not characterized by fortified settlements. While the Aksumites were known to sacrifice prisoners of war, they generally recognized that people were a valuable resource to be relocated (like the Beja), not slaughtered when they proved too troublesome. In the early days, when links were stronger with Sabaea, the people of the Ethiopian plateau revered the same deities as the Sabaeans. These included Astar (Venus), Ilmuqah (the moon), Habas (related to the moon), and two deities who were probably associated with the summer and winter sun, respectively, Dhat Himyam and Dhat Ba'adan. The Aksumites revered Astar, whom they associated with fertility; Beher, who may have been linked to the sea; and Mahrem, who was a war god and possibly connected with the sky. Mahrem was considered the father of Aksum and protector of the royal family. Recent archaeological work near Asmara in Eritrea has uncovered large numbers of small statues of bulls' heads that might indicate a cult similar to Canaanite beliefs. The name Aksum has several interpretations; one, that it came from the unvocalized Sabaean word *ksm*, meaning the people of Kush. As in Sabaea the first Aksumite kings held the title of *mkrb*, possessing royal and priestly power. Later kings were titled *mlk* and had high priests serving them.

The kingdom of Aksum developed large urban centers at Aksum, Adulis, and Metera, which visitors from the Mediterranean said matched their own cities. Its prosperity relied on agriculture, domestic and wild animal resources (cattle, sheep, camels, elephant, rhino), and Red Sea and Indian trade. Aksum exported ivory to India, Persia, Himyar, and the Roman Empire. Gold came from Sasu, Gojjam, and perhaps Eritrea, and was obtained by gold panning not from mines. Iron, silver, lead, and tin were mined, but there is no record of copper except as an import, along with bronze.

The Aksumites policed the Red Sea and the land route to Egypt. In the Christian era they became increasingly involved in the affairs of southern Arabia. Exports included ivory, rhino horn, hippo hides, tortoise shell, monkeys, emeralds (from the Beja), incense, sugar cane, salt blocks (from Danakil), and slaves. Imports from Rome and India included raw iron, iron tools and weapons, precious metals, glassware, fabrics, wine, oil, spices, and coins. Arab writers said that even after the decline of Red Sea trade with Byzantium, Aksum still remained a rich and powerful state. This is because, despite foreign trade, the economy of Aksum depended on *agriculture*. Foreign trade only provided luxuries for the ruling elite.

The Aksumite king first associated with Christianity was Ezana (ca. A.D. 330). He began his reign as a pagan. Coins made during the king's early years depicted the disk and crescent representing the sun and moon and bore the words "Son of the invincible god Mahrem." The story goes that during a period of political instability both in Rome and in Aksum a

Roman crew was massacred in an Aksumite port, and that the two young Christian Syrian survivors were taken as house slaves to Aksum, where one of them, Frumentius, became the Greek language tutor of the infant prince Ezana and won the confidence of his mother, the regent. Frumentius then went to Alexandria to have a bishop appointed to Aksum but was himself chosen. Ezana is reported to have converted to Christianity. The disk and crescent (also a Canaanite symbol) on the coinage were replaced by the Christian cross and a new inscription: "Son of Ella Amida, never defeated by the enemy." Ezana's later coins had the same standard weight as those issued in Rome by the Emperor Constantine after A.D. 324. Aksum's supposed genesis as a Christian state is dated to the mid fourth century A.D., when Frumentius was appointed the first *Abun* (bishop) of Aksum, ca. A.D. 330. His successors were Coptic Egyptian monks appointed by the patriarchs of Alexandria. Sometimes the king of Aksum quarreled with the Alexandrian church leaders, so no Abun was sent for some time. No local Abun was appointed until the 1950s. An Ethiopian tradition says that books of the Old Testament were translated from Hebrew into Ge'ez during the Queen of Sheba's reign. Frumentius, usually identified as one and the same as the Abba Salama of Aksumite tradition, was credited with bringing the New Testament, in Latin, to Aksum where it was translated into Ge'ez before the Nestorian heresy and Council of Chalcedon of A.D. 451 (see below). Another tradition, however, states that Frumentius translated "the Scriptures" from Arabic. This might explain why the names of biblical patriarchs in Ge'ez have been influenced by Arabic forms.

It is likely that the Aksumite court had pre-Coptic church contacts not only with Judaic-Christian sects but also with the Nazarenes, a Judaic sect dating from the time of Ezra (whom they opposed), and a sect to which Christ himself belonged. Whatever the truth of this matter, which will be elaborated upon later, Aksumite Christianity was clearly influenced early on by Israelite practices.

Not much is known of the history of the church in the early times of Aksum. Ezana may have only been a nominal Christian in order to ally himself with the Roman emperor. After his death it is not at all clear if the Aksumite monarchs retained the faith. According to Greek Orthodox Church sources of the fourth century A.D., the Aksumite kings were descended from Solomon and the Queen of Sheba. Solomon and Christ were both from the House of David. So too, according to the *Sheba-Menelik Cycle*, were the rulers of Aksum. When Christ was proclaimed God at the Council of Nicaea in A.D. 325, it was inevitable that Aksum, with a recent history of its kings already being associated with a god (Mahrem), would find the idea of association with the divine Christ attractive. However the Aksumite belief that they were close relatives of the divine Christ did not make an impact on their kings until the late fifth and early sixth centuries when the Nine Saints (Syriac-speaking Monophysite scholar-missionaries from southern Arabia) convinced the Aksumite king Caleb to assume a global role using his supposed royal Davidic relationship with Christ to powerful political advantage.

Christianity in Aksum has always been associated with the monarchy - the precedent established in Rome. Christianity became the Roman Empire's official religion in the reign of the Emperor Constantine the Great (A.D. 312–337). As discussed earlier, all but two of the assembled church leaders at the Council of Nicaea in A.D. 325 signed the document agreeing that Christ was of "one substance" (*homoousios*) with the Father and the Holy Spirit in a divine Trinity that had existed since the beginning of time. The Council of Nicaea denounced the Alexandrian theologian Arius for heresy, condemning his contention that Christ was subordinate to the Father and had a human not a divine substance. Despite this agreement at Nicaea, controversy continued and at the Council of Chalcedon in October A.D. 451, the problem of the relationship between the Father, Son, and Holy Ghost in the Trinity again threatened to split the church. This time between five to six hundred bishops attended and drew up a new statement of faith, the *Chalcedonian Definition*. Not only was the Arian standpoint repudiated but also that of Nicaea, for Christ was proclaimed to have been a single being with *two* natures, human and divine. The Syrian, Armenian, Egyptian, and Aksumite churches refused to accept this ruling, adhering to the Monophysite doctrine of Nicaea, that Christ had a *single divine* nature, a ruling passionately supported by the *Kebra Nagast*. The theological dispute of the single or twin natures was exacerbated when discontented peoples in the eastern provinces used it to distance themselves from Byzantium and its taxes. Indeed, Byzantium* had been reluctant to take drastic measures against the Egyptian Monophysite Copts because of the imperial dependency on Egyptian corn supplies. In A.D. 482, the Byzantine emperor Zeno (A.D. 474-491) tried to appease the Monophysites by introducing a

---

* The Roman Empire had been divided into two, West and East. The Roman Empire of the West fell in A.D. 478 when Rome was captured by Germanic invaders. From then till 1453 the Roman Empire was ruled from Byzantium (Constantinople).

theological formula known as the *Henoticon*, which, avoiding the mention of the word "nature", not only incited the Monophysites but also angered the Roman popes. The result was a thirty-five year breach between the patriarchs of Constantinople and Rome, and the Constantinople mob's successful demand that Zeno be succeeded by a Chalcedonian emperor, Anastasius (A.D. 491-518).

Anastasius was succeeded in A.D. 518 by Justin, who was controlled by his own nephew, Justinian, who succeeded Justin in A.D. 527. Justinian's wife, Theodora, who ruled jointly as empress, was sympathetic to the Monophysite cause and personally supported a Monophysite monastery, a policy that discouraged her husband Justinian from meddling with the issue until Jacob Baradaeus, appointed Bishop of Edessa by the Monophysite patriarch of Alexandria, began a Monophysite resurgence in the eastern provinces. Justinian's efforts to seek a solution again incited the Roman pope, whom he had earlier placated. Justinian died in A.D. 565 without resolving the Monophysite issue. His successor, his nephew the Emperor Justin II, had been brought up as a Monophysite, but in A.D. 571, afflicted by an escalating mental illness, he began widespread persecutions of the Monophysites that continued until his death in October A.D. 578. This cost the empire support from the eastern provinces, which fell quickly to the Persians when war broke out. The Persians captured Jerusalem in A.D. 614, when they overran Syria and Palestine. Egypt and Libya followed in A.D. 619. The Byzantines fought back to recover territory in Anatolia and Armenia, destroying the main Zoroastrian shrine. Nevertheless, the mutual exhaustion of the Byzantines and Persians made them both vulnerable to the Islamic onslaught from Arabia. In such circumstances Monophysitism seemed irrelevant.

Monophysitism was certainly not regarded as irrelevant when the *Caleb Cycle* of the *Kebra Nagast* was written. It was regarded as the means whereby Aksum would rule the world. The process had already been underway before Nicaea. The expansion of the Roman Empire brought increased Red Sea trade, and the Aksumites became more involved in the affairs of southern Arabia. The Aksumite king Gdrt (Gadarat) sent troops ca. A.D. 220-230 to occupy parts of southern Arabia to control trade and to counter the power of the Himyarites. At first Aksum was allied with Sabaea, but later alienated it when it became more powerful. In A.D. 267-8, the Aksumites invaded Himyar to seize control of the incense trade. They were repulsed and by A.D. 295 had been pushed back to small coastal enclaves.

Mutual hostility simmered between the two states and came to a head around A.D. 520.

The rivalry between Aksum and Himyar was of long standing. It appears their royal houses had a common Sabaean origin and sometimes shared the royal title as rulers of the Sabaeans. The Yemenis shared the Sheba-Menelik tradition, believing that Solomon and the Queen of Sheba had a son who was raised as an Israelite in southern Arabia, assisted by Israelites whom Solomon had sent. The rivalry between the royal houses had taken a severe turn when Dhu Nuwas (Yusuf As'ar Yath'ar), the Jewish king of Himyar, proclaimed himself the king of all peoples in Yemen (*mlk kl `s²cb*). A tradition states he came to the throne in a way similar to one of the traditions concerning the Queen of Sheba. The ruler of Lakhnia, Yanuf Dhu Shanatir, either murdered rivals or sodomized them to ensure the shame would bar them from any future leadership role. Dhu Shantir had murdered Hassan of the Tubba dynasty, whose father Tiban Asad Abu Karib had encouraged Jewish conversion. Hassan's younger brother Yusuf (Dhu Nuwas) was an extremely good-looking young man. When Dhu Shanatir summoned him, Yusuf had taken the precaution of concealing a knife under the sole of his foot. He beheaded Dhu Shanatir and was proclaimed king.

The Aksumites regarded it their right to approve southern Arabian monarchs. Tensions rose when Yusuf's subjects embraced Judaism. Yusuf slaughtered Aksumites in Zafar, the Himyarite capital, and Christians in Najran. A similar rebellion broke out in northern Mesopotamia, at that time part of greater Armenia. In both cases the Jewish militants hoped that Zoroastrian Persia would help them destroy the Byzantine and Aksumite Christian empires. Yusuf adopted a Messianic posture. The Jewish *Apocalypse of Baruch* had foretold that the Messiah would arise in the last years of the Roman Empire and demolish it, and that a military Messiah named Ben Joseph (Yusuf) would also fall in battle. Yusuf's mother was a Jewess from Nisibis (Armenian Turkey); and southern Arabia, Yusuf's paternal homeland, was a target for militant Jewish proselytizers from Tiberias in Galilee. The area had already seen the martyrdom of a prominent Christian named Azqir in the mid fifth century A.D. at the hands of Sharahbil Yakkuf, the Jewish ruler of Saba, Raydan, Hadramawt, and Yamanat. Accounts of Yusuf may have been also inspired by references to Sheba in the book of Isaiah. Yusuf's proselytizing Judaism and his claim to rule all peoples in Yemen were direct challenges to Aksumite traditional dynastic claims in the area, for it ushered in a new order where religious affiliation (Judaism), not tribal groupings, was the basis of the state.

This move to create a supra tribal militant religious identity was in keeping with the times. The world had entered a new phase: the era of expansionist totalitarian religion. It was no longer enough to impose political and economic control over large swathes of territory and disparate peoples. Christianity had been declared the sole religion of the Roman Empire in A.D. 392. Rulers now sought to dominate and to direct their subjects' thoughts and beliefs and therefore, through force of arms, demonstrate that their theology was superior to those of their enemies. In this the Zadok priesthood had been ahead of its time.

Aksum's quest for world domination may seem today to have been a sad delusion but it certainly was not ill founded. Substantial numbers of missionaries, including the Nine Saints, came to Aksum in the late fifth century, many of them fleeing persecution from fellow Christians in the Roman Empire. Important monasteries, such as that at Debra Damo, were founded by the sixth century A.D. The Nine Saints quickly converted the whole of the Aksumite kingdom to Monophysite Christianity and gave it a world vision. Ostensibly the Aksumites were the allies of the Eastern Roman Byzantine Empire, but Monophysite Christianity was also the mark of Byzantine subjects dissatisfied with Byzantine rule. The Monophysite world view, even as late as the sixteenth century, was the creation of a Monophysite empire stretching from Aksum through Egypt, Arabia, Palestine, Syria, and Anatolia to Armenia. This empire would be ruled by the king of Aksum, with a political center in Aksum, a priesthood drawn from Egypt, and proselytizing prophets from Syria.

The Monophysites were not alone. Rivaling the desire for a new empire in the same area, the borderlands of the Byzantium and Persia empires, were militant Jewish movements based in Mesopotamian Armenia, Yemen, Galilee, and possibly the Arabian Hijaz. It was the Galilee Jewish activists who inspired Yusuf in Himyar.

The *Caleb Cycle* was most probably written for King Caleb of Aksum by Monophysite missionaries who arrived in Aksum at the end of the fifth century. They would have used the historical precedent of the Zadokites and King Josiah of Judah.

As mentioned earlier, the Zadokites had "discovered" a "lost" sacred text, probably the book of Deuteronomy, using it to enhance their own and Josiah's position. The *Caleb Cycle* did the same for Caleb and the Monophysite missionaries. The missionaries had brought Syrian, Greek, and Arabic sacred writings with them (these may have included the *Sheba-Menelik Cycle*) and set about preparing the Aksumite monarchy for its destiny. In return they were encouraged to spread the faith among Caleb's subjects. The missionaries obviously encountered powerful local traditions that they had to accommodate within Christian theology. Primary amongst these must have been the story that the Aksumite monarchy had been founded by the son of Solomon and Sheba. This was theologically awkward for the missionaries, who would have preferred a faith free of substantial Judaic connotations in order to present the king of Aksum as the defender of true Christianity and to combat the Himyarite Jewish Messiah. How could they explain that the king of Aksum was an Israelite but also the world's most important Christian ruler? The answer was the *Caleb Cycle*.

It is not too difficult to see inside the mind of the author or authors of the *Caleb Cycle*. They were in the court of a monarch influenced by powerful Israelite traditions. The belief in the presence of the Ark in Aksum and the link to Solomon through Sheba must have been too strong to ignore. The missionaries wanted their Monophysite faith to triumph in the Byzantine eastern provinces and to counter Jewish Messianic movements in the same area. They had at hand the *Sheba-Menelik Cycle*, a purely Israelite document stating that Aksum was the inheritor of Solomon's kingdom. Christ and Solomon were of the royal House of David; so too was the king of Aksum. In their view, the Old Testament led to Christianity, not Ezra's Judaism. They would therefore take the *Sheba-Menelik Cycle* as their centerpiece but blend it with these additional ideas showing that Aksum was the true Israel. The True Faith (Christianity) followed the path of Solomon through Menelik to Christ. The False Faith (Judaism) followed Solomon through Rehoboam to Ezra and was not only deluded but also evil and marked for destruction. Monophysite Christianity was the true creed. Christ existed even before Creation as part of the divine substance. Aksum's kings had inherited this substance through Adam's Pearl (see below), and by implication they were semi-divine through their familial relationship with the divine Christ. Aksum was God's Holy City. This philosophy is encapsulated in chapter 95 of the *Caleb Cycle* section of the *Kebra Nagast* under the title *How the Honorable Estate of the King of Aksum Was Universally Accepted* and included the following phrases:

> We [the Aksumites] believe that only a king of the Orthodox Faith [Monophysitism] shall rule us. .... The Jews were scattered across the world, their kingdom destroyed and they must be rooted out wherever

they are found [because] they killed Christ. .... For sure in all truth the King of Aksum is the greatest of all the kings of his guardianship of Zion [the Ark of the Covenant] .... the Chosen Ones of the Lord are the people of Aksum. There is where God lives, the place of Zion, the resting place of God's Law and His Covenant.

King Caleb of Aksum ruled ca. A.D. 520-40. His original name was Ella-Atsbeha and he was the first king of Aksum to have a biblical name. Tradition says that Ezana, not Caleb, was the first Christian ruler of Aksum but it appears that Christianity did not take a firm hold in Aksum and Ezana's successors reverted to paganism as the fortunes of the Roman Empire went into temporary eclipse. The Nine Saints who had led the mass conversion of Aksum pinned their hopes on Caleb to make Monophysite Christianity a world power.

Unfortunately the *Caleb Cycle* makes very difficult reading, for its author was certainly not as gifted as the writer of the *Sheba-Menelik Cycle*. It seems to have been written before the Caleb's crusade against Jewish Himyar, with the result that the text is almost completely theological. The *Caleb Cycle* is the text within the *Kebra Nagast* that utilizes the vast majority of the 364 references, allusions, or possible influences in that work linked to the Old Testament and 176 linked to the New Testament. It interprets Old Testament material as New Testament symbolism and prophesy and returns from time to time to an unconvincing scenario whereby the 318 church leaders at the Council of Nicaea hung on every word of Gregory the Illuminator (who never attended the council) and unanimously agreed that Aksumite imperial claims took precedence over all else. The *Caleb Cycle* nevertheless contains valuable insights into the psyche of the Aksumite ruling class in the first part of the sixth century A.D. It is just unfortunate that it was so badly written. In mitigation the author may have been using reference works developed in isolation from those different traditions that later became the standard texts of the Old Testament and New Testament. Similar theories have been put forward for the compilation of the Qur'an. Josephus used ancient texts now lost; Paul of Tarsus appears to have drawn from texts that he may have discovered during his three years in Arabia, which were probably known to the Aksumites. Despite this, while historians should be eternally grateful to the author of the *Caleb Cycle* for saving the *Sheba-Menelik Cycle* for posterity through inclusion in his work, the reputation of the *Sheba-Menelik Cycle* has suffered by its association with the painful style, unconvincing arguments, and inaccuracies of the *Caleb Cycle*.

The *Caleb Cycle* of the *Kebra Nagast* is sometimes dated between the reign of the eastern Roman (Byzantine) emperor Justin I (A.D. 518-527) and before madness overcame Justin II (A.D. 571). The reasoning behind this is that the *Caleb Cycle* treats the death of the eastern Roman emperor Marcian (A.D. 457), last of the male imperial Theodosian line, as a consequence of his convening the Council of Chalcedon (A.D. 451) that rejected Monophysitism. It refers to Justin I as a co-religionist, hence a Monophysite, but makes no mention of Justin II's later years when his insanity had advanced to such a stage that he had himself wheeled round in a small cart so he could bite his subjects' legs. If the *Caleb Cycle* had been written during or after this time, it would have used this madness as an example of the consequences of rejecting Monophysitism. However, references to both Justins and to Marcian come at the end of the *Kebra Nagast* in the same section as the fourteenth century monarch Amda Seyon. In addition, the references to Marcian and other issues are inaccurate, so it is probable that the whole of this late section was written in the early 1300s not in the 500s as is the rest of the *Caleb Cycle*. The *Caleb Cycle* speaks of the emperor Marcian as being vanquished by the Persians. The writer seems to have confused Marcian, who suffered no such fate, with a later ruler. During and after the Himyarite War the Byzantines were in frequent diplomatic contact with Aksum, but it seems the authors of the *Kebra Nagast* did not have access to pertinent records. The *Caleb Cycle* states Justin I and Caleb met before launching their campaigns against the Jewish movements in Armenia and in Himyar. Such a meeting never took place, and Justin's name may have been confused with Julian, an envoy whom the Emperor Justinian (A.D. 527–565) dispatched to Aksum. The *Caleb Cycle* also confuses Justin's Armenian campaign with the Persian campaign against the Jewish state of Mahoza. It is Mahoza that was linked to Yusuf's rising in Himyar/Yemen. Justin's campaign was in the region of modern Armenia and Georgia, where there were demographically insignificant isolated Jewish groups, including blacksmiths of African descent in Colchis, whose ancestors, according to Herodotus, had been exiled by the Assyrians. These Jewish groups do not seem to have led a major rebellion against the Byzantines. The confusion between Justin's campaign and the Persian campaign must have been partly due to references to "Armenia," whose boundaries once included much of modern Turkey and Iraq. Lastly, the *Caleb Cycle* only briefly refers to Caleb's crusade against Jewish Himyar, although other highly detailed Monophysite accounts in Syriac exist. All this evidence points to the bulk of the *Caleb Cycle* being written at the beginning of Caleb's career - before the Himyarite War. The short account mentioning the war would therefore belong to the final chapters of the *Kebra Nagast* written in the early fourteenth century A.D.

Before discussing the Himyarite war here is the content of the *Caleb Cycle*. The first part of the *Caleb Cycle* (chapters 1-21A of the *Kebra Nagast*) is set at the Ecumenical Church Council of Nicaea from 20 May to 19 June A.D. 325. Records indicate that around 300, mostly eastern church leaders, attended obeying the summons of Emperor Constantine. The *Caleb Cycle* gives the figure as 318 and states that Gregory the Illuminator explained the Aksumite worldview to the 318 church leaders.

As mentioned, Gregory the Sun, or Illuminator, of Armenia, which became a Monophysite stronghold, did not attend the Council of Nicaea, but his son did and Gregory enthusiastically hailed his son's report of the council's decisions.

It is not known whether Gregory's son presented his father's views at the council. If indeed he did so, they would not have resembled the argument presented in the *Caleb Cycle*. The Council of Nicaea was concerned with standardizing Christianity. Gregory, according to the *Caleb Cycle*, harangued the council about the divine destiny and glory of the Aksumite kings. That is why the *Kebra Nagast* (The Glory of the Kings) is so titled.

The *Caleb Cycle* then proceeds to give a short history of the Old Testament, allocating a chapter each to Adam, Cain, and Abel, then from Seth through to Noah, the sin of Cain, the story of Noah, the Flood, the Covenant of Noah and the relationship between Zion and the Ark of the Covenant (chapters 3-10). The *Caleb Cycle* argues that the Ark of Noah is a symbol of the Ark of the Covenant, adding that God will keep faith with Israel if they obey His Law, and that likewise He will watch over the keepers of the Ark of the Covenant (Aksum). The 318 Church leaders then agree that the Ark of the Covenant was the first of God's creations, and that it also represented the Virgin Mary (chapters 10 and 11). The narrative continues with a chapter each given to the apostasy of Canaan, Abraham's rejection of idolatry, his Covenant with God, the story of Isaac and Jacob, Rueben, the Glory of Zion, and the construction of the Ark of the Covenant (chapters 12-17). The 318 church leaders (chapter 18) agree again to everything in the previous chapters, and then they discuss the discovery of the *Sheba-Menelik Cycle* (chapter 19). Discussion of the division of the earth between the kings of Rome and Ethiopia then follows (chapter 20).

> The Emperor of Rome will rule the area from the center of Jerusalem northwards and to the south-east. The Emperor of Aksum will rule from the center of Jerusalem southwards and to the Indian frontier in the east.

The first part of chapter 21 speaks of Christ's words concerning the Queen of Sheba, stating she would arise on Judgment Day to bear witness against those who refuse to recognize Christ. The second part of chapter 21 introduces the narrative of the *Sheba-Menelik Cycle*. The *Caleb Cycle* occasionally interrupts the *Sheba-Menelik Cycle*, vilifying the Jews for rejecting Christ (chapter 30), reminding the reader that the king of Aksum is the keeper of the Ark of the Covenant (chapter 44) and determining when it is permitted to criticize a king; Old Testament priests could do so but Christian kings were answerable only to God (chapter 44).

The *Caleb Cycle* resumes in the second part of chapter 63 with criticism of Solomon's marriage to pharaoh's daughter, which resulted in the spread of idolatry throughout the kingdom. Solomon's practice of bedding women, hundreds of them, is contrasted with David's marriage to Bathsheba after arranging for her husband's death. Solomon's bed is then compared with Christ's church, the many women who passed through it symbolizing Christ's acceptance of gentiles into the church (chapters 65 and 66).

Chapters 67 and 68 concern the divine destiny and divine relationships of the Aksumite kings. Solomon is said to have fathered three sons: Menelik, Rehoboam, and Adrami. Chapter 68 introduces the concept of the Pearl, which originated in Adam and was some sort of mark of divine grace. The pearl, however, did not automatically pass from parent to child. It is used in the *Caleb Cycle* to link Adam to Solomon and Christ, who were both from the House of David (chapter 71). This association raised the Aksumite kingship above all others. Elaboration follows on the nature of the world's kings. The *Caleb Cycle* states that all the important monarchs in the world were Semites descended from Shem. These included the Roman and Byzantine emperors (descended from Adrami, son of Solomon), the rulers of Medyam and Edom (through Esau), the rulers of Babylon, Moab, Amalek, the Philistines (through Delilah's son by Samson), and Persia (through Perez, son of Tamar). Enhanced already through his association with the pearl, the king of Aksum - descended from Menelik, Solomon's eldest son - was proclaimed most senior of the Semitic kings. The *Caleb Cycle* dismissed the line of Rehoboam, son of Solomon, as doomed because of its refusal to accept Christ. Rehoboam fathered the kings of Israel, who were then destroyed by the Roman emperors, identified in the *Caleb Cycle* as the descendants of Adrami (chapters 67, 70-83, and 95). This strange claim may refer not to the Imperial Roman/Byzantine emperors but the Palmyra and Petra Arabs, who, being Roman citizens, were often referred to as Romans.

Chapters 84, belonging to the *Sheba-Menelik Cycle*, has an interpolation from the *Caleb Cycle* stating that the Queen of Sheba's capital became the Christians' chief city. The *Caleb Cycle*'s attitude towards its ideological enemies is typified by its interpolation in chapter 93 of the *Sheba-Menelik Cycle*, its second half given over to a *Caleb Cycle* diatribe affirming the Holy Trinity and condemning Arius and Nestorius. Arius was the leading critic present at the Council of Nicaea. Nestorius's views were wrongly confused with those of Arius but were similar to those adopted at the Council of Chalcedon in the year of his death (A.D. 451). To distance themselves from their Byzantine enemies, the Persian Christians adopted Nestorianism and established a theological center at Nisibis, the home of King Yusuf of Himyar's mother. This is one of a handful of references in the *Caleb Cycle* to the great intellectual discussions that followed Nicaea, and readers are left with the conclusion that the author of the *Caleb Cycle* had little or no understanding of the issues involved and treated his readers as simpletons willing to accept unquestioningly that the Christian world stood in awe of the Aksumite emperor's divine destiny. Rival schools of thought were dismissed using character assassination. Opponents were equated with Old Testament characters such as the seventy critics of Moses who met appalling fates (chapter 97). Chapters 108, 114, and 115 are particularly virulent against the Jews, rejoicing at the thought of their perpetual punishment. Evidence in the Old Testament such as the Burning Bush, the Rod of Moses, the Rod of Aaron, the Horns of the Altar, and the Ark of Noah are all taken as signs foretelling the coming of Christ (chapters 96, 103, and 104). Chapters 105 and 106 state that the major Old Testament figures such as Abraham and Solomon all acknowledged that the world was waiting for Christ. This message was embellished (chapter 99) by a parable of a Just Master (Christ) with two servants (Adam and Satan) and other allusions mixing Old Testament history with New Testament theology (chapters 100-102, 109-112). This was not as strange as it might appear. The Monophysite standpoint at Nicaea was that Christ had existed from the beginning of time and had therefore lived through the events of the Old Testament.

Missing from all this was any reference to the theological and social implications of the life of the Queen of Sheba. In the first part of the *Sheba-Menelik Cycle* she had been portrayed as vibrant and intelligent; in the later part, world weary, cynical but strong willed. In the *Caleb Cycle* she was reduced to a mere conduit to enable the Israelite royal house to rule Aksum. The process of the Iron Age states' subjugation of women to an inferior status to men had perverted and downgraded her memory. In Jewish tradition she was remembered merely as an appendage to the greatness of Solomon. Later, the same heritage would transform her into a hairy-legged demon. The new Christian religion gave her a new role, that of a sexual temptress.

A peculiarity of the new Christian religion was its monasticism, founded largely on the premise that sexual abstinence, extreme isolation, and self-denial were conducive to spiritual development and insights to the human condition - spiritual and earthly. Some scholars have linked Christian monasticism with the work of Buddhist missionaries and have also drawn attention to earlier forms of monasticism among the Jews. The father of organized Christian monasticism is generally held to be Anthony of Egypt (ca. A.D. 251–356), a Monophysite Egyptian monk who witnessed extraordinary visions and severe psychological torment during his fifteen years of isolation as a hermit. Among his visitations was the spirit of the Queen of Sheba. Anthony, like his monastic successors, seemed to be incapable of interpreting any female contact from the present or spirit world as anything other than sexual. The queen, thereafter, became associated in Christian tradition with sexual attraction, despite Christ's reminder that she sought wisdom. Culture is constantly reinforced by images of success, but when they are neglected, denigrated, and suppressed they can no longer serve as a model for new generations to follow. The inspirational model of a beautiful and brilliant young woman roaming the earth for knowledge had long been stamped out in the Aksumite and southern Arabian collective memory. Intellectual development had become concomitant with the priorities of a purely male-directed society whose reasoning was often allied to self-inflicted physical abuse and the real threat of ostracism, exile, or execution for deviation.

In Aksum there are two Monophysite cathedrals. One dates from the sixteenth century, following the destruction of a very prestigious older edifice by the Muslim leader Ahmad Gran. The other cathedral is very large and was built by Haile Selaisse. Between the two cathedrals is a small sanctuary with a green-domed roof housing the Ark of the Covenant or its remains (Gran may have destroyed it too) in an underground chamber. Across the road are the famous stelae marking the graves of Aksumite kings, and beyond them is a great hill where the old city stood. A stream passes near the stelae. Beside it is a road to a dam containing an ancient pool known as the Queen of Sheba's bath. Rows of seats have been carved into the cliff overlooking the water. The road quickly deteriorates and becomes a rocky track. On one side of the track is a small hut containing an ancient stone block covered in Sabaean inscriptions. The track continues up a hill to an open space overlooking valleys. There are large underground tombs built with huge cut stones. One of them is the tomb of Caleb, reached by descending a flight of stone steps into a spacious stone-lined tunnel containing several rooms with stone coffins. But Caleb is not buried here. He died and was buried not far away; in a monastery where he had retired to seek peace from terrible humiliation.

Caleb and Aksum once hovered on the verge of global political power. But for an extraordinary natural disaster, the name of Caleb might have been as well known today as the Prophet Muhammad. The chance came when Yusuf, King of Himyar, provoked a holy war.

There had been earlier Jewish-Christian disturbances in Himyar at the beginning of the sixth century. The second, ca. A.D. 520, was far more serious. Yusuf attacked an Aksumite garrison in Zafar and then campaigned against Aksumite troops and Christian communities elsewhere, particularly Najran. Refugees brought horrendous stories of persecution, murder, and the destruction of churches. Whatever the truth, Yusuf expected retaliation and blockaded the Arabian ports with chains against Aksumite warships and troop transports. Caleb seems to have accepted a co-king named Alla Amidas to rule in Aksum while he invaded Himyar.

From the very beginning the war was a religious and dynastic one. Yusuf was a Messianic figure intent on restoring the greatness of Israel and creating an empire. He adopted the title of Masruq, which the Sheban rulers used in pre-Aksumite Ethiopia, but it was also used to insult his Christian Aksumite enemies, for it could also mean "stolen," a reference first to the Aksumite theft of the Ark of the Covenant, and second to Christians as a whole for allegedly stealing Christ's body from the tomb in order to convince doubters that he had risen from the dead.

Caleb defeated Yusuf, who died riding his horse into the sea rather than face capture. Caleb's Monophysite proselytizing priesthood interpreted the destruction of the Jewish state as the first step to empire. The road to the conquest of Arabia lay open. However, it was not to be.

In late March A.D. 536 a great cloud of ash rose up in the east and swept across the sky. For eighteen months it blotted out the sun to such an extent that only a dim light shone for four hours a day. In Mesopotamia there were huge snowfalls, and throughout the Mediterranean and Middle East the harvests failed. The cause has convincingly been linked to the volcano at Rabaul on a Papua New Guinean Pacific island now called East New Britain. It is estimated that eleven cubic kilometers of pumice and ash were thrown into the atmosphere and carried west by the March-October southeasterly monsoon. [5] Aksum, which relied on two harvests a year, was hit hard. The rains also failed so there was no annual torrent to carry away the Ethiopian topsoil to the Egyptian Nile flood plains, where harvests also failed. Gerbils, deprived of their usual food supplies in the grain fields of Aksum, raided the grain stores and urban areas, bringing with them, according to the Syrian historian Evagrius Scholasticus (A.D. 536 – ca. 594), the plague. This plague, known in history as the Plague of Justinian, was caused by the bacterium *Yersina pestis*. From Aksum it moved on to Egypt (A.D. 540), and Constantinople (A.D. 532), where it killed over 230,000. The sixth century A.D. Palestinian-born historian Procopius of Caesarea described the plague as "a pestilence by which the whole human race came near to being annihilated." The plague swept on to Italy, Syria and Palestine (A.D. 543) and crossed into Gaul (France) and the Persian Empire (A.D. 544). It recurred throughout those areas for the next 250-300 years. Close knit communities, in particular the army and monasteries, suffered appalling losses. By A.D. 600 the population of the Roman Empire had shrunk to about 60 per cent of its A.D. 500 total. While the Persian Empire also suffered huge demographic losses, the plague had little or no effect neither on the Arabs of the Arabian peninsula nor on the nomadic Berbers of North Africa, a people who later provided most of the Islamic troops that invaded Spain in A.D. 711.

Caleb's viceroy in Himyar, Abreha, appointed around A.D. 525, took advantage of the distress across the Red Sea and rebelled against Aksumite control. Caleb sent a 3000 strong force to crush him, but this army mutinied and killed its commander, one of Caleb's relatives, before going over to Abreha. Caleb sent a second force, this one also defeated. With manpower resources crippled by plague and with imperial grain surpluses decimated by the atmospheric catastrophe, Caleb was unable to recapture the situation. Humiliated, he abdicated around A.D. 540 and retired to a monastery where he died and was buried, leaving his place in the huge royal tomb unfilled. By A.D. 543, Abreha was recognized as an independent king.

The Monophysite dream of world domination was not yet dead. Abreha consolidated his hold on southern Arabia and then attacked north to secure the lucrative pagan religious pilgrim center and marketplace of Mecca. In A.D. 552, his army, accompanied by an elephant, was repulsed. In A.D. 542, the Great Dam at Marib, 680 meters wide and built in the eighth century B.C.E., broke, and Abreha used a labor force of 20,000 to restore it. However, in A.D. 570, the dam was washed away in a great flood that rendered it irreparable until the late twentieth century. The loss of the dam brought an end to the high culture of southern Arabia, whose ruling elite depended on control of the dam's water surplus and the revenues from the agricultural prosperity it sustained.

But for the plague, world history might have been very different. Caleb and Yusuf ruled highly organized agricultural and trading states that were more than 1500 years old. To them it seemed inevitable that one or the other would conquer the whole peninsula and impose his religion on the Arab inhabitants. Whether or not this would have led newly converted and united Monophysite or Jewish Bedouins, like the Arabs between A.D. 632-711, to abandon Arabia attacking westward to Spain and eastward to India, is highly questionable. Islam ignited the Arab Bedouin soul to an extent Judaism or Christianity never had, irrespective of the economic factors that propelled them away from Arabia in search of better conditions. Monophysite or Jewish conquest of Arabia from Yemen would have broken the power of the Meccan shrine and installed co-religionists in power in the urban areas but probably would have been unsuccessful in converting, let alone uniting and inspiring, the desert tribes. Islam was particularly suited to the aggressive nomadic way of life, while Christianity, with its ambivalent passivism and dependence on an agricultural peasantry maintaining a large church hierarchy and edifices, was not. The Israelite faith of Moses' desert wanderers seemed better suited to the Bedouins, and some tribes were already Jewish; but the faith's racial exclusiveness and hereditary class system militated against Judaism becoming an Arab mass movement. It is likely that a Monophysite or Jewish victory in Arabia would only have delayed the rise of Islam. Nevertheless, the possibility was always there that Caleb or Yusuf could have been leaders on a global scale.

Few could have foreseen the rise of Islam, in particular its success in uniting a people obsessed with blood feuds and petty rivalry, let alone the exhaustion of the Byzantine and Persian empires due to mutual conflict. Their exhaustion and decimation by plague enabled the Islamic Arab armies to pour out of the peninsula and not only take control of the area

Caleb and Yusuf had seen as their future empire but much more besides. Within a few years, the Arabs, a people dismissed as being of no consequence for generations, swept across North Africa into Spain and across Persia to the frontier of India, dooming Aksum and Yemen, which for one short span of time had stood on the verge of true empire, to political insignificance.

While the plague appears to have upset the demography of the Semitic Aksumites, changing trade patterns forced them to reassess their economic interests. The Persians overran southern Arabia in the last years of the sixth century, severely disrupting Aksumite trading relations. The triumph of Islam as a world power exacerbated the problem even though traditions say that Islam behaved cordially towards Aksum for its past kindness to members of the Prophet Mohammad's family when they fled to Aksum during the early persecutions. Whenever the Islamic Empire was based in Damascus or in Baghdad, the Red Sea declined literally and metaphorically into a trading backwater. This only changed when Fatimid Egypt asserted its independence in the eleventh century.

After the rise of Islam, the Aksumites turned southwards and began expanding into Africa to exploit new resources. A temporary capital was established at Ku'bar, probably near Lake Hayq on the escarpment edge overlooking the plains towards Djibouti. The expansion into the interior provoked fierce resistance. Tradition holds that in the mid tenth-century Yudit, a Hebrew or pagan-Hebraic queen of the Bani al-Hamwiyya from Damot (a name reminiscent of ancient D'mt), a realm overlooking the Blue Nile gorge, defeated and killed the king of Aksum, pillaging the area, severely weakening the state. Yet another capital was established in the Cushitic speaking area southeast of Aksum, although Aksum remained the ecclesiastical center. It is usual to refer to the Aksumite empire after this date as Ethiopia because the city of Aksum was no longer its political center. As time went by the Cushitic-speaking Agaw people became increasingly influential in the army and in the government. Eventually the "Solomonid" ruling house was replaced by a dynasty known as *Zagwe* (from the word *Agaw*), whose kings (ca. 1030-1270) traced their ancestry to Moses. The Zagwe king Lalibela (ca. 1185-1211), responsible for strengthening Christianity, built impressive churches such as the subterranean rock structures at the New Jerusalem (Lalibela) and established cordial relations with Muslim-ruled Jerusalem. Despite these successes, the Aksumite clergy led a campaign that terminated Zagwe rule and reinstated the Semitic Solomonid dynasty under a leader named Yekunno Amlak.

The final part of the *Kebra Nagast* was written in the first years of the fourteenth century shortly after Yenno-Amlak's reign for a purpose similar to that when the bulk of the *Caleb Cycle* was written 800 years earlier. The leader of the team responsible for drawing up the final edition of the *Kebra Nagast* was Isaac, a senior church official in Aksum who knew Arabic almost as well as Ge'ez and worked with four other translators and redactors named Yemharana Ab, Andrew, Philip, and Mahari Ab. Isaac acknowledged inspiration from Gregory Thaumaturgus, Domitius of Antioch (or maybe Constantinople) and from Cyril of Alexandria. The work had been commissioned by the governor of Aksum, Yabika Egzi, and from its references it is certain that the document was put together between A.D. 1314 and 1321, during the regency of Amda Seyon, the last ruler mentioned in the king list. Its purpose was to prove that the king of Ethiopia (the successor state of Aksum) was divinely ordained not only as the inheritor of the Israelite royal tradition but also as the world's most respected Christian monarch, the keeper of the True Faith (Monophysitism). It seems that Isaac's team added very little to the *Sheba-Menelik Cycle* or to the *Caleb Cycle*. Isaac states that his team translated it from an Arabic original that had come to the kingdom during the reign of Gabra Maskal (Lalibela), the famous Zagwe ruler responsible for enhancing Ethiopian Christianity. Isaac stated that the document was not translated into Ge'ez during the days of the Cushitic Zagwe because of its message that *Semitic*, not Cushitic, monarchs were God's chosen rulers. Other researchers have claimed that the *Sheba-Menelik Cycle* was discovered in Nazret in Ethiopia as an Arabic text at the end of thirteenth century, and that Isaac and his team used it to write what became known as the *Caleb Cycle*. However, this theory is untenable given the nature of the content of the *Caleb Cycle*, which is so obviously from the end of the fifth century and beginning of the sixth century. Had Isaac and his team written an original document in the early fourteenth century they would have dealt with contemporary theological and political issues such as usurping the Zagwe kingship, and the Muslim threat. By A.D. 1314 Byzantium's political alliances quoted in the *Kebra Nagast* had no value, and it became a remote and almost irrelevant power, falling in 1453. Despite the tradition that Isaac undertook the production of the *Kebra Nagast*, it seems most likely his team merely copied out an older text, half of it already translated from Arabic, and then added the last section of the *Kebra Nagast*, probably chapters 113, 116, and

117, with their inaccurate references to the fifth and sixth centuries, and their mention of Caleb's retirement (chapter 117) and Zagwe rule (Colophon following chapter 117). However, so far as the Queen of Sheba is concerned, historians must be grateful for the Aksumite/Ethiopian theological and dynastic interest in her life. Although the queen's importance to medieval and modern (until 1974) Ethiopia diminished to such an extent that she became merely the woman Solomon used as a means of establishing a successor state, the Monophysite priesthood's work in preserving and copying the *Sheba-Menelik Cycle*, has ensured the possibility of solving ancient mysteries.

In the *Sheba-Menelik Cycle* we not only have a plausible explanation about the loss of the Ark of the Covenant and an insight into the queen's character, but we also have a key to solving the most contentious issues of Old Testament archaeology and history. As mentioned above, the references in the *Sheba-Menelik Cycle* do not fit Palestine, but they make sense if applied to western Arabia. This only became possible with a late 1970s geographical survey. Indeed, one eminent Arab historian, Kamal Salibi, published *The Bible Came from Arabia*, drawing heavily on this survey. Unfortunately he was ahead of his time. Biblical archaeologists had not yet come to terms with the implications of finding no evidence in Palestine. Despite this, his work should be considered as the main breakthrough in Old Testament studies, for among other things, it provided a map that appears to match the narrative of the *Sheba-Menelik Cycle*.

CHAPTER SIX

Western Arabia and the *Sheba-Menelik Cycle*

In western Arabia there is a wealth of evidence from trade routes, state building processes, linguistics, place names, traditions, mineral deposits, environmental change, archaeological sites, religious development, an ancient Ark culture, and an extraordinary passage in the *Sheba-Menelik Cycle* of the *Kebra Nagast* that indicate this area and not Palestine was the true home of the Old Testament.

Today the inhabitants of Arabia are known collectively as Arabs, although they have a mixed origin. According to their own traditions, the Arabs are descended from two groups of peoples; a sedentary group in the Yemen and nomads from the north central Arabian Desert. In the west and south the population has a substantial African element, while the east has admixtures from India and Persia. The earliest known languages of the southwest were Sayhadic (Sabaean, Qatabanian, Hadramatic, Minaen). Arabic developed among the desert nomadic pastoralists and today covers all of Arabia except where about 200,000 people speak six non-mutually intelligible non-Arabic languages [1] in the Yemen-Oman borderland, the island of Socotra, and isolated pockets such as at Jebel Fayfa near Jizan on the Saudi-Yemen border.

The language spoken in ancient western Arabia has puzzled linguists. Arab traditions state that the western Arabians migrated northwards from Yemen and tend to group them with Yemenis. However, western Arabian has, in the words of Oxford University scholar Chaim Rabin, "surprising similarities and parallelisms ... with Canaanite." [2] Since Canaanite is generally held to have had a Palestinian origin this does not seem to make sense. Logically the western Arabians must have originated in the north and migrated south, bringing their Canaanite language with them. Other linguistic evidence will be forthcoming to show that it is more likely that

Canaanite developed in western Arabia and spread north, just as Arab traditions maintain. The Arabic text *Kitab al-Aghani* (Book of the Narrative Poems) has an account of the early history of Arabia. It reiterates the widely held Muslim tradition that the earliest known inhabitants of Hijaz were "true Arabs" called Amalekites, who were attacked and annihilated by an Israelite force sent by Moses, an event absent from the Old Testament but later recorded in Jewish rabbinical traditions. The Kitab al-Aghani states that the victorious Israelite forces settled at Yathrib (Medina), a city of Egyptian foundation.

The Old Testament (Numbers 24:20) describes the Amalekites, who were extremely wealthy, as the original inhabitants ("first of nations") and also states that the Israelites were intent on their elimination. Saul's failure to accomplish this mission, described as God's Will, cost him the throne. Gordon Darnell Newby, author of *A History of the Jews of Arabia* (1988) dismisses the account in the Kitab al-Aghani as appearing "to have little historical content, although some Western scholars have regarded it and other similar accounts as reliable sources of Arabia's earliest past." Other Arab traditions exist concerning an early Israelite presence in Arabia. The Rwala Bedouin, who claim Israelite ancestry, believe that in the remote past the Israelites occupied the mountains of Hijaz and were the first people to domesticate the camel at a time when the Arabs themselves were exclusively desert nomads.

It is a mistake to accept the Zadokite-Ezra-Masoretic tradition as the sole authority on Israelite religion and early Judaism even though its legacy is modern Judaism. The Old Testament's viewpoint is overwhelmingly that of the kingdom of Judah and the Zadokite-Ezra priesthood. Omri's kingdom of Israel may even have rivaled Solomon's kingdom in wealth and influence, for his kingdom controlled the vast majority of the Israelites – the ten tribes. Moreover, Omri, unlike Solomon, is commemorated in contemporary inscriptions. The Old Testament is disparaging of Omri; his kingdom's theological heritage remains today the pitifully small Samaritan sect that augments its numbers through mail-order brides.

It is not difficult to find historical parallels to the sudden disappearance of a national creed or ideology. Most instances concern the departure of a foreign occupier or an assimilated regime associated with an alien creed. These include the 300-year Portuguese rule of the coastal area of modern Kenya and Tanzania, and the 700-year Islamic occupation of Portugal. In both cases the subject peoples had no wish to remember the religion of their former overlords (such was the reputation of the Portuguese among East

African Muslims that in Pemba Island the Virgin Mary was mistaken for a war goddess). In other cases a modern political ideology may become discredited for any number of reasons, and its former adherents would be hostile to its memory. Both ancient Israel and Judah fell to invaders, and at the very least their hierarchies were taken into exile, leaving the bulk of their subjects behind. In the case of Judah, the tenacity of the Zadokite priesthood enabled them to launch a revival, although there is no evidence to suggest it occurred in their original homeland. Nevertheless, through them remnants of the two tribes, Judah and Benjamin, not only survived but revived and modified the old religion. While nothing is known what happened of the other ten, very powerful clues exist.

Old Testament history commentators who accept the historical record nevertheless do not attempt to explain how an impoverished drought stricken marginalized piece of territory like tenth century B.C.E. Judah could have suddenly created a wealthy and powerful empire. There is simply no economic reason why it should have occurred in such a place. At the same time there were indeed immense economic reasons for such a state to rise not in Palestine but to the south in western Arabia.

The life blood of Middle Eastern states in the 10th century B.C.E. was agriculture, trade and Iron Age technology. Immense profits could be made in luxury items – gold, ivory, incense, perfumes, gemstones, exotic animals, and slaves. Domestication of the camel enabled long-distance trade to traverse inhospitable regions. The trade routes from Mesopotamia to Egypt and to the Levant passed along two great crescent-shaped routes, avoiding the Syrian Desert (*see Map 5*). The southern crescent route was the major highway from Mesopotamia to western Arabia until the twentieth century A.D. and the route that pilgrims took to Mecca after A.D. 632. Old Testament history speaks of one major raid by Egypt on Judah and Israel but conquest and destruction by Assyria and Babylon. The Egyptians were badly located to intervene in western Arabia but not in Palestine. The Assyrian and Babylonian attacks on Judah and Israel suggest it was more likely they were on the major western Arabian trade routes to Mesopotamia rather than in Palestine. With its sparse pastures Palestine had no commercial importance and was unable to control any major trade routes. On the other hand Arabia contained several major routes, and it was here not Palestine that large cities developed at oases and grew wealthy from taxing and serving the camel caravans. Solomon and Omri's states could only have achieved rapid wealth through control of lucrative trade routes, losing it when those trade routes changed direction or were taken over by rival powers. In addition, they were Iron Age states, which meant they would have had a powerful impact on a fragile environment.

An example of the Iron Age effect on the environment can be seen opposite Arabia across the Red Sea in Sudan as the railway line from Khartoum to the north passes by some curious flat-topped pyramid structures in a barren desolate landscape. These date from the ancient kingdom of Cush (or Kush), an African kingdom that not only absorbed much of Egyptian culture but also provided a ruling dynasty. The pyramids, which have a distinct style of their own, built with a sharper angle than the Egyptian model, stand over subterranean royal tombs. The Sudan has other structures, also resembling squat flat-topped pyramids. These were constructed by the ancient iron smelters of Cush and Meroe. The area once produced so much iron that European historians referred to it as the "Birmingham of Africa" after the English industrial center. It seems unbelievable to realize that long ago this desolate area, now exposed, was heavily forested, providing charcoal for the iron-smelters. The forests vanished, the iron smelters could no longer operate, and the whole countryside was reduced to desert.

A similar pattern seems to have occurred in Saudi Arabia, where the Tehama mountain ridge was once heavily cloaked in giant junipers. Agricultural clearing, shipbuilding, and house construction disposed of many of these huge trees, but the presence of iron deposits in the Jeddah region suggest most of them were reduced to charcoal for iron-working, which ultimately devastated the landscape as in Sudan. It is significant that the Qur'an refers to David and Solomon as great armorers. Certainly there is nothing in Palestinian archaeology to support the presence of an ancient iron industry of such magnitude, although McGovern's research in the Transjordan uncovered an iron smelting center that utilized oak forests in the Baq'ah Valley. McGovern concluded that this development had been uninfluenced by societies west of the Jordan, i.e. Palestine.

Much further to the west, in the western African savannah, is well-recorded historical, economic, and geographical evidence that serves as a model of what must have happened in western Arabia in earlier years. Medieval European coins were made from the red gold of western Africa. The western African savannah was a belt of territory on the southern edge of the Sahara desert free of malaria and insect-borne horse disease. The western African savannah peoples lived between rock salt-producing desert northerners who wanted gold, and gold-producing forest southerners who wanted rock salt. The savannah, which was also served by the navigable

Niger River, provided the market places to exchange goods and tax both commodities. The wealth from this tax enabled the savannah peoples to build large empires between ca. A.D. 400 and 1600. The nuclei of these empires were dependent on the trade routes. The first empire, ancient Ghana, was to the west as the gold trade passed to Morocco. The nucleus of the next state, Mali, was more to the southeast to escape desert raiders and to maintain firmer control on new gold fields. Then the gold trade shifted eastwards to Tunisia, and the next empire, Songhai, was centered more in that direction although it controlled the areas where ancient Ghana and Mali had stood. Eventually, in A.D. 1571, the Moroccans invaded Songhai in an attempt to redirect trade back to the northwest. The invasion fatally weakened Songhai but killed the trans-Saharan gold trade. The European arrival to the African west coast then totally reoriented trade southwards, and much of the savannah became a commercial and political backwater.

Supratribal monotheistic religion played a vital role in the savannah. Ghana was a pagan state but had a large Muslim population living in segregated urban areas, and the desert Muslims eventually drove Ghana's rulers south. Mali also began as a pagan state but converted to Islam, establishing a literate bureaucracy, a university, and international trade links. The pilgrimage to Mecca by the Mali ruler Mansa Musa in A.D. 1324 was so magnificent (he took 80 camels, each carrying 300 pounds of gold) that his generosity devalued the price of gold in Cairo. A shift of the trade routes to Tunisia brought prosperity further to the east to Gao, and it was this region that usurped Mali's power and established the empire of Songhai. Songhai's founder seems to have been a syncretic Muslim, but later rulers were devout Muslims who used the wealth of the empire to build Qur'anic schools, universities, and a high culture in cities such as Timbuktu, Jenne, and Gao. The Moroccan invasion was a setback for Islam, and for two hundred years there was a reversion to paganism. In the first years of the nineteenth century the Fulani, a people dispersed throughout the savannah in urban and pastoralist groups and previously excluded from power, initiated an Islamic Holy War (*jihad*) that not only revived Islam but made it the religion of all classes throughout the savannah.

The western African savannah belt today is a poor arid area prone to the encroaching desert. The trans-Saharan routes exist for small amounts of traffic and the mud-built cities still retain a certain faded grandeur. Although the emirates founded by the Fulani jihad are a power within Nigeria, the area of old Ghana, Mali, and Songhai are to the north, and it is unrealistic to believe that such an area will regain its eminence as an important part of the European economy, let alone become the center of any powerful state. Despite the collapse of the old savannah empires, the British colony of the Gold Coast at independence in 1957 chose the name *Ghana*, claiming that migrants from the old empire had settled in its territory. In 1960, a part of former French West Africa took the name *Mali* from its own past. Later another territory that had taken the name *Dahomey*, after a famous militaristic state in that area, changed it to *Benin*, the name of an old empire very firmly centered far away in Nigeria's midwest. The history of western Africa's empires and their legacies are therefore most illuminating when considering the histories of Old Testament Judaism, western Arabia, the rise of Islam, and the A.D. 1948 establishment of the state of Israel. They contain the same ingredients – a prosperous trade with shifting routes, a monotheistic religion that provided bureaucracy, literacy, urban development, empire, and a divine mission. This was then followed by external aggression, impoverishment, and decline. After a long period there was a revival under the leadership of a close-knit highly educated religious elite who appealed to their ethnic kinsfolk to take control of the political and commercial process from which they had been excluded. Lastly, after freedom from imperial alien rule, there was the pride in the remote past, which encouraged the new communities to associate themselves with prestigious empires with which they had an exceedingly nebulous link.

The archaeological evidence reveals that Palestine in the era of Solomon was a peripheral area in which petty chiefdoms vied for local supremacy in a drought-afflicted land frequently plagued by maritime raiders. In contrast, western Arabia not only possessed all the elements associated with an empire's prosperity – control of highly lucrative trade routes and oases where urban areas developed and where wealth from trade sustained a literate bureaucracy and high court culture - but also political timing.

Solomon ruled one of the earliest Iron Age empires. His state was able to assert itself because of the fluctuating political fortunes of its powerful neighbors. The Egyptians had failed to inflict a decisive victory over the Assyrians and had withdrawn to Africa. The Libyans were encroaching into western Egypt while the Sea Peoples devastated the Levant and the Nile Delta. Copper and silver supplies were cut off. Official documents of the period frequently bore a sentiment reflecting widespread pessimism: "I am all right today; tomorrow is in the hands of God." In ca. 1075 B.C.E. Egypt was split into two states with capitals at Tanis in the delta under the

Twenty-first Dynasty, and Thebes in the south under priests. As for the Assyrians, they spent the period of David and Solomon's reigns combating Aramean population movements. Authorities agree that if Solomon's state did exist, it would have taken advantage of Egypt's withdrawal from Asia and Assyria's domestic disorder. It would therefore have been centered in an area controlling valuable resources or trade routes. Palestine had neither. The area to the north, known as Phoenicia, had a long history of commercial activity. We do not know for certain what the Phoenicians called themselves, although traditions say it was a word that meant either *Canaanite* or *merchant* or both. The Egyptians established control over the area around the fifteenth century B.C.E., and when they withdrew the Phoenicians enjoyed some freedom until the Assyrians moved against them in the ninth century B.C.E. Although the Phoenician southern border was Palestine, the Phoenicians had no record of Solomon's kingdom, nor did trade between the Phoenicians and Egyptians pass through Palestine. It was sea-borne and the Phoenicians traded widely, not only throughout the Mediterranean, but also as far as Britain and West Africa. Since the Phoenicians had a hold on the trade with the Near East, the only alternative for Solomon's state to gain wealth would have been to the south, in Arabia.

There is evidence of a rich and highly organized state in the southwest of Arabia, in Sabaea, and the same kind of civilization must have flourished further along the trade routes between Sabaea and Taima, a city that Solomon is believed to have controlled. If Solomon, despite the total lack of evidence, had ruled from Palestine, the prosperity of Judah would have continued after the kingdom split because of his control of the Taima trade. However, since it was *Israel* not Judah that experienced great prosperity after the split the indications are that the northern trade that sustained Solomon's united kingdom had passed to the northern kingdom. Since Judah was supposedly in the south and controlling Taima, this makes no sense at all. The Assyrian attack of 721 B.C.E. on Israel would have been logical if Israel were in western Arabia, but not if it were in Palestine.

The Old Testament and other records speak of military expeditions by the Libyan-Egyptian leader Sheshonk (ca. 945-924 B.C.E.), the Assyrian Sennacherib (ca. 704-681 B.C.E.), and the Babylonian Nebuchadnezzar II (605-562 B.C.E.). The first expedition was undertaken against Judah in the days of turmoil after Solomon's death and provided an opportunity for the Kingdom of Israel to break free of Judaean control. Sheshonk overwhelmed several Judaean cities but Rehoboam bought him off, thus sparing the capital. Fragments of a list of Sheshonk's conquests survive at the Temple of Ammon at Karnak on the Nile, but none can be equated with any certainty to locations in Palestine. The name Jerusalem does not appear but may have been in one of the lost lists. Strategically an Egyptian expedition of such magnitude against tenth-century B.C.E. Palestine would be senseless, and it almost certainly never took place. No pharaoh, raised in Middle Egypt with his capital way down the Nile at modern-day Luxor, which is closer to Jeddah than to Jerusalem, would undertake a major military expedition against a desolate unproductive sparsely populated, poverty-stricken part of Palestine, beset by petty tribal squabbles; but he would certainly take advantage of dynastic problems in a major trading area. Western Arabia not Palestine would have been his target, and his decision to accept tribute from Jerusalem would have kept trade flowing. If Jerusalem had been in Palestine at that time the only tribute the inhabitants of that area could have offered to buy Sheshonk off would have been goats and not very many of them at that.

The next major attack came in 721 B.C.E. by Assyria against Israel, the extremely prosperous northern kingdom. It is logical to assume that Israel controlled lucrative trade routes, and the obvious choice would be those around Taima, enabling Israel to prosper at the expense of Judah, which nevertheless would have still gained wealth from the southern Arabian routes. The Assyrians annexed Israel but fell to the plague when they moved against Judah. The Babylonians completed the rationalization of trade route control 134 years later when they captured, then destroyed Jerusalem. Its destruction was partly caused by displeasure with the rebellion of the Babylonians' own appointed ruler, but there may have been an economic reason to discourage any rival state building in that area. Western Arabia's continuing prosperity convinced the Babylonians to move their capital there but soon afterwards the Persians seized control of Mesopotamia. The Jews' exile to Babylon also casts light on the true location of ancient Judah. Moses' Exodus reportedly involved over 600,000 *men* (the entire host must therefore have been over a million) and these entered an already settled country. The labor needed to construct Solomon and Omri's respective public works programs attests to a large population. When Judah fell in 586 B.C.E. it is likely its population was at the very least higher than at the Exodus level. Archaeological remains in Palestine testify to scattered villages and cattle posts. The population, no matter Judah's real location, must have been substantial because of the impact it made in Babylon, its new exiled homeland. Nabodinus chose Taima as his capital, so it is probable that the Babylonians deported the population from that area to ensure security. The nature of the Babylonian settlement indicates the exiles entered the country by the southern crescent route. Standard works such as Martin Gilbert's *Atlas of Jewish History* do not mark Arabia let alone the Arabian routes when discussing the dispersions of 721 and 686 B.C.E., merely drawing arrows from Palestine to Egypt, and to Mesopotamia through the northern crescent. If these dispersals were correct, the Jewish settlements in Mesopotamia would have tapered from the north southwards. Instead they are concentrated in the south and taper northwards in agreement with an arrival from Arabia from the routes linking Taima, Medina, and Taif. The demographic evidence of the Babylonian settlements therefore supports a western Arabian rather than a Palestinian location for the pre-exilic Old Testament. C. J. Gadd, analyzing the Babylonian inscriptions concerning the capture and settlement of Taima by Nabodinus, who used Jewish assistance (556-539 B.C.E.), concluded "that Jews, whether from among the captives of Babylonia or from those remaining in their own homeland, were strongly represented among these soldiers and settlers in Arabia." [3] This indicates that the "captives of Babylonia" returned west along the southern crescent route. It may also suggest that those referred to as "remaining in their own homeland" may have been Hijaz Jews who were not from Palestine.

If the exiled Israelites had been so useful to the Persians, why did the Persians not allow them to re-establish themselves in their old kingdom? First, Judah may have no longer have been economically viable. The Old Testament speaks of it as a desolation. Reoriented trade routes may have passed it by. The Sabaeans were active in Ethiopia in this period, maybe because they were seeking other routes to escape political pressures in the north and to share the prosperity of the Upper Nile. The Cushite ruling dynasty of Egypt lost power and moved south around 656 B.C.E., founding a new capital at Meroe on the Nile south of Napata, the Cushites' former center that Pharaoh Psamtik II would sack in 590 B.C.E. Meroe was in a fertile, more secure location, controlling the trade routes south and east and developing into a powerful wealthy kingdom. The area between Yemen and Taif would therefore have become commercially marginalized, more so because it was excluded from the Persian Empire.

Second, a high proportion of the returning Judaean exiles were priests and may not have been welcome in their former land for their spectacular failure in the divine mission. In addition, it is unlikely a newly impoverished, dislocated, and defeated population would accept the re-imposition of a ruling priest caste and temple cult with its concomitant financial demands. The exiles found themselves in a similar position as the Jews of the nineteenth and twentieth centuries who were offered opportunities, and in some cases attempted, to form homelands in the USA, Canada, Argentina, the Caribbean, Australia, Madagascar, the Kenyan-Ugandan border, Crimea, Siberia, and Vietnam besides several locations in the Middle East and in North Africa. Life in Babylon for the Jews was relatively prosperous and free, but as with many religions and political ideologies there was always the desire to establish or re-establish what is dreamed or what has been lost, irrespective of location. The Zadokites wanted their own state and the offer of New Jerusalem, despite its poor land, meager resources, mixed population, and dismal infrastructure, presented the best opportunity of having it.

If by an extraordinary set of circumstances and despite all the evidence it was found that ancient Israel and Judah were indeed located in Palestine, a great mystery would hang over the Saudi provinces of Hijaz and Asir, because the history of the trade routes and the presence of numerous archaeological ruins indicate there must have been powerful rich states in the area between ca. 1000 and 500 B.C.E. Sabaea and Aksum, too far from Assyrian and Babylonian control, continued to prosper and to expand in the same era, fueled by the same factors that would have sustained states in Hijaz and in Asir during the same period. Instead we have a detailed record of powerful, rich states of that era - ostensibly in *Palestine*, a poverty-stricken commercial backwater. It is too coincidental. Judah and Israel must have been in western Arabia.

The development of Judaism in line with Ezra's doctrines, the establishment of the New Jerusalem after the Babylonian exile, the brief period of Jewish independence under the Hasmonean dynasty, the life of Christ, the Roman destruction of Jerusalem and forced dispersal of the Jews from Palestine have made Palestine the focus of Jewish history from ca. 450 B.C.E. to the mid second century A.D. Despite the comparative wealth of Jewish historical material from this area during that time, it is nevertheless important to understand the nature of that Jewish society. The Old Testament traditions emphasize that the New Jerusalem community was a theocracy with a high proportion of settlers from the priestly houses among the returnees. The Persian province of *Yehud* was small, approximately seventy kilometers from east to west and forty kilometers from north to south. It had poor agricultural land and was distant from any important trade route. The coast was under the control of the Phoenicians. The Greek historian Herodotus failed to notice either Jerusalem or the Jews when he visited Palestine ca. 450 B.C.E., reporting only that the area was inhabited by Syrians who were similar to Phoenicians. Karen Armstrong suggests that Ezra may have begun his mission after Herodotus's time, around 398 B.C.E. But whatever the date the Jerusalem community was very small and did not make much impact on its neighbors until about 125 B.C.E.

The post A.D. 135 Jewish Diaspora saw thousands of survivors settling around the Mediterranean, but Galilee inherited, and Babylon's already Ezra-ite Jews were bolstered by, the intellectual traditions of New Jerusalem's Judaism. These centers were characterized by the theological elitism and exclusion associated with Ezra and the Pharisee rabbis. The priesthood's historical successes had been achieved through alliances with ruling dynasties, foreign and local. The spread of Judaism as a mass movement in Palestine had been brief, from ca. 152 B.C.E. to A.D. 135. When the nature of Palestinian Jewry in this period is compared to the Jewish societies of the western Arabian Hijaz and southern Arabian Yemen, it becomes difficult to accept theories that Arabian Judaism was introduced by Palestinian refugees fleeing from Roman suppression.

Persian, Greek, and Roman records have little on the history of western Arabia between 500 B.C.E. and A.D. 632. The Persians established limited control, and the Romans built forts in an attempt to control the incense trade.[4] Greek sailors have left informative accounts of the Red Sea trade; and Greek culture, as part of the Byzantine Empire, was influential in Aksum. As a whole, western Arabia declined as an area of strategic and commercial importance. This was because Aksum upstaged the lower Red Sea area as the dominant commercial and political power, while Persian, Greek, and Roman developments saw the trade take the northern crescent routes. Sabaea still remained a very wealthy country but it appears the region between Yemen and Taif became politically and commercially marginalized. During this period the Arabic-speaking nomadic pastoralist Bedouin people of the Saudi peninsula began a series of struggles for political domination. They gradually infiltrated and then came to dominate the western Arabian cities where they lived side by side with a considerable Jewish population whose origins are still very much a matter of heated dispute.

These Jewish populations became the focus of attention when historians analyzed the reasons for the rise of Islam in the early seventh century A.D. Monophysite Christianity, Persian Zoroastrianism, and other religious groups made limited inroads into Arabia prior to Islam, but

Judaism seems to have been the most pervasive. The Himyar state of Yusuf (Dhu Nuwas) in Yemen has already been mentioned, but by Muhammad's time there were substantial Jewish settlements in Hijaz in a line stretching from Fadak through Taima, Khaybar, Yadir, Yathrib/Medina, Mecca, and Taif. It is estimated that on the eve of the Islamic era, half the population of these cities was Jewish, and there were also Jewish Bedouin tribes in the surrounding oases. Two of Medina's largest tribes, the Nadir and the Quaraiza, were referred to as *Kahinani*, meaning they were of the priestly tribes of Israel. The Jews of the Taima-Khaybar area and Yemen were still fiercely independent and indulged in raiding as late as the end of the twelfth century A.D.

Palestine-oriented commentators ascribe the Jewish presence in Hijaz and Yemen to the descendants of refugees from Palestine. Jewish Talmudic sources explain this presence, saying that 80,000 priestly children fled to the Arab areas after the destruction of the First Temple. However, while it is indisputable that there was contact between Palestine and Hijaz, no tradition substantiates significant migration. Babylonian inscriptions (ca. 555-539 B.C.E.) mention the presence of Jews both in Taima and Yathrib. It is significant that Khaybar's population has historically been mostly black. This may be further evidence that Israel - the Samaritan northern kingdom and home for the ten tribes who endured forced labor - was situated in this area. As already mentioned, the Hebrew word *kushi* means both Samaritan and Black African. If many of the original Hebrew were African, and racialism already existed, it could explain why the Egyptians enslaved them. The Yibir of Somalia may be a surviving remnant of the original Hebrew, a landless, wandering but technically useful Red Sea tribe set apart by their beliefs and often enslaved by other more powerful sedentary peoples.

Gilbert's *Atlas* portraying Arabia in A.D. 750 marks a large area around Taima and Khaybar as "possible area of independent Jewish tribes, or Wild Jews, who fought successfully against Muslim domination." This slightly zoological reference typifies a somewhat snobbish attitude towards groups that do not fit Palestinian centered doctrines of what constitutes true Judaism. David Ben Gurion was not entirely correct when he stated,

> You see, we were Jews without a definition for the last 3,000 years and we will remain so. There are several definitions but the thing existed before any definition was given and after many definitions were given to the same thing. By one definition the Jews are a religious community, and there are a number of Jews that accept that definition. There is a

definition that Jews are a nation, and there are a number of Jews that accept that definition. There are a number of Jews without any definition. They are just Jews. I am one of them. I don't need any definition. I am what I am.[5]

In fact, Jews *have* been defined since the days of Ezra, often as "real" and "not quite real" Jews. The kings of the House of Herod, the Roman client rulers of Judaea at the beginning of the Christian era, were regarded by the Jerusalem Jews as semi-Jews, recent converts, Arab Jews, or Edomites (Idumeans), descended from Esau, with an origin just south of the Holy Land. They may in fact have been Arabian Israelites previously unaffected by the claims of the Jerusalem priest-caste. The Idumeans were prepared to build the Second Temple in 19 B.C.E. under Herod the Great on a grand scale, with 18,000 workmen under 1,000 artisan priests who used stone blocks weighing between two and five tons. While the Idumeans may have been part of a Jewish Bedouin population outside the control of Jerusalem community that were migrating north from Hijaz, much of the population of Palestine were descendants of non Israelites forced by the Hasmoneans to convert to Judaism. When Roman rule was established many of these reverted to their former beliefs. Commentators have included the Idumeans among the forcibly converted, but at the very least they had been exposed to Israelites in Arabia from a pre-exilic background.

One of the major reasons for the explosion of Islam from Arabia into the Fertile Crescent and the corn lands of North Africa was to escape from the deteriorating Arabian environment. People *left* Arabia; they did not flee to it. After the dispersal of Jews from Palestine in the first and second centuries A.D. Jewish communities were established all over the Mediterranean world to such an extent that but for the rise of Christianity there was a possibility that a liberal form of Judaism may have become the majority urban religion of the Roman Empire.

Even before the Diaspora there is evidence of Jewish intellectual life in Arabia. Paul, after his Damascus vision, went to Arabia for three years, where he seems to have acquired information and ancient texts relating to Christ's background and early life that assisted his later mission. Waraqah Ibn Nawfal, a relative of Muhammad's wife Khadijah, appears to have possessed ancient Judaic documents concerning the life of Christ. These were known to the Ethiopians but are now lost.

The Prophet Muhammad was born ca. 570 A.D. in Mecca. His father died before his birth and his mother and grandfather when he was respectively six and eight. Although his guardian uncle was head of a prominent Meccan clan (the Hashim), under Arab law, Muhammad, a minor, could not inherit. His early years were spent being cared for by a Bedouin family in the desert, and then he became involved in the caravan trade. Mecca was an important trading center and pagan shrine where rival groups could meet on neutral ground. Mecca controlled Syrian and Yemeni trading caravans carrying Aksumite and Indian goods north and Mediterranean produce south. In A.D. 595 Muhammad married a widowed business woman, Khadijah, and took no other wife until her death in A.D. 619.

In about A.D. 610 Muhammad began experiencing a series of revelations which eventually numbered 650. He was encouraged by his wife and her cousin Waraqah Ibn Nawfal, who recognized him as the long awaited Arab prophet. He attracted a small group of followers before commencing public preaching in A.D. 613. He quickly developed a new creed, *Islam*, with a following mostly drawn from younger men. Much of his appeal came from his criticism of the breakdown of traditional values, particularly the care of the less fortunate, which was a consequence of individual acquisition among the commercial clan leaders. His revelations included a strong element of the feeling of exclusion and class oppression that characterized both the rise of Buddhism and Christianity.

> Believers, many are the clerics and the monks who defraud men of their possessions and debar them from the path of God. To those that hoard up gold and silver and do not spend it in God's cause, proclaim a woeful punishment. The day will surely come when their treasures shall be heated in the fire of Hell, and their foreheads, sides and backs branded with them. They will be told: "These are the riches which you hoarded. Taste then what you were hoarding."

Muhammad's uncle and protector, the clan leader Abu Talib, died in around A.D. 619 and his successor, another uncle named Abu Lahab, was no longer prepared to protect Muhammad from the powerful merchants he criticized. Muhammad's insistence on strict monotheism alienated those who believed in and profited from the pagan shrines. Eventually Muhammad arranged to quit Mecca for Yathrib (Medina), where disputing Arab clans invited him to arbitrate among them. Muhammad first moved to Taif, where the situation proved unsatisfactory, and then arrived in Medina in A.D. 622 in a move celebrated as the *Hijrah*, a final cutting of all links with kinship. Medina was a Jewish settlement with the best land under

Jewish control, but Arab immigrants were more powerful. Muhammad established himself as a judge among the eight or more Arab clans (the Jewish population was allocated to the clans) but he held no formal position except as prophet. The spread of his new faith was very much dependent on the concept of jihad, the obligation to make holy war. The Muslims launched sporadic unsuccessful attacks on the Meccan caravans headed for Syria, but a Muslim attack in A.D. 634 on a Yemeni caravan bound for Mecca was a violation of the general truce Arabs respected for the city. At the same time Muhammad broke with the Jews following their refusal to accept the primacy of his message which thereafter became militantly Arab. The Muslim setback at the hands of the Meccans at the Battle of Badr in A.D. 624 obliged Muhammad to take stronger measures to consolidate his position in Medina, and he also contracted several dynastic marriages. In A.D. 625 the Meccans attacked in strength but despite mauling the Islamic forces did not achieve the success they had publicly predicted. A siege of Medina in A.D. 627 by a 10,000-strong Meccan force failed, and a peace was concluded whereby Muhammad married the daughter of the Meccan leader. The truce failed to last and Muhammad moved against Mecca, which surrendered without a fight in January A.D. 630. The Persians had been defeated by Byzantium in A.D. 627-8 and their territories in Yemen and the Gulf went over to Muhammad, who also defeated a hostile confederation of Bedouins at the Battle of Hunayn. At the end of A.D. 630 Islamic troops traveling north raided Syria thus completing the unification of the Arabian peninsula. In A.D. 632 Muhammad unexpectedly died, but the new religion not only survived this shock but in twenty years also succeeded in overrunning areas from Central Asia to the Oxus River and the Indian frontier to the east; and North Africa to Tripoli in Libya in the west, establishing Islam as a world power.

Commentators have linked Muhammad's extraordinary career to Christian and Jewish influences, although it is clear that the formative years of his frenetic career was spent largely in interaction with young idealistic Arabs from the merchant class. When Islam first galvanized Byzantine attention after A.D. 632, it was interpreted as Christian heresy but, despite references to Christ and the Virgin Mary, Islam is far removed from Christianity. It is an astonishing experience to move from reading the *Caleb Cycle* of the *Kebra Nagast*, with its emphasis on the Hellenic world, Christian Monophysitism, and the controversies of Nicaea and Chalcedon, and enter the world of the Qur'an a hundred years later. It is like being transported back to an ancient time, when the Old Testament patriarchs were setting out again on an alternative spiritual journey. The Islamic Qur'an, compiled through revelations and other material, is in part a divine dialogue discussing numerous incidents, ideas, and personalities from the Old Testament and, to a much lesser extent, the New Testament, taking for granted they were part of Arab cultural heritage and did not need elaboration. In addition, many of the allusions to the Old and New Testaments do not follow the versions recorded in those books. The Joseph story is more detailed, and the Virgin Mary is a far more formidable and fascinating individual than she appears in the New Testament. It seems that Muhammad was not so much drawing on strong local Jewish traditions but on an ancient common Semitic folk culture. Muhammad himself stressed he was not creating a new religion but purifying the creed of Abraham. Solomon and the Queen of Sheba figure prominently in the Qur'an and appear to reflect Arabian not Palestinian traditions. In the Qur'an, as in the *Sheba-Menelik Cycle* of the *Kebra Nagast*, Judah and Sheba seem to be close neighbors. Other geographical details, such as Moses' reference to "where the two seas meet" (the Red Sea and the Indian Ocean) also add weight to an Arabian setting for the Old Testament. The overall impression gained from the Qur'an is of a shared Semitic historical and theological experience that the Muslims believed had been led astray by Judaism. Muhammad speaks of the patriarchs, Abraham and Moses, as if they were as much part of Arab heritage as they were to the Jews. None of his enemies disputed it.

To Christians with knowledge of Christ of the Gospels, Muhammad's knowledge seems ill-informed and inaccurate, but this overlooks that Christians based their own assumptions on extremely scanty Palestinian evidence surrounding Christ's early life. The Islamic contribution to historiography is probably not well known in the West. The Muslim writers realized that their message could not be imposed merely by force of arms. They had to appeal to the intellect. Therefore, after the Prophet Muhammad's death, they set about trying to write an accurate account of his life and work, even if this meant discussing setbacks and changes of mind. Therefore, the Muslims not only did vital pioneering work for good history writing, particularly analysis; they also wrote excellent biographies of "the Prophet" and his times. In some ways they were more fortunate than the early Christians who, being persecuted and scattered, worked underground and in the shadow of what seemed in the early days to be a very unsuccessful cause whose adherents were falsely accused of cannibalism and often committed suicide to reach heaven. Moreover, the

Christian philosophy was developed under political pressure by a recently converted pagan Roman emperor. Islam was almost immediately a successful world religion, and Muslims could write with confidence about their origins and development from recent eyewitnesses and from easily accessible documents. It is probable that they had a better knowledge of certain aspects of Christian history than the Christians themselves had.

According to Yemeni tradition, Nazarene Judaism was founded about 400 years before Christ in Najran by a virgin named Mary (sic). [6] The Qur'anic description of the Virgin Mary is of a strong-willed Levitical priestess who chastised the temple priesthood for doubting her son Isa had been fathered by *Ruah* (the Holy Spirit). This extraordinary tradition is of interest considering the nebulous nature of Christ's mother in the New Testament and the fact that her *sister's* name was Mary, something most unsatisfactorily explained by Christian commentators who suggest they had the same father but different mothers. This tradition will be discussed later in the chapter concerning Israelite influences in Ethiopia, another area sharing a general Semitic cultural heritage.

Islam appealed deeply to the Arab psyche, particularly through the beautiful poetic nature of the Qur'an. The Arabs had long despaired of having their own prophet. The revelations and dictates of Muhammad ultimately evoked a pan tribal fiercely nationalistic spirit and to ascribe this to Jewish influence would be a mistake. Charles Cutler Torrey (1863-1956), professor of Semitic Languages at Yale suggested in his book *The Jewish Foundations of Islam* (1933) that there was a substantial Jewish presence in Arabia that was highly influential in Islam, stating that "both in its beginning and its later development by far the greater part of its essential material came directly from Israelite sources." The Qur'an does in fact state (7:156) that Muhammad took the Hebrew Torah as his model for his own code of law but revised and improved it for the new circumstances and the Arab tradition. It is however highly noteworthy that Muhammad's legislation does not reflect the post-exilic form of Judaism, indicating that the type of Judaism in Hijaz was from an Israelite tradition outside that of the restored Jerusalem community. Jewish Bedouin women were veiled, and Babylonian Jews acknowledged Hijaz Jews were outside their jurisdiction but nevertheless respected their differing customs and spoke well of Simeon, a Jew from Taima, as a theological scholar. There are only 80 references in the Qur'an to laws, as opposed to 613 in the Torah. Muhammad made judgments according to his revelations and his own logical conclusions, a flexibility continued by his successors when they developed the Islamic code of law, the *Sharia*.

One legislative innovation struck a crippling blow not only to the inspirational example of the Queen of Sheba but also to the status and aspirations of millions of women thereafter. According to the Arab historian al-Tha'labi, Muhammad despised women rulers,[7] despite the assistance, advice, and financial backing of Khadija and the presence of Arab queens. The rise of Islam followed the pattern of much earlier states, condemning women to an inferior role through Holy Writ.

In his revelations Muhammad never heard a voice. He interpreted visions and feelings, ascribing them to divine inspiration. Sura 4:34 of the Qur'an declares:

> Men have authority over women because God has made one superior to the other, and because they spend their wealth to maintain them.

The same Sura gives permission for men to use violence against women, the only instance in sacred texts:

> Good women are obedient. They guard their unseen parts because God has guarded them. As for those whom you fear disobedience, admonish them and send them to their beds apart and beat them.

Reinhart Dozy (see below) suggests that Jews came to Mecca during the days of the Babylonian exile and established an Israelite cult in Mecca, which explains why they differed from the postexilic New Jerusalem community. The Arabs themselves believed that Abraham was linked to the Islamic sacred shrine of the Ka'bah, and that the Israelites had a very early association with Arabia. Charles Cutler Torrey dismissed these traditions as "fanciful tales ... all worthless for our purpose."

Khaybar has always possessed a large African population. This has been ascribed to slavery, but it is more probable that the area was from early times inhabited by an African people. The Hebrew word for African and Samaritan is the same – *kushi* – so the high percentage of African Jews in Khaybar may support the contention that the Khaybar Jews were a remnant of the northern (Samaritan) kingdom of Israel. Medina to the south, also a center for urban and desert Jews, had an ancient Egyptian origin (Yathrib), which may add weight to the argument that the Hebrew captivity took place in an Egyptian colony not in Africa itself. Spencer Trimingham summarizes the theories surrounding the origins of Hijaz Jews:

The question as to whether they derived from arabized Jews, descendants of immigrants, or were judaized Arabs, has not been satisfactorily resolved. But it is clear that the outlook and social organization of the Jews settled in these oasis communities was quite different from that of Aramaic-speaking Jews in Babylonia. ..... if they were originally Arabs, any consciousness of relationship had evaporated in consequence of their having absorbed a Jewish exclusivist outlook.

Behind most of the theories on the origins of the Arabian Jews is the preconception that Palestine was the location of the Old Testament. This is understandable given that it is only since the 1990s that demographic studies and comprehensive archaeological surveys have revealed that ancient Palestine could not possibly have sustained the high culture and economy of Ancient Judah and Israel. Torrey dismissed Arab traditions that Mecca could have been settled by Israelites in Old Testament times, because he could only envisage *Jewish* influence in late Old Testament times, moving south from Palestine to the settlements of Hijaz - Taima, Khaybar, and Yathrib (Medina) - whereas it is possible that they had been in the Mecca-Medina area since the time of Moses.

Another school of thought suggests that Hijaz Jews were descendants of Yemeni Jews. Although genetically they are identical to Yemeni Arabs, the Yemeni Jews have several traditions about their origin. One story states that some Hebrew rebelled against Moses and fled to Yemen. Their descendants told the Queen of Sheba of Solomon's wisdom. A second account states the Yemeni Jews are descendants of Israelites whom Solomon sent to Sheba, while others say their ancestors left Judah forty-two years before the destruction of the First Temple and spurned the prophet Ezra's call to return to rebuild it, foreseeing further torment. Finally, one tradition says the Yemeni Jews are descendants of Jews who fled from Palestine after the two uprisings against Roman rule that were brutally crushed in the first and second centuries A.D. If the latter story is true it would be logical to see a tapered pattern of Jewish settlement stretching from Palestine through the Arabian peninsula with larger settlements closer to Palestine. Torrey summarized the frustrating evidence "The investigator is disappointed by the scarcity of Israelites in one place [northern and central Arabia], and scandalized by their apparent multitude in the other [Yemen]". Torrey concluded that "In the absence of a plausible theory of extensive immigration, the hypothesis of converted Arab tribes seemed the only recourse." Others have disagreed. Margoliouth believed that Arabs and Israelites had a common origin in Arabia and evidence exists from Sabaean and Minaen inscriptions (ca. 1000 B.C.E.) of monotheism, a theological innovation usually associated with Judaism, but which may have evolved from a local pagan cult. During Muhammad's time, there was evidence of a monotheist Arab faith associated with Abraham. Margoliouth, nevertheless, remained unconvinced of a substantial Old Testament Jewish political presence in Yemen, stating that if "a Jewish kingdom ever held sway in South Arabia, it left little impression on the North Arabian mind."

A reason for this may have been the failure of the Israelite kingdoms. The Old Testament is the work of a priestly hierarchy supporting a political state and a divine mission. By the end of the Old Testament this hierarchy was seriously disturbed at the seeming failure of the divine mission, the destruction of the state, and the dispersal of its people (ten of the twelve tribes are forever "lost"). Yet even during the zenith of political fortunes it was clear that the Israelite religion and hierarchy did not receive overwhelming popular support. The population was conquered and its religions suppressed, but their pressure was still strong. Solomon tried to win support from his diverse subjects, who hated his high taxes, by seeking to accommodate their religious beliefs, and contracting numerous dynastic marriages, but his legacy soon collapsed and the united monarchy, wracked by dynastic quarrels and external aggression, split into two and, after Omri, were never again of significance up until their destruction by the Assyrians and Babylonians. In contrast, Sheba's Yemeni realm and the Aksumite kingdom continued to prosper and remained highly respected in Arabia until the advent of Islam.

Any Israelite kingdom intrinsically linked to a briefly triumphant exclusive Hebrew elite claiming God's divine favor could not serve as a model for an Arab state so long as the divine message was for Jews alone, who, after Ezra, made conversion a difficult process. The Old Testament very much reflects the views of the priestly class and the court circle and cannot be accepted as the outlook of the population as a whole. From their point of view the Israelite states were the creation of unpopular foreign invaders with a over demanding alien religion. It is most probable that when Judah was overwhelmed and its leadership deported, the population as a whole did not regret it.

The first academic to suggest a long-established Israelite presence in Arabia was Reinhart Dozy in his book *Die Israeliten zu Mekka von David's Zeit* (1864). Dozy believed that Mecca and other major western

Arabian settlements had been populated by Israelites since King David's time, basing this conclusion on Arab sources and the Old Testament (1 Chronicles 4:38-43) that state sections of the Israelites massacred the Amalekites and took their land. Subsequent commentators have dismissed Dozy's views but have still not come to terms with the reasons for widespread Jewish settlement in Arabia. Other writers noted that Hijaz Jews spoke a dialect known as Judeo-Arabic, phrases from which Muhammad himself quoted in the Qur'an, a factor that seems to militate against Torrey, Winckler, and other authorities' conclusions that the Arabian Jews were converted Arabs.

Nothing can be ascertained for certain until discovery of archaeological evidence or ancient documentation. Most likely important evidence exists in Mecca and Medina; but since both are closed Islamic cities it is out of the question that any Judaic research can be undertaken in either of them. The picture that emerges from the dawn of Islam is of large Israelite or Jewish communities in Yemen and Hijaz, both of unknown origin and antiquity but with little known about the territory between them.

Linguistic evidence, though certainly not conclusive, has provided interesting pointers for further research. Arabic is now the language of the Arabian peninsula. In Yemen there are six non-Arabic dialects, and elsewhere there are local dialects that differ sharply from the Standard Arabic taught in schools and used in the media. The local Arabic dialects are the result of modern Arabic absorbing local languages. Many examples of this phenomenon exist among English speakers who retain parts of grammar of unrelated languages spoken by their ancestors several generations earlier. Speakers of Caribbean English sometimes interchange *he/she* and *him/her* irrespective of the gender of the subject. This is because the language of their West African ancestors did not differentiate the gender of the third person singular (for example, in East Africa the Swahili for "he/she is asleep" is identical – *analala*). When some Africans switched to English they carried through the genderless grammar (other African languages like Maasai and Tigrinya mark the gender in verbs) and passed it on to their descendants. A British English example would be "I don't know nothing," which is from an Anglo-Saxon dialect where the double negative was used (like some modern Flemish dialects and Afrikaans). Through *error analysis* (mistakes made in the adopted language) researchers can reconstruct part of the former language's grammar. Other findings can be gleaned from vocabulary for local items such as fauna and flora and specialized activities (English has many Dutch nautical words such as *deck, yacht, skipper, and boom*).

There are several major Arabic dialects in western Arabia, each containing subgroups. The main groups are Yemen, Himyar, 'Azd, North Yemen, Hudhail, Hijaz, and Tayyi'. The major work comparing them to Hebrew/Canaanite was undertaken in Hebrew (1946) and English (1951) by Chaim Rabin, Cowley Lecturer in Post-Biblical Hebrew at the University of Oxford. Rabin quickly noted the "surprising similarities and parallelisms of West Arabian with Canaanite." Rabin's generation took for granted that the homeland of the Old Testament and of Hebrew/Canaanite was Palestine and he therefore remarked: "A northern origin [of West Arabian] would certainly supply the easiest explanation." Rabin took the Yemeni dialect of Arabic and found a number of words similar to Hebrew such as *devil, lord, furrow, wooden poker, firewood, thick clay, a small axe, to romp, to hoe, sycamore, deep river gorge, to sit,* and *to shine*. He stated "the list is too long to be taken as mere coincidence." He also noted that Ge'ez "agrees in some points of vocabulary with Hebrew against all other Semitic languages." Here at last is linguistic evidence that seems to support the inscriptions near Mekele stating that Hebrew and Sabaeans once lived together under Sabaean rulers. Wolf Leslau, the renown scholar of Ethiopian religion, traditions, and languages, discovered an extraordinary number of similarities between Hebrew and Amharic, geographically the furthest removed of Ethiopia's Semitic languages from Hebrew. In addition, Leslau investigated contributions from Ge'ez and South Arabic to Hebrew. He noted that Gafat, an extinct language once spoken in Blue Nile area (the alleged location of the Hebrew Damot state of Queen Yudit), had words similar to Hebrew, e.g. *bäsärä* (meat), *mäce* (when), which do not occur in Amharic. Leslau also discovered that some Hebrew words were identical in Cushitic. Leslau's work unfortunately does not draw any conclusions, probably because Leslau dismisses any notion that the Old Testament occurred in western Arabia.

In linguistics there is a basic list of 100 words developed by Morris Swadesh (1909-67). Critics believed that 100 words were insufficient for linguistic analysis; but when a further 100 were added, the results were the same. Swadesh reasoned that on average two languages from an ancestral language would retain 86 per cent of the basic words after a thousand years of separation. Studies accomplished among the languages of the Caucasus gave 48 per cent for 2290 years; 30 per cent for 3990 years,

MAP 8

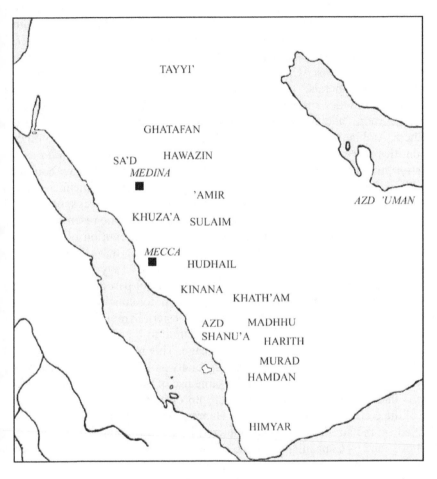

Arabic Dialects of Western Arabia (Tayyi' and Azd 'Uman speakers originated in Yemen)

and 11% for 10,260 years. Problems would of course arise if these diverging groups of languages were affected by unrelated languages, hence the difficulty in ascertaining the origin of Vietnamese and Korean, both heavily influenced by Chinese dialects. The Semitic languages, however, are largely free from external mixing although some words come from Sumerian in the east, Cushitic in the west, and Indo-European in the northwest peripherals. Leslau's *Comparative Dictionary of Ge'ez* fortunately provides material for further analysis, showing that Ge'ez, an language more ancient than Amharic and one geographically close to southern Arabia, is indeed close to Hebrew. Rabin drew attention to other similarities to Hebrew from the northern Yemen dialect's use of *dha* as a question marker and the construction of the demonstrative *that* without an article *a/an* or *the* both in Canaanite and in Northern Yemeni as "too remarkable to be accidental." When reviewing Hudhail a dialect spoken just east of Mecca, Rabin observed that with sound changes "the resemblance to Canaanite developments is striking." He dismissed the notion of a certain sound change as being general to Semitic, emphasizing that it was specific to West Arabian and Canaanite/Hebrew. In the case of Tayyi', the language of a Yemeni tribe that migrated to the northern central part of Arabia, Rabin noted similarities with Canaanite that led him to conclude: "We must therefore assume that part at least of the Western Arabians remained in close enough contact with speakers of Canaanite to be affected by a sound change which took place within that language. This is not the place to work out the historical implications of this, especially as it affects the darkest part of Arab history." Finally he found the same use of *dhu,* a relative particle in Tayyi' that brought "the Tayyi' dialect into clear connection with at least one of the constituent elements of the Hebrew language." Rabin was clearly puzzled by the similarities he encountered between the dialects of western Arabia and Canaanite/Hebrew. The evidence suggested that Canaanite/Hebrew had once been spoken in western Arabia as far south as the Yemen border and, from Leslau's work, even more probably in the Ethiopian/Eritrean highlands. This evidence is totally against the Old Testament scholastic traditional in which Rabin had been raised, yet thankfully he made no attempt to explain it away.

Next there are the ruins of western Arabia. Some archaeological excavation has been accomplished on the coast near Jizan that reveals a society with strong African links dating back to the second or even third millennium B.C.E. Pottery here is related to that of the same era in Hamasien, and in Nubia on the Nile. Jizan used to belong to Yemen, but

Jizan province along with Asir were annexed in a 1930s Saudi military campaign by the future King Faisal. Driving out from Jizan, you will encounter a wadi or gulley stretching up to Abu Arish, where a dam has been built to provide irrigation for agriculture. Along the way there are small volcanic cones, the area strewn with lava. At one point a massive lava flow (its significance will be discussed later) has blocked the wadi and just beyond that there is an abandoned *tell* (a hill composed of the accumulated ruins of successive settlements) overlooking a small village. The tell is quite high and at its summit there are lots of broken blue pottery pieces. No one knows what lies further down. The tell is just one of many unexplored ancient settlements dotted over the southern part of Saudi Arabia.

From Jizan the main road follows the coastal strip, and then climbs up the spectacular jagged escarpment to Abha in highland Asir. Here again are a substantial number of untouched archaeological remains. The early history of the area has always been a mystery, yet it must have once prospered from its control of the land trade routes from India to the Mediterranean through Sabaea.

In 1977, a three volume *Gazette of Place Names* was published in Saudi Arabia.[8] It not only listed place names but also the locations of Saudi tribes and clans. Its publication prompted Christian Arab historian Professor Kamal Salibi of the American University of Beirut to examine it for clues to the southern region's early history. To his astonishment he found himself looking at hundreds of biblical place names in an area approximately 600 by 200 kilometers, not in Palestine but in the southern part of modern Saudi Arabia in the provinces of Asir, Jizan, and Hijaz. The names of several Saudi tribal groups also matched ancient Hebrew ones. Salibi took the unvocalized place names of Saudi Arabia and compared them to the unvocalized Old Testament Hebrew names. Naturally there was not a perfect match because of *metathesis*, the linguistic process described earlier, which has probably been responsible for many changes. Salibi is a scholar with a considerable international academic reputation to defend and did not reach his conclusions lightly. He is also a very courageous man who, during the most dangerous and lawless period in Beirut's history, publicly denounced the kidnapping of foreigners in Lebanon. Salibi systematically re-examined the unvocalized Hebrew text and plotted events of the Old Testament narrative against the map references he had obtained from Saudi Arabia. His conclusions, though startling, make a lot more sense of biblical history, particularly because the place names occur in exactly the same area

Rabin found so many Hebrewisms. Salibi is apparently not aware of Rabin's work.

In 1985, Salibi published his initial findings as *The Bible Came from Arabia,* suggesting that it was likely that the events of the Hebrew Bible, until the Babylonian captivity, took place in western Arabia. Salibi suggested that one or more of the tribes that eventually became known as the Hebrew originated in the volcanic area of northern Yemen and then controlled a major East-West trade route across central Arabia. There they came into conflict with an Egyptian colony based in Wadi Bishah in western Arabia. The Egyptians enslaved the Hebrew, who, led by Moses in the Exodus, eventually reached the area just north of Mecca where they united with an Aramean people into "all Israel." The suggestion of the Israelite identity belonging to Joshua's time matches Noth's 1930 hypothesis. Salibi placed the original homeland of six of the "lost" ten tribes (Reuben, Simeon, Levi, Dan, Gad, and Issachar) in the Hijaz area around Jeddah and Mecca. Significantly his location for the tribe of Judah, eponymous to the southern Israelite state, was on the escarpment and wadis south of Taif. The tribe of Benjamin (*bn ymn*) was also assigned the same area, not surprisingly considering that the name means *Son of the South.* The Queen of Sheba, ruler of Yemen, was later referred to as the Queen of the South.

After consolidating their strength the Israelites expanded southward under Saul and then under David and Solomon until they had overrun much of the territory where their ancestors had originally been enslaved. The southern advance took them to the frontier of Sheba (Sabaea), and traditions say that Solomon proceeded further south to overrun Yemen itself.

As mentioned earlier, archaeologists had already expressed exasperation over the lack of evidence supporting the Old Testament. However none of these critics questioned the Masoretes' work in vocalizing place names that would occasionally match the locations where (e.g. Ararat) they were writing. Salibi challenged these assumptions, insisting that the Masoretes were geographically and historically biased towards their own homelands, and he insisted the unvocalized Hebrew text be re-examined. He reasoned that the word *H-yrdn*, translated in the Hebrew Bible as the River Jordan, was not a river at all but the Tehama mountain ridge that rises sharply from the Red Sea coastal plain. He placed Old Jerusalem, the City of Zion, and the City of David at separate locations, Jerusalem near An Nimas south of Taif, and stated that the "Egypt" and

"Ethiopia" of the Old Testament mostly did not refer to those countries at all but to two cities named *Msrm* and *Kws* (Cush/Kush). These were all situated in the highland area controlling trade routes from Yemen to the north. Salibi had other fascinating suggestions. He identified Al Junaynah as the Garden of Eden, hypothesizing that it was a center for a priesthood known as *krbym* (Cherubim), a name reminiscent of the Sabaean *mkrbm* priest-kings. As for Sabaea itself, he placed the city of Sheba at Khamis Mushait in Asir, quite far away from Marib, the later capital. And the wadi blocked by lava near Jizan? In Salibi's opinion it was the probable site for Sodom and Gomorrah, cities believed to have been overwhelmed by a volcanic eruption.

The story of Queen Esther has never been seriously considered by biblical scholars because it was assumed to have been set in the Persian imperial court, which has no record of a Jewish queen. Salibi suggested that the story was instead centered not in the Persian imperial capital but in the Taima region of western Arabia. In a letter to this writer, 31 March 1989, he explained:

> Right now, I am studying the extremely problematical books of Esther and Daniel, which have the same geographical and historical setting. While I remain in no position to say anything conclusive about them, one thing seems to me already clear. The Kings (Ahasuerus in Esther, and the enigmatic Darius son of Ahaurus the Mede in *Daniel*) were not Persian emperors, but viceroys in charge of an Arabian province of the Persian empire centering around Taima, in the northern Hijaz, with its fortress (h-byrh) capital at a Susa, which is today Shusha, a short distance south of Taima. It was this province which comprised 127 districts....The satrapies of the Persian empire never number more than about 30, from an original of about 20. Between Hadiyya and Kuthah (hdw to kws in Esther 1:1 – translated in the Old Testament as "India to Ethiopia") in Saudi Arabia the number of recognized imarat (traditional tribal districts), at present, is about 130.

Salibi's ideas are indubitably attractive, because if they are accepted, the events narrated in the Hebrew Bible become comprehensible. For anyone who has studied the economic geography of the sort of state Solomon ruled, Old Testament maps are very unsatisfactory. Blobs of territory are marked "Moab," "Samaria," or "Judah," with no logical economic or geographical explanation of how such states sustained themselves. Salibi's determination of ancient Israel and Judah as states controlling the trade routes of western Arabia makes more sense.

Kamal Salibi had intended his hypothesis to provide an answer both to the dilemma of Old Testament archaeology and to the unexplained ruined cities astride the ancient trade routes that followed the escarpment edge in Saudi Arabia. He probably expected his suggestions to be taken as courteously and seriously as his past publications on Lebanese history. Salibi's work was certainly not warmly received. Strong opposition came from Israel, where Salibi's work was interpreted as an attempt to undermine the basis of the Jewish state. From other quarters, John Day, the editor of the *Oxford Bible Atlas*, condemned Salibi's hypothesis as "total nonsense" while Cambridge University's Professor John Emerton and London University's Tudor Parfitt's stand against Salibi rested on their somewhat curious assertion that Hebrew had never died out as a living language. Pennsylvania's Professor James Sauer denounced Salibi's book before he had read it and stated, "Jerusalem and Hebron are exactly where the Bible says they are."

Philip Hammond of the University of Utah, in 1991, criticized Salibi for reaching historical conclusions by examining, primarily, linguistic and archaeological evidence. He concluded:

> A proper review of this book would unfortunately subject the reader to a volume far larger than the one being reviewed. The sheer enormity, page by page, of "identifications," transmutations, blatant historical error, misconceptions, and similar problems with the scholarship, preclude considerations within the scope of any "review." It is difficult to understand how such a volume could have been foisted upon an unsuspecting public. Perhaps the scholarly reader will find a certain degree of amusement in appreciating the skill of the author in his attempted linguistic exercises, but the lay reader might, regrettably, be misled by the appearance of the "scholarship" presented. To assume that similar, or even identical, place names are proof of "identity" between two places is palpably absurd. To declare that archaeology, with its modern chronometric techniques, cannot place occupations correctly is contrary to fact. To ignore the linguistic analyses of Biblical Hebrew from the Masoretes to modern scholarship is presumptuous. To dismiss casually all modern scholarship in the field is unscholarly in the extreme. To display ignorance of published archaeological and other data in favor of selected, "favorable" quotations is likewise not the way knowledge is advanced. In short, this reviewer can see no reason why this volume was published, either in its original German edition, or in English translation.

W. Sibley Towner of Union Theological College in Richmond, Virginia, in 1988, felt that "The weight of millennia of tradition and all of modern scholarship...all work powerfully against his thesis" and found it "not credible that the collective memory of Israel was so short that no recollection whatever was preserved of an old 'Jerusalem ... in the heights of Nimas, just across the Asir escarpment.'" The Saudi Arabian government was harshest of all, destroying the sites Salibi had identified as possible major Old Testament locations and giving newspaper space to an Egyptian commentator to abuse Salibi while ignoring his arguments. Salibi, the commentator declared in 1997 in an article that baffled readers, was like a man searching under a street light for a coin he had lost elsewhere, because it was easier to search by its beam.

Bruce Dahlberg, in 1994, criticized Salibi for working alone:

> The fact is ... that in the early 1980s in Beirut Salibi was for practical purposes isolated from contact with Hebrists and biblical scholars elsewhere. It can be noted in his Bible/Arabia book that there is virtually no reference to or dialogue with any scholar at all. Whether this isolation contributed to the tangent he took, or was caused by the latter, or whether the circumstance is relevant at all, I have no idea. It may well have been a vicious circle.

Jonas Greenfield (1994), agreed:

> To call what he does 'biblical studies' makes our field in the broadest sense a travesty, and one may truly wonder about good Fulbright money being spent in this manner. It is also a bit ridiculous to say that he couldn't have contact with scholars in Beirut then since Bill Ward was at AUB, and there were indeed others there. One wonders.

Salibi's book and the reviews preceded Thompson's devastating survey of Palestinian archaeology. Hammond insisted that:

> I argue on the basis of evidence from Palestinian archaeology – which rests upon rather firm cross chronologies, stratigraphic sequences, ceramic progressions, epigraphic developments, and other factors – that his hypothesis is wrong.

Salibi's work drew attention to demarcation and lack of cross discipline research in biblical studies. Arabia south of Jordan is overwhelmingly ignored and is considered an area belonging to Islamic studies for isolated specialists such as Spencer Trimingham and Irfan Shahid, renown for their work on Monophysite Christianity; and Chaim Rabin, renown for his linguistic work on ancient West Arabian, of which Philip Hammond, whose reviews emphasize his expertise as a Semiticist, was embarrassingly ignorant. Hammond, who used "contrary to fact", "unscholarly in the extreme," and "presumptuous," to describe Salibi's work, revealed lamentable linguistic knowledge and ignorance of Chaim Rabin's work, implying that Arabia in ancient times possessed only two languages:

> If Hebrew was not the language of the "Hebrews," but a language "widely spoken in western Arabia" why are there differences between it and Arabic, not to mention, in earlier times between it and both northern and southern Arabic?

Few scholars can compare with Shahid, whose knowledge covers both the Ethiopian and Arabian past, and there are almost none who can add the Hebrew past to encompass all three. Salibi is unusual, for as a Christian Arab his world view of the past is not cut off at the Jordanian border like his Western contemporaries. His scenario of a Hebrew past connected to the Arabian peninsula should not have been rejected out of hand, particularly when leading archaeologists such as Kenyon had already shown that an ancient Hebrew presence on the lines of the Old Testament was most unlikely. Salibi later stated:

> Biblical scholars and historians of the ancient Middle East have come to form a closed circle, which resents unsolicited intrusion into the field. They have built an edifice based on foundations, which are, in most cases, assumptions, which they attempt to pass for facts, while refusing any radical re-examination of the subject matter.

In the November 1991 issue of the International Journal of Mideast Studies, Professor John Joseph of Franklin and Marshall College, Lancaster, Pennsylvania, commenting on Philip Hammond's 1990 review of Salibi's work, wrote:

> We owe it to ourselves as well as to him [Salibi] .... to scrutinize his thesis and the mass of detailed evidence that he has carefully gathered to defend it ....Five years after the publication of this controversial book [The Bible Came From Arabia], perhaps MESA [Middle East Studies Association of North America] should devote a special issue its Bulletin, if not of IJMES [International Journal of Mideast Studies], to an expert and fair evaluation of Kamal Salibi's arguments and approach. In the meantime, perhaps Hammond would enlighten those of us who do not have the expertise to judge for ourselves, but have students to teach and seminars to conduct, what at least some of the most "blatant" errors are that he seems to have found throughout the book and correct them.

No such debate has eventuated. Despite this, commentators have continued to debate Salibi's ideas, mostly on the Internet. Chris Khoury, writing on February 25, 2003, aptly summarized the situation:

> Upon scouring whatever journals I could for book reviews and commentary on Salibi's work, I found much ridicule, scorn, and disregard but virtually no substantive criticism.

The same year the University of Arizona's William Dever, Professor of Near Eastern Archaeology, published his *Who Were the Early Israelites and Where Did They Come From?* in which he dismissed Salibi's work as,

> "a notorious book ... thoroughly discredited, of course, by critics on all sides." [9]

During his career Dever received over US $1,300,000 in grants to dig at sites believed to be from ancient Israel, in particular Gezer, and served as director of the Albright Institute (1971-75). He had vast experience in academic editorial, lecturing, supervisory, and research work, and publishing, yet the word *Arabia* does not appear once in his eighteen page résumé. He and others with deep but exceedingly narrow experience are in no position to judge research on subjects in which they have never professed any interest and of which they are profoundly ignorant. Any scholar with an elementary knowledge of Arabian Judaism would have responded in a more academically professional manner to Salibi's ideas.

Salibi elaborated on his ideas in three later books: *Secrets of the Bible People* (1988), *Conspiracy in Jerusalem: the Hidden Origins of Jesus* (1988), and *The Historicity of Biblical Israel* (1998). He placed the development of the early Israelite religion in the "ring of fire" volcanic region of Yemen and the Egyptian captivity not in Egypt itself but in an Egyptian colony in Arabia, in either the Asir or Jizan regions in the south.

The beginning of the Hebrew captivity has been assigned to either ca. 1800 or ca. 1600 B.C.E. The Egyptian Middle Kingdom rulers Amenemhet I (ca. 1938-1908 B.C.E.) and his son, co-regent and later monarch, Sesostris (ca. 1918-1985 B.C.E.) re-established the capital at Thebes. From there they annexed the south as far as the Second Cataract and perhaps had some involvement in their Asian borderland. Speculation spurred by biblical interest points to Palestine, but economic logic suggests it is more likely that the Egyptians were more focused on controlling the Hijaz trade routes to ensure luxury goods were channeled towards the Red

Sea ports serving Thebes rather than continuing northwards to the Nile Delta and the Levant. It was during this joint reign that written Egyptian was standardized and a code of conduct drawn up for the monarchy, the *Instructions for Merikare*. Sesostris III (ca. 1836-1818 B.C.E.), continuing the work of bringing uniformity and central control, created a standing army and centralized bureaucracy, and also established fortresses with garrisons. He, too, was active in extending control in the south and on the Asian frontier.

If the Hebrew had been brought under Egyptian control in this period they would most likely have been within striking distance of Thebes, either in Nubia or Hijaz. The Egyptians never developed a systematic administrative system outside their homeland, let alone in a colonial settlement; but place names in western Arabia such as *Yathrib*, Medina's former name, indicate a substantial presence, most likely a military one. Salibi lists twenty locations in western Arabia named after ancient Egyptian gods, six named after "two lands" (*t'wy*) the name of Egypt itself, and others bearing the Semitic name for Egypt, *msrm* (Arabic) and *msrym* (Old Testament Hebrew). Many of these place names are centered on the Khamis Mushait area of Asir province in Saudi Arabia. Saudi television had often displayed Egyptian artifacts discovered in this area but ceased doing so once Salibi's book linked them to Israelite history. If captivity and the Exodus occurred in Arabia, it is likely the Egyptian garrisons withdrew soon after Moses led the Hebrew to freedom. The Egyptians later appear to have launched raids or punitive expeditions against western Arabia. Unlike other ancient empire builders, the Egyptians were disinterested in establishing permanent control and colonies outside their home area. Salibi places the main thrust of Sheskonk's military campaign against western Arabia, not Palestine.

If the captivity commenced ca. 1600 B.C.E. it would have been associated with the Delta-based Hyksos dynasty (ca. 1630-1523 B.C.E.) when a wave of new technology swept into Egypt from Asia, introducing new techniques and improvements in bronze-making, weaponry, weaving, and pottery. Horse-drawn chariots made their debut. This was a time for an influx rather than an exodus. The aftermath of the reign of Akhenaton (ca.1379 – 1362 B.C.E.) was marked by chaos, as the new dynasty erased his heretical religious beliefs. His new capital was abandoned and Ramses I (1292-1290 B.C.E.) re-established the old capital in the Delta. Dynastic and religious disputes, combined with a change in the political and economic geography, would have made it easier for the Hebrew to break free if they were under Egyptian control in a peripheral area. This points to Nubia or Hijaz. As mentioned earlier, Salibi believed that the Exodus passed along the Red Sea coastal strip before ascending the Tehama defiles near Taif. In 1997, archaeological remains in the coastal plain of western Yemen revealed that, contrary to previous conclusions, the area was occupied between about 1400 and 800 B.C.E. Edward Keall, director of the Canadian Archaeological Mission of the Royal Ontario Museum, commented: "We don't know what was keeping people in this terribly marginal desert area." What he found extraordinary was that, sometime between 2400 and 1800 B.C.E., this unknown people had constructed enormous granite megaliths. Three were still standing, each eight feet in height and approximately twenty tons in weight. His report stated that about fifteen others were scattered around the area including a twenty-foot-long megalith rising from the ground at a slant. Keall was at a loss to explain why monuments of this magnitude had been placed in such a desolate place. The pillars, which date from a time that includes the Exodus, stand below a volcanic area and are in the path where Salibi places the Exodus. It is also of interest to note that the book of Exodus 24 states that the Israelites erected pillars to represent the twelve tribes. Preliminary findings, however, point to occupation by a *Bronze* Age people. The area was then abandoned and remained uninhabited between 800 B.C.E. and A.D. 800.

The Tehama (or Sarwat) escarpment is Salibi's location for *H-yrdn*, (the Jordan of the Old Testament). In his latest book on Arabian Israel, Salibi discusses in detail the probable position of Mt. Nebo, Moses' vantage point as he gazed on the Promised Land he would never enter. Salibi points out that if the Palestinian site of Mt. Nebo is accepted, it is quite extraordinary that the Old Testament description makes no mention of the Dead Sea, which is a short distance southwest.

Salibi's four books have a mass of speculative detail not only on the true location of Old Testament sites but also on biblical symbolism. The amount of detail in Salibi's work enabled critics to attack possible small inaccuracies in an attempt to destroy the thesis as a whole. Salibi had not only pointed out geographical controversies in the Masoretic text but also made suggestions for other sections. In one place in the Song of Solomon, where the conventional translation is "O my dove, in the clefts of the rock, in the covert of the cliff ... ," Salibi deemed the correct version to be "O my dove in Jarf Sala, behind Madrajah," indicating a willingness to take the Old Testament text as a geographical guide even when poetry alone was involved. Following *The Bible Came From Arabia*, Salibi's next book was

Secrets of the Bible People, suggesting that Abraham and Moses were composite characters drawn from several other people, and interpreting some of the Old Testament stories as allegories about folk deities. Salibi suggested that the tale of Joseph was a myth symbolizing the death of a sacrificed god, thus subverting one of history's greatest stories. These small points do not detract from the main thrust of his compelling argument that the Promised Land was in western Arabia.

Salibi's initial investigation was prompted by the extensive archaeological remains in Asir, Jizan, and Hijaz. It is obvious that they were part of the ancient past's cyclical international trading network, which linked southern Arabia and Mesopotamia to the Mediterranean world, prospering and declining in relation to the volume of traffic. The Saudi Arabian government has never had an encouraging attitude towards archaeology, the regime celebrating its seizure of power in 1927 by destroying the mile-long tomb of Eve in Jeddah. So until archaeologists have access to the ruins Salibi's hypotheses will be untested.

Salibi introduced his work by stating that its inspiration had come when he was shocked to find that the 1977 *Saudi Gazette of Place Names* revealed astonishing numbers of place names too similar to those in the Old Testament narrative to be dismissed as coincidental. This admission led many of his critics to attack his conclusions on the grounds that they had been reached in the same way as, for instance, Revivalist Christians claiming the Israelite tribe of Dan migrated to Denmark (*Danmark* in Danish); or the Motu people of Papua New Guinea wondering if they colonized Zanzibar because the Swahili words for *deceit* and *quickly*, respectively *koi-koi* and *haraka-haraka*, are identical to theirs. Later, Salibi's work was bracketed with Iman Jacob Wilkens' 1990 book *Where Troy Once Stood*, which argues that the events of the Trojan War described in the Iliad had occurred in the Gog Magog Hills, Cambridgeshire, England.

Salibi's conclusions were based on far from superficial evidence. Unfortunately when he published his first book on the subject in 1985, few mainstream archaeologists had concluded that the Old Testament was not an accurate account when applied to Palestine. When Salibi eventually cited Thompson and other archaeologists' findings in 1998, his opponents had developed a new strategy for dealing with him. Unable to refute his hypothesis they simply ignored him. Axel Knauf, who studied the North Arabian evidence, felt that Salibi's hypothesis was not convincing yet it is clear that Knauf, like many others, had not taken into account the Ethiopian and Sabaean evidence. Knauf wrote that in his opinion the Queen of Sheba did not exist, [10] overlooking the nearly thirty-year-old published evidence of the Ethiopian Sabaean inscriptions and the deep animosity of the Zadokite priesthood towards her. Ancient commentators denigrated what they opposed.

We know very little about Christ, but it is a sure sign he existed when a Jewish tradition disparaged his claim to kingship, saying he was the bastard son of a Roman soldier. Only one Jewish tradition linked to Palestine's 2nd Century A.D. Rabbi Jonathan, claims the Queen of Sheba did not exist, stating that it was a king not a queen who ruled. Lou Silberman, (1974) cites the opinions of Krauss (1972) who argued that this was an attempt to dismiss the Ethiopian claim that its monarchs were descended from Solomon and the Queen of Sheba. [11]

In taking the place names and examining the topography and other evidence, Salibi suggests that the Hebrew people emerged from the volcanic ring of fire in Yemen, making reference to an Arab tradition that the Israelites original home was destroyed by a volcano. He believes that the Promised Land of Abraham was on the Red Sea coastal strip below the Tehama range north of Yemen (*see Map 3*).

Salibi's work offers logical solutions to the bewildering Old Testament references to Ethiopia and Egypt. The Old Testament text refers to a people known as the Cushites (*h-kwšym*), which is usually taken to mean Ethiopians. 1 Chronicles speaks of the Cushites living next to the Hebrew tribe of Simeon, while 2 Chronicles has an account of King Asa of Judah (ca. 908-867 B.C.E.) repelling an attack by the Cushite leader Zerah. Ancient Egypt's Cushite ruling dynasty belonged to a much later date (ca. 716-656 B.C.E.) and had its origin in Nubia above the Fourth Cataract of the Nile in what is now the northern part of the Sudan. Salibi identified three urban settlements near Abha, the capital of Asir province, as Msrm, Kws, and Sheba. Msrm is understood in the Old Testament to mean Egypt, while Kws (Kush) is understood to refer to either or both Ethiopia and Sudan. Salibi suggested they were more likely references to settlements near Khamis Mushait, a modern-day Saudi air force base, that Salibi sites as the location of the old city of Sheba. These three cities were close together and if Salibi is correct, Josephus is also vindicated for saying the Queen of Sheba was also the queen of Msrm and Kws, incorrectly translated as Egypt and Ethiopia. Moses was also reported to have married a wife from Kws (probably near the coast) and led the Msrm army against Kws (in the highlands).

Salibi places the Philistines' original homeland also in Arabia, a view supported by the ancient geographer Herodotus, and points out that references to Lebanon and Tyre in the Old Testament were really *lbyn*, (an area on the Asir/Yemen border noted for giant juniper trees), and *sr*, (a settlement near Najran). In Salibi's opinion the Old Testament monarch Hiram ruled Sr not Tyre on the Mediterranean coast, where there are no records of a king of that name. Hiram's *ships* (*'wnywt*) were more probably ships of the desert – *camel trains*. The *Cedars of Lebanon* Solomon used for his vast public works program must have been junipers. Unlike junipers, the famed cedar trees of Lebanon make poor building material. In Salibi's opinion the boundaries of the Promised Land from the *nhr msrym* to the *nhr prt* were not references to the Nile and the Euphrates but to two rivers in Asir. Matching Old Testament place names with those of the Saudi Gazette was of great interest as he concludes that Eden and its garden were at Al Junaynah in Wadi Bishah.

Salibi discusses theological development, suggesting that the Israelite religion had emerged from respect accorded to several western Arabian mountain deities, *Yahweh, El Sabaoth, El Shalom, El Shaddai,* and *El Elyon*. He believes the division of the Israelites into Judah and Israel reflected religious as well as political differences, and that while there may have been a geographical division of Israel to the north and Judah to the south, there were settlements near each other owing allegiances to rival cult centers and monarchs. He initially placed Jerusalem at An Nimas south of Taif, but has since revised his views, saying that it is more probable Jerusalem was an area not a specific city, and that the City of David and the City of Zion were separate cities. He believes the "lost tribes" were not at all lost but had been absorbed into western Arabian society. He gave one example of the biblical tribe of Joseph with its two branches as being the origin for the Saudi Bani Yusuf tribe, which claims descent from two separate groups.

Salibi discussed the problems of vocalization of the Old Testament text by politically motivated Masoretic scholars, although he admitted that documents surviving from ca. 200 B.C.E. reveal that the Jews believed the Promised Land to be Palestine. He took the details of Sheshonk's invasion to show that the place names made more sense if applied to western Arabia than to Palestine and devoted a detailed section concerning the home towns and villages of the Babylonian exiles (Ezra 2:3-36) that indicate a western Arabian rather than a Palestinian origin. Other sections of his book deal with lack of findings and exaggerated claims by archaeologists in Palestine, theories about the development of monotheism, and the instances in Arabic traditions that supported the ancient presence of Israelites in Arabia. Among the latter were passages in the Qur'an that give an alternative geographical reference to an Old Testament location; for instance in the Old Testament Moses was called by God to Mt. Horab (*hrb*) whereas the Qur'an speaks of the Tuwa Valley (*tw*). Salibi found place names of *hrb* next to *tw* in Jebel Hadi, a previously active volcanic region in Asir.

Salibi's books are highly detailed and are accompanied by a few maps but no photographs. Further research on the ground will have to substantiate his meticulous conclusions. At present the hostile attitude of the Saudi government rules that out. However, Salibi's work can be supported by the very discipline he admits he knows little about – the Ethiopian/Eritrean evidence and in particular the *Sheba-Menelik Cycle* of the *Kebra Nagast*.

As already stated, the *Sheba-Menelik Cycle* was translated from an Arabic text into Ge'ez. This Arabic text must have drawn from a purely Israelite document or oral tradition most probably dating from the tenth century B.C.E. because it makes no mention of events after that time and contains only the most ancient parts of the Torah. If the *Sheba-Menelik Cycle* had been originally composed rather than edited in the sixth century A. D. or in the fourteenth century A.D., the geographical references would have been much clearer. What seems to have happened is that the Ge'ez Christian-era scribes found the geographical references puzzling and therefore made some changes in an attempt to make the final publication acceptable to Christian-era Ethiopia. The result, as remarked upon earlier, is complete geographical nonsense.

Below are the transliterated texts from the first part of chapter 53 and extracts from chapters 55, 58, and 59 of the *Kebra Nagast*. They concern Menelik's escape route carrying the stolen Ark and Solomon's unsuccessful pursuit. The relevant place names have been highlighted, followed by a translation. The Ge'ez text is in the Appendices.

The method of transport mentioned in the text is not entirely clear. It is possible Menelik's party used a camel train. This may explain why the text uses "let down" and "rose up" when referring to their transport, which translators have termed *wagons*. The text states that divine intervention enabled the party to travel "in the air" but, for reasons given below, this seems to be a fanciful later addition. The text emphasizes the speed of Menelik's escape. Camel trains could make 40 miles (64 kilometers) a day, lightly-laden camels considerably more.

Ge'ez has three forms of the letter S, two for D, H, T, and P as well as two gutturals marked as ' and '. Š is pronounced as SH. The a and ā are respectively pronounced as short and long versions of the a in father while e is pronounced as a long version of ai in bait, e as in let, i as a long version of i in machine, o as a long version of oa in boat, and u as a long version of oo in boot. [12] According to the *Sheba-Menelik Cycle* Menelik's party traveled from Jerusalem to Gaza. Then they passed to the border of Mesrin (Egypt) and river of Ethiopia. The Romanized text reads:

Chapter 53 (first section)

Xeba tawhba saragala la'ityopya

Wabaxeba xedarusa **gāzā** hagara 'emu laneguš zāwahaba soba tmas̱u'e xecēḫu neguš salomon lanegušta 'ityopyā. Wa'emhya bas̱hu ba'ahati 'elat westa dawala **gebes̱** 'enta smā **mes̱rin** wasoba r'eyu daqiqa xeyalāna 'esrā' ēl kama ba'ahati 'elat bas̱hu mḥwāra 13 'elat wa'idakmu wa'irxbu wa'is̱ab'e wa'i'enssā wakwilomu kama zasobē s̱agbu wastyu 'a'imaru wa'amnu 'emuntu daqiqa xeyl kama 'emxeba 'egzi'abḥēr konat zati waybēlwe lanegušmu nāwrd saragālate 'esma bas̱aḥna māya '**ityopyā** zāti y'eti **takazi** 'enta tward 'em'ityopyā watsaqi **falaga gebes** wa'awradu saragalātihomu hjya watkalu dabāt rihomu. Wahoru xbura daqiqa xeyl wasadedu kwilo 'aḥzaba. Waybēlwo lanegušmu nngrkanu nagara la'ema tkl ta'agšo waybēlomu 'ewa 'ekl wala'ema tbēluni 'eska 'elata motya 'iyawad̲'e wa'iyāš'e.

The translation reads:

How the transport of the Ark reached Ethiopia

They halted at **Gaza**, the city of the king's mother, which King Solomon had given to the Queen of Ethiopia when she visited him. From there they took a single day to travel to **Gebes** (Egypt), the name of which is **Mesrin**. When the children of the leaders of Israel saw that they and their animals had taken one day to travel a distance that usually took thirteen without getting tired or hungry or thirsty and indeed felt that they had eaten and drunk their fill, they believed it was God's work. They spoke to their king (Menelik) "Let us put our loads down for we have arrived at the **waters of Ethiopia**. This is the **flow** that comes from **Ethiopia** and waters the **Brook of Gebes** (Egypt)." And so they let down their transports [made their camels kneel?] and pitched their tents.

Chapter 55 (extracts)

Ba'nta zatafashu sab'a ityopya

Watanš'u saragalātni kamu qadimu wagēšu ba<u>s</u>bā<u>h</u> y<u>h</u>ēlyu lāti watalā'lu kwilomu ma<u>t</u>ana 'emat 'enza yastafānwwomu sab'a bhera **Gebe<u>s</u>** xelafu baqdmēhomu kama <u>s</u>lalot wasagadu lomu sab'ā b<u>h</u>era **Gebe<u>s</u>** 'esma r 'eywā 'enza traw<u>s</u> kama <u>dh</u>ay bawesta samāy wakwilomu yrawsu basaragalā 'enza yrawsu baqdmēhā wabedxrēhā. Waba<u>sh</u>u **Ba<u>h</u>ra 'al 'A<u>h</u>mar** 'enta y 'eti **Ba<u>h</u>ra 'Ireterā**....... la**bā<u>h</u>ra 'Ireterā** walasab'a 'tyopya wawad'u bāhra wata fa<u>sh</u>u fadfāda 'emna 'esrā'ēl soba ywad'u 'mgebes waba<u>sh</u>u 'an<u>s</u>ra **dabra sina** waxedr westa **qādēs**....... Wa'emhiya <u>s</u>a'anu saragalātihomu watanš'u we<u>h</u>oru wuxelafwā lab<u>h</u>ēra **mdyām** wabu<u>sh</u>u **hagara bēlontos** 'enta **hagara 'ityopya** ...

The translation reads:

How the people of Ethiopia rejoiced

Then the transports [camels?] rose up early in the morning and left and the people sung praises to Zion and they were all raised up to the height of a cubit. They passed by like shadows and the people of **Egypt** called out their farewells and the people of **Egypt** paid homage to Zion as she flew above them by accompanying her transport before and behind. Then they came to the **Sea of Al-Ahmar**, which is the **Sea of Eritrea** (the Red Sea)....... And the Sea of Eritrea was joyful as too were the people of **Ethiopia**, who went to the sea and celebrated mightily with a greater pleasure than did Israel after the escape from Egypt. They arrived opposite **Mount Sinai** and stayed some time in **Qades**....... And then they loaded their transports, rose up and departed, passing to the land of **Mdyam** and then the city of **Belontos**, a city of **Ethiopia**....

Chapter 58 contains the account of Solomon's pursuit.
Chapter 58 (sentence four onwards)
Xaba tans'a salomon yotlomu

Waḫoru wabas̲ḫu hagara **msr** xaba ta'yanu hya sab'a ityopya msla negušomu waxabahi tasalamwa las̲yon watafas̲ḫu waḫatatu kiyahomu ḫara neguš waybēlwomu sab'a bhēra **gebes̲** 'emrhuq maw ā'el bazya xlafu sab'a **'ityopyā** 'enza yraws̲u basaragalā kama malā'ēkt wayqallu 'emna 'ansrt bawesta samāy waybēlwomu mā'azē 'elat xalafu 'emnēkmu waybēlwomu yom tasu'e mawa'el bazu xalafu 'emnēna. Wabo 'emnēhomu 'ela gab'u wanagarwo languš salomon kama xalafu tasu'a mawā'el 'emza xalafu 'e**msr wa'abyās̲inasa** horu kama yxeššu 'eska **baḫr 'irtrā** wanhnasa gabā'ena kama nngrka zanta 'esku xali lalika neguš ba'elata sanuy 'emkama wad̲'u emxabeka bas̲ḫu bašalus xaba **falaga takazi hagara msr** walanani soba fanawkana 'em**'iyarusālēm** basāhna ba'elata rāb'e xalikē batbab matana ybas̲ḫu 'emuntu sab'e.

Watam'a neguš waybē 'axezwomu xamstihomu 'aska nrakb s̲dqa qālomu. Wa'aftanu ḫawira neguš wasarawitu wabas̲u **gaza** wattas'elomu waybelomu ma'azē xalafa waldya 'emanēkmu. 'Aws'u waybelu xalafa y'eti šalus 'elat wasoba sa'anu saragālatihomu 'albo zayahawr mal'elta mdr 'alā basaragalā squlān mal'alta nafus wayqallu 'emna 'ansrt zawesta samay wakwilu nwayomu yaḫawr mslēhomu mal'elta nafās basaragalā walanasa masalana za''anta rasayka lomu batbabka kama yhoru basaragalā mal'elta nafās. Waybēlomu bonu zahalawat syon tabota hgu la'egzi'abḫēr mslēhomu weybēlwo ālbo zar'ine.

The translation is:
How Solomon rose up to kill them

And Solomon's cavalry sped on and reached the **city of Msr** where the men of Ethiopia had camped with their king and where they had made peace with Zion and rejoiced. And Solomon's troopers questioned the people and the men of the **region of Gebes** told them "Some days ago some Ethiopians passed through here and they traveled swiftly in wagons like angels and faster than eagles." And the king's men asked, "How many days ago did they leave?" And the men of **Gebes** told them nine days had passed since they left. Then some of the troopers returned to Solomon and told him, "It's been nine days since the Abyssinians left **Msr**. Some of our detachment have gone to look for them at the **Sea of Eritrea** but we came back to report the situation. Consider the matter, my lord. On the second day they left your territory and on the third they reached the **river Takazi** at the **city of Mesr**. And after being sent out by you from **Jerusalem** we arrived on the day of the Sabbath. And we returned today, the fourth day of the week. You can estimate just how far those men have traveled." At this the king became extremely angry and ordered the five cavalrymen to be seized and held until their story was checked. Then the king set out with troops for **Gaza** where he asked the people when his son had left. They replied that he had departed three days earlier, adding "and having loaded their wagons, none of them traveled on the ground but in wagons suspended in the air. And they were swifter than the eagles in the sky, and all their loads traveled with them in wagons above the winds. As for us, we thought you had in your wisdom, enabled them to travel in this way." But when the king asked them if the fugitives were carrying Zion, the Tabernacle of the Law of God, they replied they had seen nothing.

Chapter 59 appears mostly to be an interpolation but the reference to a three day journey to the Brook of Egypt is probably genuine.

Chapter 59 (first section)

Xaba hatato lagbsawi gabra far'on
Waxalafa 'emhya werekebe 1 makwanna 'emakwānnta **gebes** zaneguš far'on zala'ako xabēhu mslā 'amxā wamlu'e nwāy mslehu waba**sh**a wasagada laneguš. Wa'aftano hatita salomon neguš za'enbala yahab 'amxāhu wamal'ikto waybēlo bonu zar'ika sab'a 'ityopya 'enza yg'ezu 'emhya. Wa'awš'a waybēlo mal'aka far'on laneguš **h**yaw 'anta neguš la'ālam, le'akeni 'egzi'eya neguš far'on **'em'eskndryā** xabēka wanawa 'ayad'ka zakama ma**s**ā'eku; wasoba ma**s**ā'eku **'em'eskndryā** bo'eku **qāhrā** westa hagaru laneguš wabab**sh**atya ba**sh**u hya 'elu sab'a 'ityopya zatbl; ba**sh**u 'enta xalafat šalus westa **takazi falaga msr**....

The translation reads:

How the king questioned an Egyptian, the servant of Pharaoh

And Solomon left that place, and he met an emissary from the courtiers of the Pharaoh of Egypt, whom the Pharaoh had dispatched with a gift to present Solomon along with much treasure. He arrived and paid his respects to the king. King Solomon was so anxious to discover what had happened that he began asking questions even before the emissary had presented his gift and his compliments, saying, "Have you seen a band of Ethiopian fugitives pass this way?" Pharaoh's ambassador responded to the king, stating, "Oh king, live forever! My lord, King Pharaoh, dispatched me from **Alexandria** to see you. And so, I will tell you how I have come. Having left **Alexandria** I arrived in **Cairo**, the city of the king, and there encountered those Ethiopians of whom you speak for they had arrived there too. They reached there after a passage of three days to the watercourse, the **brook of Egypt**....

According to the text, Menelik's party passed through Gaza and Mesrin to the waters of Ethiopia. Then they crossed the Sea of Eritrea to Ethiopia, opposite Mt. Sinai. There they passed through Qades, Mdyam, and Belontos. Solomon's pursuing force reached the city of Msr in the region of Gebes, where the cavalry troop was told Menelik's party had reached the Takezze River at the city of Mesr. One detachment raced for the Red Sea to determine whether Menelik had crossed. Solomon then set out for Gaza, where an Egyptian official from Alexandria told him Menelik's party had passed through Cairo and taken three days to the Takezze. This is a very unsatisfactory account. First of all Alexandria and Cairo did not exist in Solomon's time and were founded, respectively, 600 and 900 years after his death. The use of the term King Pharaoh, a tautology, supports the notion that the part of the text dealing with the Egyptian emissary is a fabrication added long after dynastic Egypt had fallen.

Second, although it is obvious that the redactors believed Menelik's party crossed to Egypt via Gaza and traveled south alongside parts of the Nile to Ethiopia, the text states that Menelik's party crossed the Red Sea to Ethiopia *after* traveling through Egypt and the waters of Ethiopia. Map 7 shows the absurdity of the text, for it demonstrates that Menelik would have found himself a very short distance from the southern border of present day Israel.

Third, there is doubt that *Mesrin, Msr,* and *Gebes* should all be translated as *Egypt*. The remark "Gebes (Egypt), the name of which is Mesrin" seems to have been a later elaboration by the Ge'ez scribes. Wallis-Budge and Bezold both translated *hagara msr* as if Msr (Egypt) were a country (Ge'ez = *beher* or *medr*; the word can also mean region, province, or district) but *hagar* is the Ge'ez word for *city*. Since Menelik's party crossed the Red Sea *after* passing through Mesrin, Msr, and Gebes, the three locations should be on the *east* side of the Red Sea, in Arabia, and the text is speaking of a city named Msr not a country.

Next there are references to *takazi*. In chapters 53, 58, and 59, Sir E.A. Wallis-Budge translated the word takazi to mean the Takezze River, which rises near Lalibela in Ethiopia and joins the Atbara River at Showak in Sudan. Bezold, considered the best authority on the text of the *Kebra Nagast*, would have been fully aware of the existence of the Takezze River but translated it as *Fluss* (*watercourse* or *flow*). Budge translated the text to mean the river watered the "Valley of Egypt," but Bezold more accurately stated that it watered the *Brook of Mesr*. In Chapter 58, Bezold again translated *falaga takazi hagara msr* as "*nach dem Flusstale in's Land Mesr*" [river valley in the land of Msr], and in Chapter 59 *westa takazi falaga msr* as "*zum Flusse, dem Bach von Mesr*" [to the watercourse, the Brook of Mesr]. These names probably do not refer to the Nile.

Next are the references to Ethiopia. The *Kebra Nagast* states that Menelik's party crossed the Red Sea and describes Menelik's people as *Ethiopians*. However, the text states they "arrived at the waters of Ethiopia" (*basahna maya 'ityopya*) before crossing the Red Sea to Ethiopia. It is probable that the original word was *Kws*, not *'Ityopya,* but the Ge'ez editors followed the examples of the Septuagint (Greek version of the Hebrew Old Testament) and Josephus by rendering *Kws*, *Cush*, and *Sudan* as well as *Aksum* as *'Ityopya* (Ethiopia). Professor Edward Ullendorf, one of the most prominent authorities on Old Testament links with Ethiopia, concluded that *Kws* probably referred to two locations on each side of the Red Sea. The Ethiopians identity with Cush/Kush, which was also the name of the Kingdom on the Nile and is the name of a settlement next to Khamis Mushait in Asir; and in the heights overlooking the port of Al Luhayyah in Yemen. Kamal Salibi identified the waters of Ethiopia (*kws*) as a wadi linked with Wadi Bishah in Arabia. In a letter to this writer on 30 August 1988, he also wrote, unaware of the place names in the *Sheba-Menelik Cycle*, that a major wadi on the present Saudi-Yemen border was called the *Brook of Egypt*, and that Mt. Sinai referred to a mountain in Yemen near the Red Sea shore. Suddenly the place names in the *Sheba-Menelik Cycle* made a lot more sense. Although there are several locations in western Arabia called *Mesr, Mesrin, Kws,* and *Gebes,* all lie in the area Salibi calls the frontier region of Judah and the realm of Sheba.

The extracts above from the *Kebra Nagast* emphasize that Menelik's party "traveled through the air" at great speed. However, since the people of Gebes were stationed in front of and behind the transport carrying the Ark of the Covenant, it seems that the references to it flying were added afterwards to explain why the party arrived so quickly at locations that the later redactors believed were far down the tributaries of the Nile. The truth was probably that the locations were near each other in western Arabia, and rather than alter the time taken to move between them, the redactors added a divine element of air travel to explain why it took a single day from Mesrin (which they believed meant Egypt) to the waters of Kws (River Takezze). The time span must have been unacceptable to the later redactors, who knew that the journey from the junction of the Nile at Atbara to the Takezze took thirteen days at approximately twenty-three miles a day. The short time it took for the cavalry detachment to report back to Solomon seems to support this. Confusion may of course arise because the exact mode of transport in unclear. Horses, camels, or wagons drawn by oxen or even elephants could have been involved.

The Shiloh–Jerusalem part of the Ark's travels and place names on *Map 9* were provided by Salibi, who had no knowledge of the contents of the *Sheba-Menelik Cycle*, yet its contents make sense. In the first part of the story the Queen of Sheba goes north with a huge retinue to meet Solomon. The Israelites had expanded southwards from the Medina-Mecca area and had reached the Sheban border, making Judah and Sheba immediate neighbors. Although Solomon, in chapter 29 of the *Kebra Nagast*, speaks to a young servant in a language the Queen of Sheba does not understand, there is no tradition of language differences between the Israelites and Shebans, giving weight to Rabin's findings that the inhabitants of that area spoke mutually intelligible dialects of a language closely related or identical to Canaanite/Hebrew.

The second visit to Jerusalem in the *Sheba-Menelik Cycle* of the *Kebra Nagast* concerned Menelik. He appears to have set out with a small retinue from Ethiopia, not Arabia, to govern Gaza. According to Salibi's map, Gaza was a strategic settlement at a pass overlooking the Red Sea to the west, and it controlled the route south to Sheba. Menelik's flight from Jerusalem with the Ark took his party to the Waters of Ethiopia, or rather the river of Cush, which would be the headwaters of Wadi Bishah in Asir. Menelik then crossed the Sea of Eritrea (the Red Sea). The account of the movements of the pursuit party is very interesting because one detachment heads for the sea and the other for Msrm (*see map*). Menelik must have been heading for a more southerly port in the region of modern Jizan, but the pursuing troops first swooped down on the nearest port in hopes he had taken that route and was still waiting for a ship. The crossing from Jizan to Eritrea is dotted with the numerous islands of Farasan and the Dahlak archipelago, which in the past contained numerous settlements with hundreds of wells, and it was probably a much easier place to obtain a ship and ensure escape. Arabic has taken many nautical words from Ge'ez, indicating that shipping in the Red Sea was primarily in the hands of Sabaeans and D'mt/Aksumites, and that was probably the case in Solomon's time as well. The *Sheba-Menelik Cycle* states Menelik landed in Africa opposite Mt. Sinai. Salibi, unaware of the *Sheba-Menelik Cycle*, places Mt. Sinai in the volcanic ring of fire in what is now the northern part of Yemen, opposite Menelik's most probable landing stage in Eritrea. Solomon's foray into Gaza was most probably to convince himself that his

MAP 9
The geography of the movements of the Ark of the Covenant according to the Salibi hypothesis

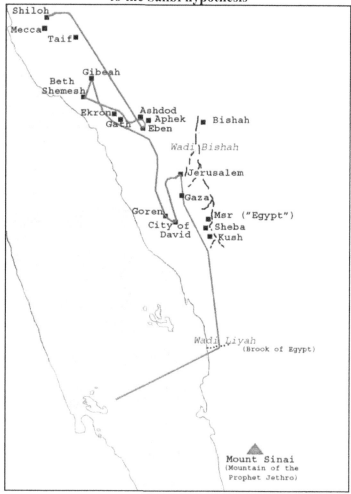

Biblical Account of the Ark's movements: Shiloh – Eben – Ashdod - Gath- Beth Shemesh – Gibeah – Goren – City of David – Jerusalem
Kebra Nagast account of Menelik's route: Jerusalem – Gaza – border of Egypt – Waters of Ethiopia – Brook of Egypt – Sea of Eritrea – arrival in Ethiopia opposite Mt Sinai

errant son and the Ark were not in the area and, that being the case, further pursuit was fruitless.

The highest mountain in Arabia is in Yemen. It is 3,666 meters high and is a very prominent landmark for sailors navigating the Red Sea. Sailing due west you reach the peninsula on the Eritrean coast that shelters its most famous port of antiquity, Adulis. The mountain is not called Mt. Sinai of course, but *Jebel al-Nabi Shu'ayb*. *Jebel* means mountain and *al-Nabi* means the Prophet. At first *Shu'ayb* seems a mystery, and few in the West would have heard of a prophet named Shu'ayb. In the Old Testament however he is referred to as *Jethro*. Shu'ayb (Jetho) is considered in Islamic tradition to be the thirteenth prophet after Adam and therefore a religious leader of some magnitude. He also had a daughter who married Moses. Jebel al-Nabi Shu'ayb overlooks Kushm, and it was probably from the people of this area that Moses took his "Cushite" wife. It is generally accepted that this wife was Zipporah, Jethro's daughter. Mention has already been made of southern Arabian inscriptions referring to a single deity, *the* God, named Rahman (the Merciful One) and the Prophet Muhammad's efforts to persuade his followers refer to the One True God as *Rahman*, the name used in southern Arabia. Salibi suggested that this area was the original homeland of the Hebrew. Arab traditions say the Hebrew were displaced by a volcanic eruption. The land surrounding Jebel al-Nabi Shu'ayb is one of the world's largest areas of volcanic activity. Plateaus exist in Yemen composed of lava flows up to 1000 meters thick. In the deepest sections of the Red Sea molten lava continues to bubble up between the African and Arabian tectonic plates. The story of the Exodus is full of references to what must have been volcanic activity. Given Qur'anic evidence, the locations in the *Kebra Nagast*, the demography of Hebraic remnants such as the Yibir, the Tigre inscriptions, the place names and linguistic evidence of Western Arabia, it seems that Jebel al-Nabi Shu'ayb may very well have been the Old Testament Sinai. If that was the case, it would appear that Moses may have obtained the Torah, other guidance and maybe tribal support during challenges to his leadership, from an already long-established religion in the area, perhaps Jethro's Kenite-Midian cult, [13] that later developed into the one associated with Rahman. Jebel al-Nabi Shu'ayb is about one hundred kilometers from the granite megaliths on the Yemeni coastal plain investigated by Canadian archaeologists in 1997. Salibi, writing before the discovery of the megaliths, suggested that the Israelite priestly clan of Levi made its home in the Jizan area, close to where the megaliths were found. The Yemeni tradition mentioned earlier maintains that the Virgin Mary, a Levite, was also from the region and launched the Nazarene sect in Najran, east of Jizan. Research is at present hampered by Saudi political considerations and Yemeni rural volatility.

The history of the Ark of the Covenant, which occupies the next chapter, is a logical extension of the Salibi hypothesis and the theft of the Ark narrative from the *Sheba-Menelik Cycle*. The Ark's nature is unknown. It was reputedly the gold-covered earthly abode of God that annihilated Israel's enemies and those of its own guardians who mishandled or defiled it albeit unintentionally. The ruling elite of Israel regarded the Ark as the symbol of their state power. It was the focal point of their religion and divine purpose.

Graham Hancock in his entertaining book on the Ark of Covenant, *The Sign and the Seal*, uncritically accepted the *Kebra Nagast* with all its interpolations, for example, the existence of Alexandria and Cairo in Solomon's time. He ignored the bizarre geographical references and explained how it was most likely that Jewish priests, not Menelik's party, took the Ark down the Nile and eventually housed it in Ethiopia. Hancock is not alone in having a touching faith in ancient customs. Take the idea that it was Menelik's companions who stole the Ark. If Solomon's state really did exist in Palestine, Azariah's theft of the Ark would have been madness. Azariah could not have hoped for many days' grace before the theft was discovered, and Solomon's centralized military would have used signal fires and cavalry to cut off any means of escape. Even if Menelik had managed to reach Egypt, the situation is very unconvincing. Can anyone seriously imagine the authorities of dynastic Egypt, a country with a large, dense, and heavily policed population, happily waving through a small band of hunted criminals fleeing from one of the most powerful monarchs in the Middle East, from whom they had just stolen the deadliest weapon known to mankind? Hancock's suggestion that Israelite priests carried the Ark south before King Josiah's time (ca. 640 B.C.E.) to Elephantine (Aswan) on the Nile is equally unacceptable. The Elephantine Jewish settlement was a mercenary garrison established by the Persians in the 520s B.C.E. The Jewish troops were Aramaic-speaking and, from their correspondence and rituals, their idiosyncratic religious practices seem related to the pagan-Israelite mix of the destroyed northern kingdom of Israel. They corresponded with the settlement in New Jerusalem but did not adhere to the laws in Deuteronomy. Their language, beliefs and social organization were far removed from the Hebraic and Israelite culture in

Ethiopia. If indeed Israelite priests had considered carrying the Ark down the Nile, their prestige was minimal and the risks unacceptable. Dynastic Egypt was a heavily policed society that did not suffer transient renegades, refugees (blameless or otherwise), and exotic strangers gladly. In the first years of the thirteenth century A.D., during the Zagwe dynasty, the newly appointed Monophysite bishop of Ethiopia, Michael of Fuwa, arrived from Alexandria. Five years later, out of favor, he struggled back to Egypt, eventually arriving stripped of his possessions and abandoned by his original retinue except for three slaves and a pet civet cat. Later, suspicious citizens forcibly drowned a West African monarch in the Nile. Such was the fate of unsanctioned travelers, and Menelik's party would have been doomed if they had chosen an Egyptian route. Had Israelite priests carried the Ark of the Covenant to the Aksum area in later years, the Sabaean rulers would have demanded an impressive demonstration of the Ark's power. Had one been provided, it would certainly have entered folklore. In contrast, the Salibi hypothesis of a western Arabian scenario is far more credible. Menelik's party had a much better chance of escape. The distances involved were short, and he would have been operating in his mother's country. Moreover, he had access to shipping; Solomon did not.

Chapter 7, the final chapter, will discuss more evidence that supports western Arabia as the true location of the Old Testament. This concerns the Ark itself, Israelite elements in Ethiopian Orthodox Christian Church and the history of Hebraic and Israelite groups such as the Beta Israel and the Qemant of Ethiopia, the Latos of Eritrea, and the Lemba of southern Africa.

CHAPTER SEVEN

The Ark of the Covenant and Israelite Influences

This final chapter discusses the Ark of the Covenant tradition in the Old Testament and in Arabia and Ethiopia. It also examines Hebraic groups in northeast and southern Africa and the Israelite nature of the Ethiopian Orthodox Church.

The Old Testament tells us that Hebrew and Arabs share the same ancestry, respectively descended from Abraham's sons Isaac and Ishmael. Hagar, Ishmael's mother, was a concubine from *Msrm*, translated in Genesis 21 as *Egypt*, but more likely a settlement in Asir, Arabia. Sarah, Abraham's wife and Isaac's mother, was angry about the birth of Ishmael, so Abraham told Hagar to leave. Desolate, she wandered in the direction of *br sb* (probably Khamis Mushait in Asir) and abandoned her baby under a bush. Then she heard the voice of an angel, who told her that she must care for the child because he would father a great nation. Arabs and Jews share many traditions, so when Muhammad began preaching Jews and Arabs alike recognized him as the long awaited Arab prophet. Muhammad declared that he had not come to found a new religion but to return the world to the faith of Abraham, from which it had deviated. For that reason the Muslim sacred text, the Qur'an, refers to the Queen of Sheba as a convert to Islam not the Israelite faith.

Until the reign of Solomon the Ark of the Covenant played a major role in the Israelite religion. There are two Old Testament accounts describing the Ark. First, Exodus states that after the Hebrew had fled from Egypt God instructed the Prophet Moses at Mt. Sinai to construct a gold-covered wooden box (Latin: *arca*), measuring 115 by 70 by 70 centimeters, surmounted by two kneeling gold cherubim (high-ranking angels) facing each other. It was here that Moses received the Ten Commandments and ordered the slaughter of 3000 Hebrew as punishment for worshipping Ba'al, symbolized by the *Golden Calf*. After the massacre, Moses climbed the mountain a second time to convince God to spare the remaining Hebrew and to replace the divinely inscribed stone tablets he, Moses, had smashed in anger. When Moses returned he had become a mysterious being whose face was hidden by a veil, and in this new frightening persona he supervised the building of the Ark of the Covenant and its ritual accouterments. The new tablets were placed inside the box and were carried by the Levites, who had massacred the deviant worshippers of Ba'al.

The second Old Testament account of the Ark is from Deuteronomy and states that it was a plain box made from acacia wood. Both Arab and Ethiopian traditions adhere to the description of a wooden box.

The story of the Exodus is marked by phenomena associated with volcanic activity; therefore it should come as no surprise that the Mt. Sinai in the Sinai peninsula near modern Israel has no record - until about the fourth century A.D. - of veneration as a biblical site. The area is igneous but lacks a volcanic past. It is more likely that the original Sinai was a part of the volcanic *ring of fire* in northern Yemen. The Hebrew set out for the Promised Land: by day guided by a column of smoke; by night, a column of fire. They believed that God himself was in the Ark. During encampment the Ark was placed in a tent of its own.

Hebrew and Arab traditions maintain that the Ark brought terrible destruction to its enemies. It was supposed to have leveled the walls of Jericho but, as Kathleen Kenyon discovered, the present site of Jericho does not correspond with the Old Testament account and was, as this book argues, in another yet unexplored location. After Joshua overran the Promised Land the Philistines captured the Ark in battle but returned it after they were decimated by plague. Other reports say that people were struck dead if they approached the Ark inappropriately or disrespectfully.

Many theories have been advanced that the Ark was a primitive but powerful device of electrocution. Some, who believe the box to have been silk-covered, suggest that it was used like a giant Van der Graaf accelerator to generate a lethal electrical charge. Others believe the sacred stones inside the Ark and at other shrines were meteorites that for a number of years retained some sort of radioactive or other destructive force such as a virulent bacillus. Arab traditions also associate the Ark and holy tablets or stones with death. Arab accounts say an Amalekite-Jurhum tribal alliance captured the Ark from the Israelites some time after Solomon's death, when the latter unsuccessfully attacked Mecca. The Jurhum threw the Ark on to a dunghill and in doing so incurred divine wrath that annihilated 200,000 Meccans, sparing only about 40 citizens who had opposed the desecration.

There are other sacred stones in Islam's most venerated shrine at the Ka'bah in Mecca. The Ka'bah is the site where Muslims believe Abraham stood in the presence of God and built a simple shrine. As time passed it became a center for pagan beliefs, a practice the rise of Islam eventually terminated. When Muhammad began preaching for a return to the One True Faith, revulsion grew against Meccan pagan practices. Consequently, venerating stones and images was condemned as idol worship; but when the Ka'bah shrine was restored and purified as the center of the One True Faith of Abraham, two stones were nevertheless allowed to remain. The first stone was known as the *Station of Abraham* and marked the spot where Abraham had stood in God's presence. This stone was kept in a box and shone with an ethereal light. In the tenth century A.D. it was reported that it bore ancient inscriptions, testifying that there was only One True God, and that this place was His House. The second stone, originally brilliant white but eventually stained by blood sacrifices, is known as the *Black Stone*. This is the stone that Muslims kiss during the rites of pilgrimage.

In A.D. 925 the Qarmatians, an Ismaili Shiite sect, captured Mecca and removed the Black Stone, intending to use it to divert the pilgrim caravans to their center at Hajar near the border of modern Iraq. Twenty years later, when the Qarmatian leader died horribly from internal flesh-eating worms, his followers returned the stone to Mecca.

Bedouin Arabs have traditions extremely similar to the Ark of the Covenant's nomadic days. Portable and permanent shrines were a common feature of pre-Islamic Arabia and echo early Hebrew history, that is, noting where the Levites carried the Ark and placing it in a tent wherever they stopped. The Hebrew Ark contained sacred tablets, and this finds parallels throughout pre-Islamic Arabia, where tribes venerated unusual stones. The Bedouin had a special red leather tent, *kubbe*, to house tribal deities. Women played a major role in caring for the kubbe, which was considered too sacred to accompany troops except in extremely important engagements. The Prophet Muhammad possessed a kubbe that stood empty, and Abraham's original shrine in Mecca was little more than a tent, a low stone structure with a cloth roof.

In A.D. 685 when the military commander al Muktar ibn Ubaid Allah exhorted his troops to avenge the death of the Prophet's grandson Hussein, he showed them a throne that he said would be for them what the Ark of the Covenant had been for the Israelites. After the rise of Islam the Bedouin continued to retain customs reminiscent of the Old Testament, carrying ark-like battle-standards. The Bedouin had three different ark-like devices. First, in the 1920s the Ruala Bedouin, who claimed Israelite ancestry, bore a kind of altar on camelback called a *markab* (ship) or *abu duhur* (Father of the Ages), accompanied into battle by a bare breasted young woman screaming exhortations to the troops. The tradition was of antiquity, and the markab had been passed from tribe to tribe as a war trophy. Another camel-borne battle-standard was called *ofte*. The markab was a large framework made from acacia wood and decorated with ostrich feathers. The ofte was a smaller but similar structure. The third kind of Ark was called *mahmal* and was similar to the camel litters for women except that it was covered with velvet cloth and silver decorations. Like the markab, a young woman accompanied the mahmal into battle. Mahmals also carried boxes containing prayers or the Holy Qur'an. The Wahhabi rulers banned mahmals in the late 1920s.

The Ark cult developed in similar ways among Israelites and Arabs. In both cases it was not so much the Ark itself that was important but God's presence and the law. The nomadic life gave way to a sedentary urban-based, centralized empire. Solomon built the First Temple to house the Ark and the sacred texts. The Muslims rebuilt the Ka'bah as a black cube measuring the same as the First Temple's inner sanctum. The rise of central government, a literate bureaucracy, and Jewish-Islamic hostility towards images probably diminished the prestige of cultic objects and enhanced the power of the written word.

The Old Testament states that the Ark of the Covenant was originally housed at Shiloh and then carried into battle against the Philistines at Eben. The victorious Philistines then took it to Ekron via Ashdod and Gath. Fearful of its powers, they returned it to the Israelites at Beth-shemesh. These Israelites found themselves ill equipped to deal with the Ark and called in the priest at Nadab in Gibeah to remove it. Later David took it via Goren to his capital, the City of David.

The City of David and Jerusalem of the Old Testament were probably not located in the same place. Kamal Salibi's place name analysis, undertaken with far more thoroughness than Edwin Robinson's mid nineteenth century survey of Palestinian Old Testament nomenclature, placed Shiloh just north of Mecca and the City of David to the north-west of Abha in Asir (*see Map 9*). Onomastic studies conclude that Solomon's name derives from the Medina area. Solomon's capital of Jerusalem was probably near Nimas, northeast of the City of David on the escarpment astride the caravan route from Sheba. It was in Jerusalem that Solomon built the First Temple and had the Ark of the Covenant placed within its inner sanctum where only the high priest could enter. Given Salibi's unawareness of the *Sheba-Menelik Cycle*, his hypothetical locations are remarkable. Whereas Shiloh was somewhat distant, both Jerusalem and the City of David were in easy striking distance of Ethiopia. This southern location is supported by a passage in the Chronicles 2:14-16 speaking of Ethiopian (probably *Kws* in Asir) and southern Arabian military campaigns against Judah. The accounts of the Cushite kingdom of Napata assisting "Tyre, Sidon, Israel and Judah" defy the Assyrians before Shabaka (ca. 712-698 B.C.E), the southern-based Cushite pharaoh of Egypt conquered the Nile Delta, cannot possibly refer to a Palestinian-Levant scenario. The Napata kingdom, based between the 3rd and 4th Nile cataracts west of what in now Port Sudan, prospered from Red Sea trade and would have intervened in western Arabia to protect what must have been its trade links with Arabian Judah that Assyria wanted to divert north.

If western Arabia was the location of the Old Testament, it explains that region's strong and ancient Ark tradition, which was finally extinguished in the late 1920s by the puritanical Islamic Wahhabi sect.

Hebrew, Arabic, and Ge'ez names for the Ark of the Covenant are respectively *tebhah, tabut,* and *tabot*. This puzzled Theodor Nöldeke (1836-1930), a German Semitic scholar who published works on Aramaic, Syriac, and Classical Arabic as well as histories of the Middle Eastern areas and Persia. He had a reputation for questioning conventional wisdom, doubting the historical existence of Abraham and his alleged home city of Ur. However, his imagination was unable to fathom the Medina dialect word for the Ark of the Covenant, *tabut*, which he termed "an atrocious monstrosity."

Despite his liberal reputation and views on Abraham, Nöldeke fully accepted that later figures in the Old Testament lived in Palestine and spoke Hebrew. The Hebrew word for the Ark of the Covenant was *tebhah*. The word *tebhah* evolved into Palestinian Aramaic *tebhotha*. Then, after the Roman destruction of Jerusalem, many Jews fled to Arabia, allegedly introducing many Old Testament traditions to the Arabs, who also adopted some of their vocabulary. When one language borrows from another, changes are made according to that language's grammar. Aramaic loan words that have endings (suffixes) in *ah* change to *ut* in Arabic. The Aramaic-speaking Jews would have passed the word *tebhotha* (Ark) to the Arabs, who would have adopted it as something like *tebhothut*. However, the Meccan Arabs used *tabut*, which meant that they had taken the word before 400 B.C.E. directly from Hebrew *tebhah* and put their own suffix *ut* on it, forming the word *tabut*. That is why Nöldeke was perplexed. More interestingly, before the prestige of Qur'anic Arabic displaced other dialects from the seventh century A.D. onwards, the word used in Medina was *tabuh*, taken directly from Old Testament Hebrew without the modification used by the Meccans. The evidence showed that Hebrew must have been spoken in the Medina region long before the Jews adopted Aramaic, and that made no sense to Nöldeke. He could not accept that Arabia had an ancient Ark culture and had taken the word directly from an ancient local Hebrew source. Chaim Rabin, writing about the ancient West Arabian language, concluded that "Ethiopic (Ge'ez), then, must have received the word (tabut/tabot) somehow via West Arabian, through channels as yet unknown to us." This supports the hypothesis that the Ark itself was from western Arabia, and, as narrated in the *Sheba-Menelik Cycle*, stolen there and taken to Ethiopia. Debate continues as to whether or not Ge'ez words may have been taken directly from ancient Hebrew vocabulary. The main candidates are *'arami* (pagan) and *'arb* (eve of Sabbath). In other cases it is difficult to distinguish between Hebrew, Aramaic, or Syriac (an Aramaic dialect) sources. Sixth century A.D. Syriac-speaking Christian missionaries, the Nine Saints, were responsible for mass evangelism and introduced new theological vocabulary. Their word for Ark was *qebuta*.

In November 1962 the late Professor Maxime Rodinson assessed the theories of all authorities concerning the word tabot, concluding that the Ethiopian Orthodox Church had adopted it after A.D. 1400 as an ecclesiastical affectation. Rodinson quoted Rabin's work in his survey so it is astonishing that he completely ignored Rabin's list of western Arabian Hebrew-isms.[1]

The Old Testament is vague about the fate of the Ark of the Covenant and consequently many explanations have been forthcoming, almost all hamstrung by the belief that the Old Testament was located in Palestine. The *Sheba-Menelik Cycle* provides the most detailed explanation for the Ark's disappearance, but there is a rival Arabian-based theory. Of the few spared divine wrath in Mecca for opposing the desecration of the Ark was a Jurhumite leader who was then appointed the Ark's guardian. The Jurhum, of Yemeni origin, controlled the Ka'bah until the fifth century A.D. and the region's other most important pilgrim shrine at Najran near Yemen, which also contained a mysterious stone. If the Jurhum did indeed possess the Ark, they may have brought it to Najran when they gave up control of the Ka'bah.

The best account of the Ark of the Covenant is by Roderick Grierson and Stuart Munro-Hay, published in 1999. They state that Yusuf, the sixth-century A.D. Jewish ruler of Himyar, may have inherited or come into possession of the Ark. If he had indeed stolen the Ark from Aksum that could explain his nickname of *Masruq* (Stolen), and it would certainly have been a matter of national and religious honor for Aksum's Christian king Caleb to retrieve it. Conversely, the Ark may have been in Najran since early times and *Masruq* was an ancient Sabaean title known to be used hundreds of years B.C.E. on the Ethiopia plateau. Grierson and Munro-Hay suggest that if Caleb had captured the Ark from Yusuf, the Ark culture of Aksum may have entered the kingdom for the first time around A.D. 520, hence the Arabic name. Another hypothesis is that Christians fleeing Himyar before Caleb's invasion brought the Arabic text of the *Sheba-Menelik Cycle* with them to prove that Aksum was the resting place of the Ark, and that Yusuf had stolen the tradition claiming he had the true Ark. If they had invented the *Sheba-Menelik Cycle*, its geography would of course been very different and matched a Palestinian setting. Therefore it is likely that arrival of the *Sheba-Menelik Cycle* Arabic text revived the Ark story rather than introduced it to Aksum for the first time.

Ethiopian culture is obsessed with the Ark of the Covenant. The main weakness of Grierson and Munro-Hay's book, from this writer's point of view, is their acceptance that Solomon's kingdom was in Palestine. Despite this, Munro-Hay is a leading authority on Aksum, and his work with Grierson demonstrates the Ark's extremely nebulous nature (unfortunately Stuart Munro-Hay died in Chiang Mai, Thailand, in late 2004, six weeks before this writer arrived to visit him). Even the account in the *Sheba-Menelik Cycle* does not describe the Ark, only the size of the wooden frame that Azariah built to replace it. The text refers to the Ark as "Our Lady," and traditions report that Azariah stole a very large tablet. The Ethiopian Orthodox Church is of course fully aware of the description in Exodus, but its Ark tradition is centered around tablets, not gold boxes adorned by cherubim.

Every Ethiopian Orthodox church possesses a tabot, a replica of the original held in the Chapel of the Tablet next to the Church of Mary of Zion in Aksum. The Ark, under the care of a monk with the title of *Atang* (Keeper of the Ark), has never been publicly revealed, but clergy have occasionally described it as a milky colored stone tablet that emits a bright light and is contained in a small gold-covered hinged box the size of a modern encyclopedia.

The Alexandrian Coptic Church uses a wooden Ark as a shelter for wine and water during services. This is not called *tabot* and resembles the Arabian walled tent named mahmal and the Ark described in Deuteronomy, not the elaborate Cherubim-adorned gold-covered version of Exodus. There is a lack of unanimity about what the tabot represents. In Ethiopia and Eritrea the altar slab rather than the church is consecrated and this is referred to as tabot. For example, the tabot for the Orthodox cathedral in Asmara, Eritrea, was consecrated in Egypt. Tabot can also refer to the chest that contains the tablets of the law, the tablets themselves, or both. Tabotat (plural of tabot) are usually made from hard timber, but prestigious tabotat have been of gold. Although Israelite in origin tabotat are often dedicated to Christian saints.

The Ethiopians refer to the Ark as the *Ark of Zion*, and there is an annual festival in Aksum to celebrate its arrival. Elsewhere tabotat are paraded under canopies at all major Christian festivals. Whatever their appearance, they are all associated with the original story of Menelik's epic journey to Ethiopia, a symbol that God decided to switch his blessing from Solomon's kingdom to the New Zion.

The desecrated memorial at Mai Bela and disparaging remarks concerning the veracity of the *Sheba-Menelik Cycle* reflect the deep nationalist and political divisions that devastated Ethiopia and Eritrea after 1952. The *Kebra Nagast*, of which the *Sheba-Menelik Cycle* is part, was used by the Ethiopian imperial ruling family from A.D. 1270 to justify its rule until its fall in 1974. It was in the imperial family's interest to emphasize its divine authority, using the *Kebra Nagast* to prove its legitimacy as successor to Solomon's kingdom and as guardian of the One Truth Faith authorized at Nicaea. As mentioned earlier the Orthodox Church at Aksum had revived its fortunes by supporting the restoration of the Solomonid royal house under Yekunno Amlak. This close relationship of church and monarchy dominated Ethiopian society thereafter. During the Eritrean war of independence the Orthodox Church was criticized for supporting Ethiopian rule because the emperor had granted it lucrative feudal land rights. Eritrean nationalist leaders tended to be members of non-Orthodox churches or Muslims.

However, self-seeking imperial policies do not explain the Hebraic/Israelite nature of the Orthodox Church nor the claim by population groups of ancient Hebraic origin who support the *Sheba-Menelik Cycle* story but have endured hundreds of years of persecution.

The Beta Israel or Black Jews of Ethiopia are usually referred to as Falasha, which is usually taken to mean a wanderer, tenant, or outsider; or as Kayla, a Cushitic word of unknown origin. The Beta Israel consider both words insulting. No other African people has been so thoroughly studied or discussed. In the 1980s and 1990s 25,000 Beta Israel were airlifted to Israel from refugee camps in Sudan. It is believed their total population in Israel is just under 40,000. The erosion of their beliefs and customs through assimilation into the highly volatile and militaristic society of modern Israel is a matter of considerable controversy.

The Beta Israel are Agaw in origin, but had overwhelmingly abandoned their Cushitic language for Semitic Amharic or Tigrinya Semitic before their exodus to modern Israel.[2] Their sacred book, the Ge'ez Old Testament, is identical to that used by Christian Ethiopians. Their knowledge of Judaism was confined to events before the Babylonian captivity and their traditions state that they had arrived in Ethiopia during Solomon's reign and later when Jeremiah warned of impending doom. One tradition claims they are descendants of Agaw who had lived in Arabia. Archaeological evidence shows that a common culture did exist on the opposite shores of the Red Sea, ca. 1500-1000 B.C.E., but no inscriptions exist to indicate their language. The Beta Israel believe they are descendants of Menelik's followers. The Beta Israel worshipped in buildings called the *House of God*, yet they venerated pagan rituals and practiced spirit possession. They faced *east* when praying, believing it to be the direction of Jerusalem, and probably never had any historical link with Palestine. They built special ritually "unclean" huts for menstruation and childbirth and practiced circumcision and clitoridectomy. Sharing Christian traditions, the Beta Israel hierarchy included monks and nuns, high priests, low priests and lay personnel. As mentioned earlier, Nazarite practices (Samson, of Old Testament fame, was a Nazarite) are found only among the Beta Israel.

However, clearly the Beta Israel, along with the Qemant, who have a weaker Hebraic tradition, are culturally almost identical to their Christian neighbors. All observed Mosaic dietary laws and had similar beliefs in a heaven for the good, a hell for the damned, angels, Satan, a first and second coming of a messiah, resurrection, and a day of judgment. The chief authority on the Qemant, Frederick Gamst, best summarized the three groups - the Qemant, the Beta Israel, and the Amhara-Tigrinya - as follows:

> The...Qemant...have a largely pagan but somewhat Hebraic religion, with Christian elements. The Beta Israel [have] a largely Hebraic but somewhat pagan religion, with Christian elements. The Amhara and Tigray practice a Christianity markedly ba-orit (following the Old Testament).

The Ethiopian church is monophysite and was under an Egyptian *abun* (archbishop) from the fourth century until 1952. In medieval times, when European contacts became more common, European observers were immediately struck by the Orthodox Church's Israelite practices, for example circumcision. Some accepted that the Ethiopians had inherited them from Solomon's kingdom through Menelik's companions; a claim seemingly supported by the book of Isaiah and the book of Zephaniah, which mention Israelites in *Kws*.

The Aksumite priesthood believes it is the *inheritor* of the Hebrew Aaronite priesthood (the Beta Israel priests believe they themselves are Aaron's *descendants*). Their churches are traditionally built on small hills in the manner of synagogues and follow the three divisions found in Israelite religious architecture rather than the basilica model used by early Christians elsewhere. The Orthodox Church has also adopted many terms from Syriac Aramaic for items specifically associated with Judaism such as *kahen* (priest), *menorah* (seven-stemmed candle holder), and words for skull cap, a priest's ritual belt, and probably a priestly breastplate modeled on that worn by the Jewish high priest. The Orthodox church denied Jesuit accusations that its adherents were forbidden to eat pork, but in practice Ethiopian Christians abhor it. The custom of rearing only white chickens - even though hawks find their yellow chicks easier to spot - may have some Hebraic ritual symbolism. Ethiopian Christians generally follow Mosaic dietary laws but have no sanction against consuming milk and meat in the same meal.

The basis of the Ethiopian legal code from ca. A.D. 1450 until 1930 was the Fetha Nagast (the Law of the Kings). It was originally a twelfth-century A.D. Arabic document compiled in Egypt by a Coptic scholar, who based the code on the Torah, the New Testament, decisions and canons of early church councils, Roman civil law, and tenets of Qur'anic law. When discussing sexual relations, the Fetha Nagast reminds Orthodox Christians:

>...tazakar za'azazaka 'egzi'abher ba'afa musi.... [...remember what God has commanded you through the mouth of Moses....].

In accordance with Mosaic Law, sexual relations are forbidden during times of fasting and when a woman is menstruating. The Fetha Nagast utilizes Leviticus 20:18, which is that part of the Torah dealing with sexual relations that is included in the *Sheba-Menelik Cycle*.

Circumcision is performed on the eighth day after birth, a custom shared only with Jews.

Two important Christian festivals and fasts are of Hebraic origin. The first is the New Year feast, which corresponds with the Jewish New Year. The second festival is Mäsk'äl, sixteen days after the New Year, which echoes the Jewish period of atonement. Mäsk'äl supposedly commemorates the granting of a piece of the true cross to King David of Ethiopia (1380-1409), the method of celebration, i.e. interpreting the smoke patterns of bonfires, indicates a Hebraic origin based on the pillars of fire and smoke of the Exodus.

Orthodox churches have large oval baptisteries for total immersion. These appear to be inherited from a pre-Christian tradition linked to southern Arabia. The temple at Yeha, the probable capital of pre-Aksumite D'mt, contains a typical example that is duplicated in Ethiopian Christian churches. There is however a Jewish ritual whereby the high priest conducts total immersions. On New Year's Day Ethiopian Christians take a purification bath in their local river to cancel the sins of the previous year; then they sacrifice an animal, a custom similar to the Israelite practice where the priest sacrificed an animal to wipe away sins. Another festival linked to Judaism includes one whereby angels inform God about the conduct of the Faithful and divine decisions are taken on their future.

Magic, sorcery, and witchcraft, a major part of Ethiopian life, are closely associated with Judaism, although they may belong to a general Semitic culture. However, as mentioned earlier, the Hebraic Yibir of Somalia, a Cushitic-speaking country, have a reputation for witchcraft and lucky amulets.

The Ethiopian church, nevertheless, appears to have made some changes to accommodate European Christian critics. Originally the church, following Israelite practice, set aside two days a week for fasting. These were changed from Monday and Thursday to Wednesday and Friday to combat Catholic accusations of Judaism. However, the subject of the Sabbath caused a major crisis.

The northern part of the Ethiopian highlands, now part of Eritrea, has always adhered more strongly to Israelite practices than the southern part. The religious leader Ewostatewos (1273-1352) chose exile and death in Armenia rather than accept Sunday instead of the traditional Saturday as the Christian Sabbath. Despite excommunication, banishment, and fierce opposition by the Egyptian bishops and the Amhara-Showan clergy in the south, the Ethiopian ruler Zar'a Ya'eqob eventually recognized that the followers of Ewostatewos were not "closet" Jews and he permitted in A.D. 1450 both Saturday and Sunday to be respected as Christian holy days. Tigre also witnessed another religious movement led by a monk named Estifanos (1394 - ca. 1450), who was highly critical of royal involvement in church affairs, a stance that provoked accusations of Judaism. Estifanos followers' exact theological views are not clear but it is believed they worshipped on Saturdays and refused to bow before the cross and images of the Virgin Mary. Some researchers believe that the Ewostatewos and Estifanos movements were Judaic-Christian.

Judeo-Christianity evolved from the beliefs of followers of Christ associated with his brother James and others who neither accepted Paul's nor Constantine's interpretations and innovations. If Judeo-Christianity were present in Ethiopia it would complete a religious continuum in Ethiopian society beginning on one end with the pagan-Hebraic Qemant, then passing on to the Beta Israel on through Judaic-Christianity until reaching Christianity at the other end. If Judaic-Christians existed in Ethiopia it would explain the lack of clear distinctions between the practices of the separate faiths.

The traditional Ethiopian account of their history is mostly the viewpoint of the Semitic ruling house, which claimed descent from Solomon and the Queen of Sheba and, despite fluctuating adherence, up to half Aksum's population followed a form of Judaism before Frumentius converted Ezana to Orthodox Christianity in the fifth century A.D. Approximately 5 per cent of Aksum's archaeological remains have been investigated. Nonetheless, it seems clear that while some pre-Christian coins were marked "King of Zion," the ruling house did not leave behind any obvious signs of a state-sponsored Israelite religion. If the *Sheba-Menelik Cycle* is correct, Solomon's hostility for the loss of the Ark would have cost Menelik any external support for building an Israelite state. Furthermore, the prestige of Solomon's state quickly dissipated after his death. No record exists of the Zadokite priestly house between Azariah's flight to Ethiopia and Hilkiah's success 300 years later in restoring

Zadokite prestige in Judah. In later years the Jurhum showed that an ousted priesthood could reassert its prestige elsewhere. The Zadokites must have had a center where they regrouped and eventually returned to power. One clue that this may have been in Ethiopia or southwestern Arabia comes from DNA testing undertaken in the late 1990's on the Lemba, a 40,000 strong southern African people (South Africa, Zimbabwe, Mozambique, and Malawi), with seemingly pagan-Hebraic customs that include a kosher diet, circumcision and ritual purity. Jewish hereditary priests, the *kohenin*, are traditionally believed to be direct descendants of Aaron, the brother of Moses. DNA testing has revealed that members of the kohenin do indeed have a high percentage of common ancestry, since 45 per cent of Ashkenazi (European Jews) priests and 56 per cent of Sephardic (Iberian, North African, Middle Eastern and Arabian Jews) priests share the same Y chromosome, exclusively passed down the male line. This Y chromosome has only a 3 - 5 per cent occurrence in Jewish populations in general and is rare or absent in other groups. Based on the study of DNA generational mutations, their common ancestor would have lived between 2,650 to 3,180 years ago (ca. 1180 – 650 B.C.E.). It is therefore more likely that the kohenin are descendants, not of Aaron (ca. 1400-1200 B.C.E.), but of a member of the priestly House of Zadok. 9 per cent of Lemba men carry the kohenin chromosome, but it also occurs in 53 per cent of the members of their priestly clan, the Buba. [3] A Lemba tradition states that their ancestors were from a place called Senna, which may be Senna in Yemen, near Tarim, the ancient capital of the Hadramawt Kingdom, and the port of Sayhut. [4]

While the Lemba priestly clan appears indubitably linked to the Israelite priesthood, their traditional customs and religious beliefs indicate that, if their culture is Hebraic in origin, it is very weak. Legends pre-dating the colonial era connect Menelik with volcanoes in Tanzania (where a legend says he died on Kilimanjaro) and the Comoros Islands (where he fled with Solomon's throne). Hebraic practices have been recorded on the Kenyan coast among the Wakilindi; and the Malagasy language of Madagascar appears to contain elements of a Semitic language that one researcher linked to Hebrew. [5] However, the Lemba have neither Old Testament oral traditions nor pre-colonial written records, and in the past were mainly regarded as a metal working artisan caste. While claiming a link with the medieval kingdoms of Mapungubwe, which flourished just south of the Limpopo river in South Africa ca. A.D. 950 – 1270; and its successor, Great Zimbabwe, ca. 1270 – 1600, the Lemba kohenin do not appear to have played a significant role in the administration or religion of either state. If Buba, the ancestor of the Lemba priestly clan, did originate in Yemen he may have been a member of the Zadokite priesthood during one of its periods either out of favor with the Judaean monarchy ca. 920-642 B.C.E., or during the period following the 586 B.C.E. Babylonian conquest when it may not have been prudent to identify with a failed and unpopular regime. The Lemba's adherence to some of the basic aspects of the Torah but ignorance of Ezra's Judaism may also indicate that Buba was a member of the Samaritans, whose priests are also kohenin, or another, unknown, Hebraic group. Whatever Buba's origin, the Lemba DNA evidence appears to support an ancient Hebraic or Israelite presence in the area of Ethiopia and southwestern Arabia. The present South African Lemba westernized assimilated elite strongly, but most probably erroneously (like the airlifted Beta Israel), identifies with modern Israel and "normative" Judaism.

The *Sheba-Menelik Cycle* may be in origin a text composed by a Zadokite priest of Azariah's line bolstering the new Israelite state in Africa. The Arabic version probably came either from Alexandria or from southern Arabia. It would be unusual if its author(s) wrote nothing else. Besides the Ark, the major candidate for possible First Temple Zadokite influence in Ethiopia is, as mentioned above, the design of Ethiopian churches. The nature of the Zadokite restoration under Hilkiah (ca. 640 B.C.E.) suggests he struck from a secure, long-established theological center. It was certainly a time of disruption. Some researchers have suggested Israelite refugees entered pre-Aksumite Ethiopia at this time fleeing Assyrian devastation. In addition, the Egyptians were taking a greater interest in the Red Sea and eventually the pharaoh Necho (ca. 610-595) dispatched a successful 2 - 3 year circumnavigation of Africa. The Judaean ruler Manasseh (ca. 687-642 B.C.E.) had horrified the Zadokites by tolerating not only paganism but also human sacrifice. Perhaps the refugees, joining other elements in southern Arabia and in Ethiopia convinced the Zadokites to seize the initiative. Had the Zadokites been in a respected but not dominant position in pre-Aksumite Ethiopia or Arabia (a situation similar later to the Persian ruled Babylonian Jews ca. 529 B.C.E.), this option would have been more attractive than occasionally having the ear of various pagan monarchs. If the Zadokites had endured 300 years in disfavor for losing or stealing the Ark, it is unlikely they would have mentioned it in the sacred texts they subsequently collected and amended to create the Old Testament.

Christianity became the mass religion of the Aksumite Empire in the sixth century through the efforts of the Nine Saints and Caleb's military success against Yusuf. Plague, the rise of Islam, and other factors weakened the Semitic population, and as they advanced deeper into Africa they allegedly encountered fierce resistance from Yudit, a Cushitic Hebrew queen, who swept into Christian territory and sacked Aksum. Demographic change resulted in the Zagwe, a Cushitic dynasty, ruling the area from about A.D. 980 until 1270, when it was replaced by the Solomonids, a Semitic dynasty, who, despite Amhara-Tigrinya rivalry, lasted until 1974.

The Cushitic element in Ethiopia was often associated with Judaism. Professor Edward Ullendorf considers that before the advent of Christianity, the Cushitic population of Ethiopia and Eritrea probably practiced a syncretic pagan-Hebraic/Israelite religion [6] that only survives today among small Hebraic/Israelite groups such as the Qemant, an Agaw-speaking peasant community living near Gondar. The Qemant accept the *Sheba-Menelik Cycle*; however, their religion, a synthesis of pagan Agaw with Hebraic practices and beliefs, has almost died out. Gamst considers that their faith was the last of the native Agaw religions and although the Qemant have converted to Christianity they still respect some of the old ways such as worshipping in sacred groves. [7] This finds parallels with the Muslim Hebraic Yibir of Somalia, who venerate trees.

The Beta Israel informed the nineteenth century German missionary Martin Flad that they were originally tribal Israelites, a claim supported by their Tigrinya neighbors. The Beta Israel high priest stated that their technical skills, which included ironworking, enabled them to establish dominance among the Agaw, with whom they intermarried. The Zagwe royal house took a similar line, claiming descent from Moses, although their Semitic rivals spread the story that the Zagwe were descendants of Solomon through the Queen of Sheba's maidservant. The Beta Israel, despite using Christian-manufactured Old Testaments, have their own separate traditions, including one describing the death of Moses. Zagwe's King Lalibela was however an ardent Christian renown for his impressive ecclesiastical architecture. His Christian zeal aroused interest among Christian Europeans looking for co-religionist allies to help attack Islam from the rear, and he seems to have been the inspiration for the legend of Prester John.[8]

The most recent major studies of the Beta Israel before their mass assimilation in Israel have been conducted by Harvard's Kay Shelemay, Fisk University's James Quiran, and the University of Jerusalem's Steven Kaplan. All conclude that the "Judaism" of the Beta Israel is a "recent" fabrication, belonging to the period after A.D. 1270.

Shelemay, an ethnomusicologist whose work on the Beta Israel has been highly praised, published her findings in 1989. [9] She makes no mention of the *br* inscriptions on the Tigre plateau let alone the important new trends in Old Testament archaeology. Worse, when she was later informed of these findings in 2006, she declined to receive details. She accepts the late Maxime Rodinson's conclusion that neither the Israelite religion nor Judaism made any significant impact in southern Arabia until around A.D. 395. She dismisses the *Sheba-Menelik Cycle* as a myth and often judges Beta Israel practices by comparing them with "normative Judaism", which is of little relevance since all Ethiopian traditions maintain that their past is Israelite not Judaic, and long predates Ezra's fifth-century B.C.E. reforms. Shelemay's work is thorough, and no one can seriously doubt her conclusion that the Beta Israel musical tradition comes from an Orthodox Christian source but, given the antiquity of their relationship, this would be expected. Shelemay is an ethnomusicologist making historical judgments and is unable to move outside the mental constraints of her Zionist beliefs. Nevertheless, given the growing doubt concerning Biblical archaeology and the need to find a plausible theory to explain Arabian Judaism, it might have been expected that Shelemay would have been alerted to the possibility that Beta Israel traditions deserved reassessment. Consequently, her final sentence - "It is difficult to dispute what we find, since one cannot argue with a song" - can only apply to the relationship between Orthodox and Beta Israel music and only fractionally to their historical past.

Quiran and Kaplan both published in 1992, [10] the same year as Thompson's survey of Israelite archaeology. Neither of them mentions the disquiet in Old Testament archaeological circles nor Professor Ali Mazrui's consideration that Salibi's hypothesis could shed considerable light on the origins of Israelite influences in Ethiopia. Kaplan concludes that Aksum was influenced by southern Arabian Judaic elements between the second and third centuries A.D. Quiran suggests they may have come from a Judaic-Christian background. They and Shelemay emphasize that the word *Ayhud*, meaning *Jew*, was often used to denigrate those who did not fully accept the tenets of the Orthodox Church, which, after 1270, became increasingly entwined with the imperial monarchy. Quiran argues that while Jews or Judaic-Christians may have been active at the court of Aksum before Frumentius's arrival, the Beta Israel are not their descendants. Quiran and Kaplan both postulate that marginalized elements in Ethiopian society chose to oppose assimilation into the imperial framework by identifying as a separate people named Beta Israel. The centuries following the 1270 Solomonid restoration witnessed the expansion of the new dynastic power. Recalcitrant groups that refused to adopt the Orthodox faith or to pay tribute lost their land and were forced into infertile peripheral areas along with heretical Christian monks. Military expeditions exacerbated the situation, and by the sixteenth and seventeenth centuries rebels were openly supporting a form of Judaism influenced by Christian monasticism and were creating their own kingdom in the Semien Mountains, nominally under imperial governorship. The Semien Mountains provided strong natural defenses. Imperial power faltered when Muslim attacks seriously threatened the empire, forcing the emperor to ask for Portuguese assistance. The Beta Israel initially welcomed the Muslim invasion but then decided to switch allegiance to the Orthodox. When imperial power revived, relations between the Beta Israel and the Orthodox broke down and eventually, after many campaigns, the Beta Israel were finally crushed in 1632.

Quiran emphasizes that caste connotations played a role in the alienation of groups from Orthodox rule. It is therefore interesting to note that once the Beta Israel had been defeated in the Semien Mountains, they rapidly gained a reputation as artisans, craftsmen, and even soldiers in the city of Gondar. The Beta Israel profited from their association with imperial public works, and despite their constitutional disadvantages as inferior citizens they enjoyed a peaceful, prosperous, existence until 1769, when the assassination of Emperor Iyo'as sparked conflict between rival feudal warlords. Artisans and peasants suffered the most, and the Beta Israel undertook despised, ritually unclean work such as blacksmithing and pottery to survive. They never recovered their former prosperity or security. The Great Famine of 1888-93 decimated their monasteries and left them destitute. They were harassed by European Christian missionaries and used as scapegoats by feudal landlords and peasants angry with government land reform. Their skills were made obsolete by Western technology, and when famine struck again in the 1980s during the Ethiopian civil war their situation deteriorated to such an extent that they accepted evacuation to Israel as their only hope. Their subsequent experience in Israel, sometimes attacked as a trade-off between economic benefits for cultural genocide, has, at least, been highly controversial.

Mention has been made of possible Judaic-Christian influence prior to the arrival of Orthodox Christianity in Aksum. This subject deserves a separate book. The New Testament account of Christ's ministry covers three years, but his origins and early life are not at all clear. Christ spoke Aramaic, but his teachings and sayings were memorized in verse and later translated and written in Greek. Christ was from the Israelite royal House of David and a direct descendant of Jehoiachin, son of the last independent king of Judah. He may have been from Galilee in Palestine or Wadi Galil/Jalil in Taif province, northern Hijaz. He had a commanding knowledge of the law, but his egalitarian attitude towards women and various exchanges with the Jerusalem priesthood in the Gospels indicate that he belonged to another sect. He was more likely a member of the Nazarene sect (the people of Wadi Jalil are still called *Nasirah*) and not from the town of Nazareth, which emerged in later times. The Arabic name for Christian is *nasrani*, and after Paul had his vision on the road to Damascus he immediately left for Arabia, where he stayed for three years.

The Qur'an contains the most detailed account of the Virgin Mary, portraying her as a powerful figure whose prestige was so great that a dispute arose when the time came to sponsor her in the temple. This portrait is in sharp contrast with the extremely hazy figure in the New Testament. According to Yemenite tradition, after the Babylonian exile a member of the Levi tribe, a virgin mother named Mary (Miriam) opposed Ezra's draconian reforms. She founded the Nazarene Israelite sect in Najran. The Yemenite account dates Mary to around 400 B.C.E. Ezra cursed the Yemeni Israelites for refusing to join his new community. There is an extremely controversial theory that Paul may have used sacred texts in Arabia to create a composite figure from two separate leaders: Isa, the son of Mary of the House of Levi; and Yeshu, the son of Joseph of the House of David. Whether or not Mary was the founder or a later adherent of the Nazarene Israelite sect, it is known that in the seventh century A.D. the Negus of Aksum possessed Christian texts now lost that matched the Qur'anic account. It is therefore possible that Nazarene Israelites had some influence at the Aksumite court before the arrival of Orthodox Christianity. Their faith would have evolved into Judaic-Christianity after Christ. If the Nazarene faith had indeed been influential in Aksum it is likely its Israelite customs would have been retained when it gave way to the more prestigious Orthodox faith with its imperial Roman connections. This would also explain why the Orthodox Church could respect Israelite customs and beliefs while displaying hostility to Judaism.

A Judaic-Christian group still exists in Hamasien, Eritrea. This is the Latos, a highly significant group of Tigrinya-speakers enjoying considerable economic and political power in Eritrea. They have priests known as *Qes* (as the Beta Israel) and a secret society called *Kansha* (probably a corruption of *kanisa* meaning *church*), based in Himbirti near Asmara, which maintains genealogical records. The Latos claim to have been the first inhabitants of highland Eritrea, particularly the former province of Hamasien with its dynastic centers of Hazega and Tse'azega. They explain that their influence is the reason the Christianity of the area has always been so heavily Israelite. It was this area that supported Ewostatewos in his fight to retain and revere Israelite practices in Orthodox Christianity. There is unsubstantiated belief that the presence of the Latos distinguished the area from Christian Tigre, a factor that Menelik II recognized when the Italians sought control over the area.

The Latos tended to covert to Roman Catholicism or Protestant creeds in the twentieth century as a further mark of their separate identity to the Orthodox Church, which supported Haile Selaisse. Despite this, past Latos migration patterns from the area were towards the Beta Israel communities in Ethiopia. The Latos issue is highly contentious given the volatile politico-religious nature of the Horn of Africa and its external, in particular Israeli, linkages. The Israeli government recognizes the Latos as Jews. The Latos are relatively prosperous and their numbers reportedly include many of the Eritrean administrative and political hierarchy including the president, Isaias Afwerki, himself. During the 1999 conflict Ethiopians referred to the Eritrean leadership as "Hamasien (Italian Latos)" and attributed the border conflict to the "supreme race mentality" of the Eritreans adding, "They call themselves 'the Jews of Africa' and the 'Black Israelis'." The Eritreans, who quoted these attacks, deny their substance. Information about the Latos has been more forthcoming from Latos families who, from long residence in Addis Ababa, have chosen to identify with Ethiopia. It is likely that they retain a better knowledge of traditions that have been considerably weakened in Eritrea by war but are now of little relevance, let alone influence.

The word *Latos* is probably a contraction of *pilatos,* the Tigrinya insult meaning a Jew (from *Pontius Pilatos* meaning "Christ killer").[11] Ewostatewos's monastery at Debra Bizen is just below Asmara, and the Mai Bela Queen of Sheba memorial stele is also in Latos territory. Hamasien has ancient iron and gold deposits, excellent agricultural land and rainfall, and controls the route to the coast as well as access to the Antseba valley, the ancient trade route to the alleged land of Punt. Very little archaeology has been undertaken in Hamasien, but it is clear that already published conclusions on the Beta Israel and Hebraic-Israelite elements in

Orthodox Christianity would be very different if the Latos had been considered. This book is the first to mention them, but they are so sensitive about their identity that they will ignore any reference to it should the matter be raised by an outsider in the presence of another Latos. Asmara has a synagogue, established by Italian settlers. It has a minuscule membership of foreign Jews, and no Latos has ever worshipped there.

The study of the Ark of the Covenant and Israelite religion in the Horn of Africa in some ways follows the pattern of Old Testament archaeology. There was initial excitement followed by growing disillusionment. The reason for both is of course related, for the solution depends on the true location of Solomon's kingdom.

Fascination with the *Sheba-Menelik Cycle* has been replaced by a false logic that dismisses the account because a Palestinian-based ancient Israel would have been too distant for such influences to make an impact so far away in Solomon's time. It has taken eighty years for biblical scholars to accept that Palestinian archaeology does not correspond with Old Testament accounts. While suggestions should be considered that the Old Testament may be fantasy or a gross exaggeration, they do not explain, for example, the link between the Hebraic Yibir and the pre-Ezra *br* inscriptions at Abuna Garima, Hebrew-isms in West Arabian, the antiquity of *tabut,* or the pre-fifth century B.C.E. texts in an ancient form of Hebrew that were incorporated into the fifth century Hebrew canon.

In the past, scholars who have been unable to reconcile their geographical preconceptions have either disparaged the narrative of the *Sheba-Menelik Cycle* or have interpreted it as an expression of "deep-lying psychological conflicts widely shared by members of Ethiopian society." [12] Old Testament scholarship is now witnessing a similar trend. The reluctance of the minimalist school of Old Testament scholarship to consider the alternative location theory may have at first have been influenced, as Thomas Thompson acknowledged, in a communication of August 21, 2000 to this writer, by ignorance of the western Arabian and Ethiopian evidence, but that situation has now changed. However, despite scholastic awareness of the ideas expressed in this book, the hypothesis of an Arabian Judah and Israel is viewed as a political, religious, and academic Pandora's Box. Since the publication of Salibi's *The Bible Came from Arabia,* a number of writers, Beta Israel, and Yemeni Jews who either support an Arabian Zion or dare to suggest that Ethiopian and Arabian Israelite traditions contain some truth have become targets of vigorous and often successful campaigns to prevent their views being published or even discussed. Beta Israel in particular have been pressured into silence by accusations of being "ungrateful" for being "saved." Consequently, "minimalist" archaeologists will probably continue to be content for the immediate future to accept the Old Testament as an inaccurate but inspirational text rather than provoke a torrent of irrational abuse (or worse) by suggesting that Biblical scholarship should start looking outside Palestine. Biblical scholarship unfortunately attracts a vast number of enthusiasts who have created a mass popular culture that has reduced it to a shallow even ludicrous discipline mixing faith, fragile psyches, and politics rather than one linked to rationality and science. Despite this, it is difficult to believe that acceptance of Palestine as the site of the Old Testament can prevail given intelligent people's constant quest for solutions, and the growing concern among serious scholars that ill-founded Judeo-Christian beliefs are responsible for humiliating Islam, causing massive political instability, and endangering world peace for the past sixty years. If the events of the Old Testament did indeed occur in West Arabia not Palestine, Judaism and Christianity must come to terms with their role in causing a monstrous historical injustice and examine the concomitant theological implications.

Another issue is the vast disparity between the immense research funding for Judaic Studies and the paltry amounts available for Ethiopian/Arabian Israelite Studies. Between 1922-6, under the direction of Francesco Da Bassano, the Catholic Church in Asmara, Eritrea, compiled a four-volume Ge'ez Old Testament drawn from printed sources and manuscripts in collections, museums, churches, and monasteries in Africa and elsewhere. This was the beginning of an unfulfilled project to analyze all important ecclesiastical manuscripts from the time of Frumentius or even earlier. Further work was frustrated by the Italian invasion of Ethiopia, the Second World War, changes in administration from Italian to British and imperial Ethiopian rule, political unrest, Eritrea's fight for independence, and further conflict.

There was a call at the 1966 Third International Conference of Ethiopian Studies, Addis Ababa, for a major international effort to continue the kind of research Da Bassano had pioneered. Hardly anything was accomplished because the champion of the Ethiopian imperial and ecclesiastical heritage, Emperor Haile Selaisse, was overthrown in 1974, tortured to death, and his Solomonid dynasty replaced by a Soviet-allied Marxist regime whose excesses led to civil war and increased Eritrean resistance. The association of the Ethiopian Orthodox Church and the

Kebra Nagast with Haile Selaisse has influenced research in the new democratic Ethiopia and independent Eritrea. There has been a swing against the imperial legacy, and archaeologists are now more interested in the general development of society than Ethiopia's links to the Old Testament. While this is quite understandable, it is also unfortunate because the time is certainly ripe for a major revival of interest in ancient Ethiopian, Eritrean, Western Arabian, and Yemeni studies to solve the problems plaguing Old Testament scholarship. This book's analysis of chapters 53, 55, 58 and 59 of the Ge'ez *Kebra Nagast* has shown even the most respected academics will alter evidence to suit their preconceptions. These chapters are but a minuscule part of the massive corpus of Ge'ez documents awaiting intense scrutiny. For example, here is an extract from a Ge'ez manuscript in the Bibliotheque Nationale, Paris, which reads:

> ...wamakebeba masahftihasa zabluy ta'alwa em 'ebraysti xaba ge'ez bamawa 'liha laNegešta 'Ezeb 'enta hawasato laSalemon...
> [...and concerning the books of the Old Testament they were translated from Hebrew into Ge'ez in the days of the Queen of the South who visited Solomon].

Whereas a decade ago such claims could be and were dismissed as myths, biblical scholarship can no longer afford such arrogant certainty. In the past support for pre-Christian-Aksumite exposure to Israelite religion came from careful researchers, including the late David Hubbard, who, regrettably, never published his doctrinal thesis on the Kebra Negast. Hubbard, who became president of Fuller Theological College, California, concluded that: "There can be little doubt that the Ethiopians were acquainted with substantial portions of the Old Testament before they knew anything about the New Testament." While most of the Ethiopian Bible seems to have been translated from Greek sources, the Ethiopian Old Testament has additional books, including Jubilees and Enoch. The latter two exist only in Ge'ez. Further investigation into the additional books, as well as other ecclesiastical documents such as the *Miracles of the Virgin Mary* (only partly published), and Beta Israel texts such as the *Death of Moses*, may provide further evidence to support a western Arabian setting for the Old Testament.

Now that even Israeli scholars are questioning the Old Testament account, it is logical, as mentioned above, for historians and biblical researchers who accept the account to be true to examine the possibility of an alternative location for the events described within its pages, reassess academic attitudes towards Ethiopian historical traditions, and encourage more universities, colleges, and high schools to include courses dealing with this subject in their curricula. The life of the Queen of Sheba is of vital importance in this process, and the queen can no longer be dismissed as a myth. If the *Sheba-Menelik Cycle* had never been written down it would probably have been impossible to make sense of the various traditions, linguistic oddities, inscriptions, archaeological remains and religious practices scattered throughout Arabia and the Horn of Africa. It is hoped that the ideas in this book, like the lectures that originally formed its nucleus, will continue to encourage new generations to investigate with a fresh perspective, free of bias and political considerations, these ancient epic stories that have had such a profound effect on world society.

REFERENCES AND NOTES

CHAPTER ONE

1. *Sunday Times (UK)*, 16 February 1997, report of conclusions of Dr. Victor Clube, Oxford University astrophysicist.

2. A modern Israeli joke has it Moses asked that *Canada* be the Promised Land, but God misunderstood his stammering as *Canaan*.

3. Antonio Arnaiz-Villena et al., "The Origin of Palestinians and Their Genetic Relatedness With Other Mediterranean Populations." *Human Immunology* 62, 2000, 889-900.

4. Benjamin Mazar, *Biblical Israel: State and People*. 1992, Jerusalem: Israel Exploration Society, 98.

5. The Old Testament calls the Arameans of this period Chaldeans.

6. Peter Marsden. *The Taliban: war, religion and the new order in Afghanistan*. London: Zed Books, 1998.

CHAPTER TWO

1. Kathleen M. Kenyon, *Archaeology in the Holy Land*. London: Benn, 1979, 240.

2. N.P. Lemche, *Early Israel. Anthropological and Historical Studies in the Israelite Society Before the Monarchy*. (Leiden, Netherlands: Brill, 1985), 386.

3. Keith W. Whitelam, *The invention of Ancient Israel: the Silencing of Palestinian History*. (London: Routledge, 1996), 231.

4. Quoted in Ranuph Fiennes, *Atlantis of the Sands – The Search for the Lost City of Ubar*, (London: Bloomsbury 1992), 26-27.
5. Miller, J.M. and Hays, J. *A History of Ancient Israel and Judah*

(London: SCM, 1986), 199.

6. *Evidence of Migration to Britain* Category N12 Sheet 2012/0302, Christian Assemblies International, Coffs Harbor, Australia, March 2002.

CHAPTER THREE

1. Bernard Berenson, *Rumor and Reflection.* (New York, Simon and Schuster, 1952) quoted in Howard M. Sachar, *The Course of Modern Jewish History* (Weidenfeld and Nicolson, 1958), 405.

2. Dr David Appleyard reports that Qwarenya is "extremely endangered, if not extinct."

3. Wolf Leslau, *Falasha Anthology* (Yale University 1951), xxi.

4. Angel Sáenz-Badillos, *A History of the Hebrew Language* (Cambridge: Cambridge University Press, 1993).

5. James Barr, *Comparative Philology and the text of the Old Testament.* (Winona Lake, Indiana: Eisenbrauns, 1987), 99-101.

CHAPTER FOUR

1, Rodolfo Fattovich, Lorenzo Petrassi, Kathryn Bard, and Vincenzo Pisano. *The Aksum Archaeological Area: Preliminary Assessment.* Naples, Italy: Instituto Universitario Orientale Napoli, 2000.

2. Gerald Obermeyer, "Civilization and Religion in Ancient South Arabia," *Bulletin of the Royal Institute for Inter-Faith Studies*, 1, no. 1, (Spring 1999) Amman, Jordan: 35-64; Andrey Korotayev, "Ancient Yemen: some general trends of evolution of the Sabaic language and Sabaean culture," *Journal of Semitic Studies*, (Oxford) Supplement 5, 1995.

3. Charles Cutler Torrey, *The Jewish Foundation of Islam*, New York: Ktav Publishing House, 1967, 18-19.

4. Sarah Marshall, "Myrrh: magi, medicine and mortality,"*The Pharmaceutical Journal (UK)* 18/25 December 2004, 919-921.

5. Chaim Rabin, *Loanword Evidence in Biblical Hebrew for Trade Between Tamil Nad and Palestine in the First Millenium B.C.E.*, Second International Conference Seminar of Tamil Studies (Madras, India), 1968.

6. Luigi Luca Cavalli-Sforza, Paolo Menozzi, Alberto Piazza, *The History and Geography of Human Genes*, Princeton: Princeton University Press, 1994. Jones, Steve. *In the Blood God, Genes and Destiny.* London: Flamingo/Harper Collins, 1997.

7. Supreme Sutra of the Pearl of Good Fortune. A Qur'anic scholar in the United Arab Emirates (*Guardian Weekly* UK May 27 – June 2, 2005) declared that female suicide bombers would be rewarded in Paradise by becoming male so they could enjoy female virgins.

8. E-mail from Bir Zeit University to this writer 28 June 1999. The full story is in Edward Fox's *Palestinian Twilight: The Murder of Dr Albert Glock and the Archaeology of the Holy Land*, London: Harper Collins, 2001. Professor Al Glock was the American director of the W. F. Albright Institute of Archaeological Research in Jerusalem from 1978 to 1980 and then of the Palestinian Institute of Archaeology at Bir Zeit until 19 January 1992 when he was shot dead. Glock told his students that archaeology would reveal only Palestinian history and nothing Israelite. However, he caused much controversy by blocking the promotion of a Palestinian archaeologist, and may also have been targeted as a symbol of what was perceived in militant circles as the US betrayal of Palestinian aspirations.

CHAPTER FIVE

1. The contents of the *Kebra Nagast* have been analyzed in David Hubbard, *The Literary Sources of the Kebra Nagast*, Ph.D. thesis, St. Andrews University, Scotland, 1956.

2. Richard Schneider, "Deux inscriptions subarabiques du Tigré," *Bibliotheca Orientalis*, 30, (1973): 385-87; Rodolfo Fattovich, "Remarks on the pre-Aksumite period in northern Ethiopia" *Journal of Ethiopian Studies* 23 (1990): 15-17.

3. Rodolfo Fattovich, "Remarks on the pre-Aksumite period in northern Ethiopia" *Journal of Ethiopian Studies* 23 (1990): 15-17.

4. Kirk, John William Carnegie. *A grammar of the Somali language with examples in prose and verse; and an account of the Yibir and Midgan dialects*. Cambridge: University Press, 1905. Information also from the Somali community in London 2001-4.

5. R.B. Stothers, "Mystery Cloud of A.D. 536," *Nature* 307, (January 1984), 344-5; Andrey Korotayev, Vladimir Klimenko, and Dimitri Proussakov, Origins of Islam: Political-Anthropological and Environmental Context *Acta Orientalia Academiae Scientiarum Hung.*, 52 (3-4), (1999): 243-276.

CHAPTER SIX

1. Hetzron, Robert (ed.) *The Semitic languages*. London: Routledge, 1998.

2. Chaim Rabin, *Ancient West Arabian*. London: Taylor's Foreign Press, 1951

3. C.J. Gadd, "The Harran Inscription of Nabonidus." *Anatolian Studies* 8, 1958.

4. Prior to the Roman arrival, the Nabataeans of Petra in northern Arabia had achieved considerable wealth and power through control of the caravan trade from the Arabian peninsula.The Jerusalem Jews were ill-placed to profit from this.

5. David Ben Gurion speaking to foreign correspondents at apress conference, Tel Aviv, 20 February 1959.

6. Salibi, Kamal. *Who was Jesus? A conspiracy in Jerusalem*.London: I. B. Tauris, 1998.

7. Jacob Lassner, *Demonizing the Queen of Sheba: boundaries ofgender and culture in postbiblical Judaism and Medieval Islam*. (Chicago: University of Chicago Press, 1993), 223, note 87.

8. Sheikh Hamad Al-Jasir, *Al-Mug'am al-gugrafi li'l bilad al-'Arabiyyah al-Sa'udiyyah*. [Gazetteer of Saudi Arabian Place Names](3 volumes) Riyadh Saudi Arabia: Saudi Government, 1977.

9. William G. Dever, *Who Were the Early Israelites and Where Did They Come From?* Grand Rapids: Eerdmans, 2003.

10. Ernst Axel Knauf, *Midian: Untersuchungen zur Geschichte Palastinas und Nordarabiens am Ende des 2.Jahrtausend v. Chr* [Investigations into the History of Palestine and North Arabia atthe end of the Second Millennium B.C.E.] Otto Harrassowitz1988, dealt with the economic conditions in northern Arabiabut Knauf, in a 29 June 1999 e-mail to the author, dismissedthe idea of an Arabian location for ancient Israel and Judah,adding, "In *Midian* you would read, concerning the Queen of Sheba, that she never existed."

11. Lou H. Silberman in Pritchard, James (ed.). *Solomon and Sheba*. London: Phaidon, 1974, 68, quoting the work of S. Krauss *Die Namen der Königin von Saba*, Berlin: Festschrift Freimann, 1937. Krauss however conceded that Rabbi

Jonathan would not have known the Kebra Nagast, and Ethiopia would not have been a Christian state in those years with a monarch proudly proclaiming descent from Solomon. However, judging from Josephus's contemporary writings, which are a summary of the section of the Sheba-Menelik Cycle dealing with the Queen's visit, it is highly likely that the Sheba-Menelik Cycle was indeed known to Rabbi Jonathan's circle. Josephusmentions nothing of the creation of an Ethiopian/Yemeni Israelite rival dynasty. Nevertheless, like the disappearance of the Ark and Zadokite priesthood, the facts were probably well known but suppressed.

12. Thomas O. Lambdin, *Introduction to Classical Ethiopic (Ge'ez)*, Harvard Semitic Studies, No. 24, (Scholars Press 1978), 3.

13. The Prophet Jethro was priest leader of the Kenites, reputedly descended from Adam and Eve through their son Cain. The Kenites were itinerant blacksmiths who worshipped Yahweh and formed part of the nomadic Midianites, who claimed kinship with the Israelites through Keturah, Abraham's second wife, and introduced the Israelites to circumcision. Moses told the Hebrew that the Kenite deity Yahweh was the True God they had forgotten. Many Kenites were later absorbed into the tribe of Judah, but others refused. One group in the 9th century B.C.E. was the Rechabites, who violently opposed Ba'al, refused to touch wine or engage in agriculture, believing nomadism a religious duty.

CHAPTER SEVEN

1. Maxime Rodinson, "Sur eth. tabot, ar. tabut, et les noms semitiques de l' Arche." (Concerning the Ethiopic word tabot and the Arabic word tabut, and the Semitic name for the Ark), *Groupe Linguistiqued'Études Chamito-Sémitiques* IX (1962): 64-68.

2. Today the Agaw (or Central Cushitic) languages, according to David Appleyard, are confined to four groups in isolated

pockets surrounded by Ethiopian and Eritrean Semitic languages. In the 1994 census 1,625 of 172,291 Qemant spoke Qemanteney. Qwarenya, the former language of the Beta Israel, is closely related to Qemanteney. Awgi (in Gojjam south of Lake Tana) and Bilen in Eritrea around Keren, still thrive. Khamtanga appears to belong to another branch of Agaw.

3. *New York Times* May 9, 1999 "Group in Africa has Jewish Roots, DNA Indicates." Report concerning research undertaken by Dr. Karl Skorecki, Dr. Michael Hammer, Neil Bradman, David B. Goldstein and others on Y chromosomes.

4. Tudor Parfitt, *Journey to the Vanished City: the Search for a Lost Tribe of Israel.* London: Hodder and Stroughton, 1992.

5. Joseph Briant, *L'hebreu à Madagascar.* (The Hebrew in Madagascar) [Antananarivo, Malagasy Republic], 1946.

6. Edward Ullendorf, *Ethiopia and the Bible*. (Oxford: Oxford University Press, 1968), 117.

7. Frederick C. Gamst, *The Qemant, A Pagan-Hebraic Peasantry of Ethiopia.* (New York: Holt, Rinehart and Winston, 1969), and subsequent postings on the internet.

8. Nicholas Jubber *The Prester Quest* (New York: Doubleday, 2005) In A.D. 1165 the Byzantine emperor, Manuel Comnenus, received a letter from a Christian monarch ruling a paradise on the far side of the encircling Islamic world. A copy reached Pope Alexander III, who instructed a monk named Phillip to contact him. Phillip never returned and the letter has been described as a brilliant hoax pandering to the foibles of the medieval European mind.

9. Kay Kaufman Shelemay, *Music, Ritual and Falasha history*. (East Lansing: Michigan State University Press, 1986).

10. James Quirin, The Evolution of the Ethiopian Jews: a history of the Beta Israel (Falasha) to 1920. (Philadelphia: University of Pennsylvania Press, 1992). Steven Kaplan, *The Beta Israel (Falasha) in Ethiopia from Earliest Times to the Twentieth Century.* (New York: New York University Press, 1992).

11. Information from my former student at Asmara University, Tiberh Tesfamariam.

12. Donald N. Levine, "Menelik and Oedipus: Further Observations on the Ethiopian National Epic." *Proceedings of the First United States Conference on Ethiopian Studies* (Michigan State University, 2-5 May 1973), 11-23.

APPENDIX A

Comparison of Subject Material Describing the Queen of Sheba's Visit to Solomon's Court

Sheba-Menelik Cycle	Josephus	1 Kings 10: 1-13
Came with gifts	Came with large retinue and gifts	Came with large retinue and gifts
Took up residence in the palace	Amazed at the palace	Questioned Solomon
Description of the wonderful food	Amazed at sumptuous apartments	Solomon answered all her questions
Was given beautiful clothes	Was shown the house known as the Forest of Lebanon	Impressed by Solomon's wisdom, palace, food, seating arrangements, attendants' clothes' wine' burnt offerings
Experienced Solomon's wisdom	Description of the daily food and its preparation	Declared she was deeply impressed
Had her questions answered	Saw beautiful clothes of the servants	Gave gifts of gold and spices
Daily given food and clothes	Witnessed Solomon's administration	Acknowledged benign influence of Solomon's God
Saw how table was prepared	Witnessed daily sacrifices	Solomon reciprocated in official and other ways
Amazed at the palace	Believed things were better than expected	
Amazed at sumptuous apartments	Believed that the Hebrew were a blessed people	

Witnessed daily burning of incense		
Converted to Solomon's religion		
Tricked by Solomon into bearing his child		

APPENDIX B

1. The Jewish Torah

The Torah in the Sheba-Menelik Cycle is listed in Chapters 41, 42, 89, 90, and 91 of the *Kebra Nagast*. This Torah seems to be that which existed when the Queen of Sheba accepted the Israelite faith. Certainly scholars are in agreement that the laws governing sexual relations are from the Holiness Code (Leviticus 17-26), one of the oldest parts of the Hebrew Bible.

It is illuminating to compare the Sheba-Menelik Torah with the 613 commandments of the Jewish Torah (available at several sites on the Internet and about 7500 words in length). The Jewish Torah emphasizes racial purity. It accepts slavery. It has highly detailed rituals and has laws relating to personal matters, urban bureaucratic centralized government, and the priesthood. It calls for respect for prophets but death for those who dissent. It gives a privileged role to hereditary priest clans, the Levites and Kohenin, and sanctions taxation to maintain them. It outlines regulations concerning kingship. The laws from Deuteronomy that enhance the priesthood, establish central control, demand racial exclusiveness and theological conformity, are listed below, followed by brief comments and the Torah of the *Sheba-Menelik Cycle* itself:

Bring all offerings to Jerusalem. *Deuteronomy* xii. 5, 6
Offer all sacrifices in the Temple. xii. 14
Bring to the Temple also the offerings from beyond the land of Israel. xii. 26
Obey the prophet of each generation if he neither adds nor takes away from the statutes. xviii. 15
Appoint a king. xviii. 1.
Obey the authority of the Sanhedrin. xvii. 11
Appoint judges in every town. xvi. 18
Destroy idolaters and burn their city. xii. 2, xiii. 16
Destroy the seven Canaanite nations. xx. 17
Blot out the remembrance of Amalek. xxv. 17
Neither fear a false prophet nor hinder any one from killing him. xviii
Never show mercy to or intermarry with idolaters or allow them to live in your land. *(Also in Exodus xxiii. 33; and vii. 2, 3)*
Never permit the marriage of a daughter of Israel with an Ammonite or

Moabite. xxiii. 3
Never offer peace to the Ammonites and Moabites in time of war. xxiii. 6
Never forget the evil done by Amalek. xxv. 19
Never leave any Levite without support. xii. 19
Never rebel against the Sanhedrin. xvii. 11
Never elect a stranger as king over Israel. xvii. 15

None of these issues are mentioned in the Sheba-Menelik Torah. On the other hand, the Jewish Torah has a section on laws relating to Nazarites, who only exist among Ethiopia's Beta Israel.

Hilkiah's success in using the book of Deuteronomy to massacre and defile the Samaritan priesthood was followed later by Ezekiel's "vision" and Ezra's draconian measures that distanced the Jewish colony of New Jerusalem from the tolerance of the earlier Torah.

The provisions of the Israelite Torah in the *Sheba-Menelik Cycle* are listed on pages 205 to 207 following:

2. The Israelite Torah According to the *Sheba-Menelik Cycle*

Chapter 41 (Kebra Nagast)
Do God's work
Have no other God
Don't get angry
Treat good people well
Criticize sinners
Deal harshly in court with violence against people
Treat poor people and orphans well and defend them
Protect and restore abandoned and unhappy people
Judge impartially irrespective of background
Never accept bribes

Chapter 42
Respect only the one true god
Don't worship material objects
Don't make a false oath invoking God's name
Respect as holy the seventh day of the week and do no work that day
Treat your parents well
Don't have sex with someone else's wife
Don't kill anyone
Don't have sex outside marriage
Don't steal
Don't give false testament
Don't desire anything belonging to another person

A man must not have sex with the following:

Sister, half sister, step sister, adopted sister
Son's daughter
Daughter's daughter
Father's sister
Mother's sister
Father's brother's sister
Son's wife
Daughter
Brother's son's daughter
Brother's wife
Woman and her daughter
Woman and her son's daughter
Woman and her daughter's daughter
A menstruous woman
Your neighbor's wife
Another man
An animal

Don't marry sisters while both live
Don't offer your children to Moloch

A woman must not have sex with an animal
"Sanctify ye your souls and your bodies to God"

Chapter 89
Love what is right
Hate deceit
Don't be fraudulent
Don't oppress
Don't make auguries from birds or signs
Don't use charms
Don't use incantations
Don't use portents
Don't use magic

Chapter 90
Don't eat the meat of an animal that died of natural causes or was killed by other animals
Keep sex within marriage
Don't use force to settle disputes
Don't rob your neighbor
Don't abuse each other
Don't oppress anyone
Don't quarrel
Return stray livestock
Report livestock in difficulties and assist in their retrieval
If you dig a well, cover it
If you build a shelter, put a roof over it
Help people carrying heavy loads
Don't cook the meat of animal in the milk of its mother
Respect and defend the rights of the poor and orphans
Don't take bribes
Refuse to be corrupted
Neither harm birds with young nor remove the young birds
Don't harvest the entire crop
Keep surplus food for strangers
Don't engage in dishonest and immoral activities
Judge fairly
Don't bully people
Don't mistreat the infirm
Don't have sex with your father's partners
Don't cheat your neighbors
Don't cause death by perverting justice for aliens
Respect your parents and don't treat them lightly
Don't worship material objects
Don't have sex with animals
Men must not have sex with other men
Don't kill innocent people
Don't worship other gods

Chapter 91
Acceptable food
Ox
Sheep
Goat
Ram
Stag
Gazelle
Buffalo
Antelope
Oryx
Any animal with cleft foot and nails
Fish with scales and fins
Birds with clean habits

Forbidden food
Pig
Camel
Wolf
Hare
Coney (rabbit or hyrax)
Water creatures without fins and scales
Birds with unclean habits
Vulture
Eagle
Osprey
Raven
Owl
Hawk
Sea gull
Heron
Swan

Ibis
Pelican
Hoopoe
Night raven
Hornbill
Water piper
Water hen

Bat
Locust
Grasshopper
Flying or springing creatures with two to six legs (nor touch their dead bodies)

APPENDIX C
The Ge'ez Alphabet

	+A	+U	+I	+Ā	+Ē	-/+E	+O
H	ሀ	ሁ	ሂ	ሃ	ሄ	ህ	ሆ
L	ለ	ሉ	ሊ	ላ	ሌ	ል	ሎ
Ḥ	ሐ	ሑ	ሒ	ሓ	ሔ	ሕ	ሖ
M	መ	ሙ	ሚ	ማ	ሜ	ም	ሞ
Š	ሠ	ሡ	ሢ	ሣ	ሤ	ሥ	ሦ
R	ረ	ሩ	ሪ	ራ	ሬ	ር	ሮ
S	ሰ	ሱ	ሲ	ሳ	ሴ	ስ	ሶ
Q	ቀ	ቁ	ቂ	ቃ	ቄ	ቅ	ቆ
B	በ	ቡ	ቢ	ባ	ቤ	ብ	ቦ
T	ተ	ቱ	ቲ	ታ	ቴ	ት	ቶ
X	ኀ	ኁ	ኂ	ኃ	ኄ	ኅ	ኆ
N	ነ	ኑ	ኒ	ና	ኔ	ን	ኖ
ʼ	አ	ኡ	ኢ	ኣ	ኤ	እ	ኦ
K	ከ	ኩ	ኪ	ካ	ኬ	ክ	ኮ
W	ወ	ዉ	ዊ	ዋ	ዌ	ው	ዎ
ʽ	ዐ	ዑ	ዒ	ዓ	ዔ	ዕ	ዖ
Z	ዘ	ዙ	ዚ	ዛ	ዜ	ዝ	ዞ
Y	የ	ዩ	ዪ	ያ	ዬ	ይ	ዮ
D	ደ	ዱ	ዲ	ዳ	ዴ	ድ	ዶ
G	ገ	ጉ	ጊ	ጋ	ጌ	ግ	ጎ
Ṭ	ጠ	ጡ	ጢ	ጣ	ጤ	ጥ	ጦ
P	ጰ	ጱ	ጲ	ጳ	ጴ	ጵ	ጶ
Ṣ	ጸ	ጹ	ጺ	ጻ	ጼ	ጽ	ጾ
Ḍ	ፀ	ፁ	ፂ	ፃ	ፄ	ፅ	ፆ
F	ፈ	ፉ	ፊ	ፋ	ፌ	ፍ	ፎ
P	ፐ	ፑ	ፒ	ፓ	ፔ	ፕ	ፖ
Qw	ቈ		ቊ	ቋ	ቌ	ቍ	
Xw	ኈ		ኊ	ኋ	ኌ	ኍ	
Kw	ኰ		ኲ	ኳ	ኴ	ኵ	
Gw	ጐ		ጒ	ጓ	ጔ	ጕ	

APPENDIX D
The Ge'ez (Ethiopic) Numerals

1	፩	11	፲፩	30	፴	28	፳፰
2	፪	12	፲፪	40	፵	37	፴፯
3	፫	13	፲፫	50	፶	46	፵፮
4	፬	14	፲፬	60	፷	55	፶፭
5	፭	15	፲፭	70	፸	64	፷፬
6	፮	16	፲፮	80	፹	73	፸፫
7	፯	17	፲፯	90	፺	82	፹፪
8	፰	18	፲፰	100	፻	91	፺፩
9	፱	19	፲፱	105	፻፭	200	፪፻
10	፲	20	፳	150	፻፶	1000	፲፻

APPENDIX E

Ge'ez transcript of sections of the *Sheba-Menelik Cycle* of the *Kebra Nagast*

CHAPTER 53	*208*
CHAPTER 55	*211*
CHAPTER 58	*214*
CHAPTER 59	*216*

Chapter 53 of the Kebra Nagast

፶፫ ዐበ ትውህበ ሰረገላ ለኢትዮጵያ።

ወበነበ ጎደራስ ጋዛ ይእቲ ሀገረ እሙ ለንጉሥ ዘወሀባ ሶበ ትመጽእ ጎቤሁ ንጉሥ ሰሎሞን ለንግሥተ ኢትዮጵያ። ወእምህየ በጽሑ በአሐቲ ዕለት ውስተ ደወለ ግብጽ እንተ ስማ ምስሪን፡ ወሰብ ርእዩ ደቂቀ ጎያላነ እስራኤል ከመ በአሐቲ ዕለት በጽሑ ምሕዋረ ፲ወ፫ ዕለት ወኢደክሙ ወኢርኅቡ ወኢጸምኡ ኢሰብእ ወኢእንስሳ ወኮሎሙ ከመ ዘሰቤ ጸግቡ ወሰትዩ አእመሩ። ወአምኑ እሙንቱ ደቂቀ ጎይል ከመ እምነበ እግዚአብሔር ኮነት ዛቲ፡ ወይቤልዎ ለንጉሦሙ ናውርድ ሰረገላተ እስመ በጸሕነ ማየ ኢትዮጵያ ዛቲ ይእቲ ተከዚ እንተ ትወርድ እምኢትዮጵያ ወትሰቂ ፈለገ ግብጽ፡ ወአውረዱ ሰረገላቲሆሙ ህየ ወተክሉ ደባትሪሆሙ። ወሐሩ ጉቡረ ደቂቀ ጎይል ወሰደዱ ኩሉ አሕዛብ ወይቤልዎ ለንጉሦሙ ንንግርከኑ ነገረ ለእመ ትክል ተዐግሦ፡ ወይቤሎሙ እወ እክል ወለእመ ትቤሉኒ እስከ ዕለተ ሞትየ ኢያወጽእ ወኢያወሥእ። ወይቤልዎ ወረደት ፀሐይ እምሰማይ ወተውህበት በሲና ለእስራኤል ወኮነት መድኀኒተ ለዘመደ አዳም

እምነ ሙሴ እስከ ዘርአ እሴይ ወነዋ ኀቤከ በፈቃደ እግዚአብሔር፡ ወኢኮ እምነቤን ዘተገብረ ዝንቱ አላ በፈቃደ እግዚአብሔር ወኢኮ እምነቤን ዘተገብረ ዝንቱ አላ በፈቃደ ኬንያሃ ወገባሪሃ ኮነ ከመዝ፡ ንሕነ ፈቀድነ ወእግዚአብሔር ፈጸመ ንሕነ ተሰናአውነ ወእግዚአብሔር አሠነየ ንሕነ ተናገርነ ወእግዚአብሔር ገብረ ንሕነ ኀለይነ ወእግዚአብሔር መከረ ንሕነ ኀቤ ወእግዚአብሔር ሠምረ ንሕነ አንጸርነ ወእግዚአብሔር አርትዐ ንሕነ ኀለይነ ወእግዚአብሔር አጽደቀ: ወይእዜኒ ኪያከ ኀሪየ እግዚአብሔር ወሀገርከ ሠምረ ከመ ትኩን ላእከ ለጽዮን ቅድስት ሰማያዊት ታቦተ ሕጉ ለእግዚአብሔር ወይእቲ ትኩንክ መርሐ እስከ ለዓለም ለከ ወለዘርእከ እምድኀሬከ ለእሞ በቀብከ ትእዛዞ ወገበ ርከ ፈቃዶ ለእግዚአብሔር አምላክከ: እስመ ኢትክል አንተ አግብአታ ለእሞ ፈቀድከ ወአቡከ ነሡኢታ ለእሞ ፈቀደ እስመ ለሊሃ: ተሐውር ገበ ፈቀደት ወኢትትነሣእ እመንበራ ለእሞ ኢፈቀደት ለሊሃ ወነያ ይእቲ እግዝእትነ እምነ ወመድኀኒትነ ጽወንነ ወምስካይነ ክብርነ ወመርሶ መድኀኒትነ ለእለ ናሰምክ ባቲ። ወቀጸበ አዛርያስ ለኤልምያኖስ ወይቤሉ ሐር አሠንያ ወአልብሳ ለእግዝእትነ ከመ ይርአያ ንጉሥነ። ወዘንተ ሰብ ተናገረ አዛርያስ

ደንገፀ ንጉሥ ዳዊት ወአንበረ ክልኤሆን እደዊሁ ውስተ ልቡ ወአስተንፈሰ ሠለስተ እስትንፋሰ ወይቤ አማንኑ እግዚአ ትዜከረነ ቦሐልከ ለጋዱፋን እለ መነንከ ሕዝብ ከመ እርአያ ለማኅደርከ ንጽሕት እንተ በሰማያት ጽዮን ቅድስት ሰማያዊት፤ ወምንተኔ ነዐስዮ ለእግዚአብሔር በእንተ ኵሉ ዘገብረ ለነ ሠናያተ እንዘ ወእምንትኒ ቦጎቤሁ ክብረ ወስብሓተ ከለለነ በጸጋሁ ከመ ናእምር በምድር ስብሓቲሁ ወንግናይ ኵልነ ልዕበየ ዚአሁ፤ እስመ ቤር ውእቱ ለጉሩያኒሁ ወሉቱ ስብሓት እስከ ለዓለም።

ወተንሥአ ንጉሥ እንዘ ያንፈርዕጽ ከመ ማሕስአ በግዕ ወከመ ሐርጌ ጽጉብ ሐሊብ እሙ፤ በከመ ፍሥሓ ዳዊት አበ አቡሁ በቅድመ ታቦተ ሕጉ ለእግዚአብሔር፤ አጽሐሰ በንገሪሁ ወተሐሠየ በልቡ ወተሀለሰ በአፉሁ።። ወምንተ እብል ሚመጠነ ፍሥሓ ወሐሤተ በውስተ ትዕይንተ ንጉሠ ኢትዮጵያ፤ ይነግሩ ጅ ለካልኡ ወያንፈርዕጡ ኵሎሙ ከመ ጣዕዋ ላህም ወይጠፍሑ እደዊሆሙ ወያነክሩ ወይሰፍሑ እደዊሆሙ ውስተ ሰማይ ወይሰግዱ በጸዑም ውስተ ምድር ወያአኵትዎ ለእግዚአብሔር በአልባቢሆሙ።።

Chapter 55 of the Kebra Nagast

፶፭፡ በእንተ ዘተፈሥሑ ሰብአ ኢትዮጵያ።

ወአነኑ ዐንዚራተ ወነቢዮ ቀርና ወከበሮ ወዕዘ ወበቃል ማሕሌቶሙ ወፍሥሓሆሙ ተሀውክት ወደምፀት ፈለግ ግብጽ ወነብሩ ምስሌሆሙ ውዉዓ ወማሕሌት። ወዎድቁ ጣዖታቲሆሙ ዘገብሩ በእደዊሆሙ አምሳለ ሰብእ ወከልብ ወድመት ወዓዲ ማኅፈደ ነዋኋት ወእለ ምስሌሆሙ አምሳለ አንስርት ዘወርቅ ወብሩር ወድቁ ወተቀጥቀጡ፡ እስመ ከመ ፀሐይ ታበርህ ወእምግርማሃ ይደነግፁ፡ ወአልበሰዋ አልባሲሃ ወጸሩ ሞጻሃ ቅድሜሃ ወአንበርዋ ዲበ ሰረገላ ካጺሮሙ ሜላተ ታሕቴሃ ወፀፈሮሙ ሜላተ በመልዕልቴሃ ወይሐልዩ ማሕሌተ በቅድሜሃ ወበድንጋሄ። ወተንሥኡ ሰረገላትኒ ከመ ቀዲሙ ወጌሡ በጽባሕ እንዘ ይሔልዩ ላቲ ወተላዕሉ ኵሎሙ መጠነ እመት፡ እንዘ ያስተፋንውዎሙ ሰብአ ብሔረ ግብጽ ጎሰፉ በቅድሜሆሙ ከመ ጽላሎት ወሰገዱ ሎሙ ሰብአ ብሔረ ግብጽ እስመ ርእዩዋ እንዘ ትረውጽ ከመ ፀሐይ በውስተ ሰማይ። ወኵሎሙ ይረውጹ በሰረገላ እንዘ ይረውጹ በቅድሜሃ ወበድንጋሄ። ወበጽሑ ባሕረ አለአሕመር

እንተ ይእቲ ባሕረ ኤርትራ እንተ ተሠጥቀት በእደ ሙሴ ወኬዱ ደቂቀ እስራኤል ውስተ መዓምቅቲሃ ዐቀብ ወቀልቀስ እስመ ኢተውህበት አሜሃ ለሙሴ ታቦተ ሕጉ ለእግዚአብሔር ወበእንተዝ ጠገዐ ማይ አረፍት በይምን ወአረፍት በፀጋም ወአንስፍሙ ለእስራኤል ምስለ እንስሳሆሙ ወደቂቆሙ ወእንስቲያሆሙ፡ ወእምድኃሬ ዐደዉ ባሕረ ተናገሮ እግዚአብሔር ወወሀቦ ታቦተ ኪዳን ምስለ መጽሐፈ ሕግ። ወሶበ ተዐዱ ጽዮን ቅድስት ምስለ እሊአሃ አሜሃ እንተ ኀቤሃ እንዘ ይሐልዩ ማሕሌተ በመሰንቆ ወበዕንዚራት ባሕርኒ ተቀበለቶሙ እንዘ ታንፈርዕጽ መዋግዲሃ ከመ ሰብ ይትበተኩ አድባር ኮዖት ወከመ ድምፀ አንበሳ ዘይጥሕር ከማሁ በገንሕ ትደምፅ ወከመ ነጐድጓደ ክረምተ ደማስቆ ወኢትዮጵያ ሰብ ይዘብጠን መብረቅ ለደማናት ከማሁ ታንጐደጕድ ወጎብረ ነጐድጓድ ምስለ ዕንዚራተ ወሰገደት ላቲ ባሕርኒ፡ ወእንዘ ይትሀወክ መዋግዲሃ ከመ አድባር ተለዐለ ሰረገላቲሆሙ መልዕልተ መዋግድ መጠነ ፫ እመት ወበዜማ ማሕሌቶሙ መንክር ተላህያ ለባሕር፡ ግሩም ፈድፋደ ወመድምም ተላህያ ለባሕር ዐዚዝ ጥቀ ወዕፁብ ተላህያ ለባሕር ወእለ ውስቴታሂ አራዊት እለ ይትዐወቁ ወእለ ኢያስተርእዩ ይወፅኡ ወይሰግዱ ላቲ ወአዕዋፍኒ እለ ውስቴታ ይጠፍሑ

በክናፈሆሙ ወይጼልልዋ ወኮነ ፍሥሓ ለባሕረ ኢርትራ ወለሰብአ ኢትዮጵያ ወወፅኡ ባሕረ ወተፈሥሑ ፈድፋደ እምነ እስራኤል ሶበ ይወፅኡ እምግብጽ ወበጽሑ አንጻረ ደብረ ሲና ወጎደሩ ውስተ ቃዴስ ወበሀየኒ እንዘ ይሴብሑ መላእክት ወያንብሩ ስብሐቶሙ መንፈሳዊያን ምስለ ደቂቀ መሬታዊያን በማሕሌት ወበመዝሙር በከበሮ ወበትፍሥሕት። ወእምሂየ ጸዐኑ ሰረገላቲሆሙ ወተንሥኡ ወሐሩ ወጎለፍዋ ለብሔረ ምድያም ወበጽሑ ሀገረ ቤሉንቶስ እንተ ሀገረ ኢትዮጵያ፡ ወተፈሥሑ በሀየኒ ወአዕረፉ እስመ ደወለ ብሔሮሙ በጽሑ በክብር ወበፍሥሓ ዘእንበለ ፃማ በፍኖት በሰረገላ ነፋስ ምስለ ጎይለ ሰማይ ወሚካኤል ሊቀ መላእክት፡ ወተፈሥሑ ኩሎሙ አድያም ኢትዮጵያ እስመ ታቦረ ጽዮን ጎበ በጽሐት ከመ ፀሐይ በውስተ ጽልመት።

Chapter 58 of the Kebra Nagast

፶፰ ነበ ተንሥአ ሰሎሞን ይቅትሎሙ፡፡

ከመዝ ተናገረ ንጉሥ ሰሎሞን ወተንሥአ በመዐት ወሐረ ከመ ይኅሥሦሙ፡ ወሰበ ተንሥኡ ንጉሥ ወመኳንንቲሁ ወኂያላኒሁ ተጋብኡ አእሩግ እስራኤል ውስተ ቤተ እግዚአብሔር ምስለ አቤራት ወደናግል ወበከዩ በእንተ ጽዮን እስመ ተነሥአት እም ኄሆሙ ታቦተ ሕጉ ለእግዚአብሔር፡፡ ወለሰዶቅኒ እስመ ገብአ ልቡ እምድኅረ ጉንዳይ ሰዐት፡፡ ወእምዝ አዘዘ ንጉሥ ከመ ይሐሩ ይምነ ወፀጋመ ከመ እመቦ ከመ ይትገሐሡ እምፍርሀተ ስርቅ፡ ወለሊሁስ ንጉሥ ተንሥአ በአሠረ ፍኖቶሙ ለሰብአ ኢትዮጵያ ወሬጠወ መባርዲን፡ ሰብአ አፍራስ፡ ከመ ያእምሩ ነበ ሀለዉ ወይግብኡ ወይንግርዎ፡፡ ወሐሩ ወበጽሑ ሀገረ ምስር ነበ ተዐየኑ ህየ ሰብአ ኢትዮጵያ ምስለ ንጉሥሙ፡ ወነበዪ ተሰለምዋ ለጽዮን ወተፈሥሑ ወሐተቱ ኪያሆሙ ሐራ ንጉሥ ወይቤልዎሙ ሰብአ ብሐረ ግብጽ፡ እምርሑቅ መዋዕል በዘየ ኀለፉ ሰብአ ኢትዮጵያ እንዘ ይረውፁ በሰረገላ ከመ መላእክት ወይቀልሉ እምነ አንስርት በውስተ ሰማይ፡ ወይቤልዎሙ ማእዜ ዕለት ኀለፉ

እምኔክሙ፡ ወይቤልዎሙ የግም ተሱዕ መዋዕል በዘ ኃለፉ እምኔነ። ወቦ እምኔሆሙ እለ ገብኡ ወነገርዎ ለንጉሥ ሰሎሞን ከመ ኃለፉ ተሱዐ መዋዕል እምዘ ኃለፉ እምስር ወአብያጺነስ ሓሩ ከመ ይኃነዉ እስከ ባሕረ ኤርትራ ወንሕነ ገባእነ ከመ ንንግርከ ዘንተ፡ እስኩ ኃሊ ለሊከ ንጉሥ በዕለተ ሰኑይ እምከመ ወፅኡ እምገቤክ በጽሑ በሠሉስ ኃበ ፈለግ ተከዚ ሀገረ ምስር፡ ወለነኒ ሰብ ፈነዉክን እምኢየሩሳሌም በጻሕነ በዕለተ ሰንበት ወገባእነ ኃቤክ የግም በዕለተ ራብዕ፡ ኃሊኬ በጥብብ መጠነ ይብጽሑ እሙንቱ ሰብእ። ወተምዐ ንጉሥ ወይቤ አነዘዎሙ ኅምስቲሆሙ እስከ ንረኪብ ጽድቀ ታሎሙ። ወአፍጠኑ ሐዊረ ንጉሥ ወሰራዊቲ ወበጽሑ ጋዛ ወተስእሉሙ ወይቤሉሙ ማእዜ ኃለፈ ወልድየ እምኔክሙ። አውሥኡ ወይቤሉ ኃለፈ ይእቲ ሠሉስ ዕለት ወሰብ ጾዕኑ ሰረገላቲሆሙ አልቦ ዘፈሐዉር መልዕልተ ምድር አላ በሰረገላ ስቁላን መልዕልተ ነፋስ ወይቀልሉ እመን አንስርት ዘውስተ ሰማይ ወኩሉ ንዋዮሙ የሐውር ምስሌሆሙ መልዕልተ ነፋስ በሰረገላ። ወለነሰ መሰስን ዘአንተ ረሰይክ ሎሙ በጥብበክ ከመ ይሐፉ በሰረገላ መልዕልተ ነፋስ። ወይቤሉሙ ቡኑ ዘሀለወት ጽዮን ታቦት ሕጉ ለእግዚአብሔር ምስሌሆሙ፡ ወይቤልዎ አልቦ ዘርኢነ።

Chapter 59 of the Kebra Nagast

፶፱ ፡ ባብ ሐተቶ ለገጻዊ ገብረ ፈርዖን፨

ወነስሬ እምህየ ወረከብ ፶ መኩኔን እመኳንንተ ገብጽ ዘንጉሥ ፈርዖን ዘለአኮ ኀቤሁ ምስለ አምኃ ወምሉእ ንዋይ ምስሌሁ ወበጽሐ ወሰገደ ለንጉሥ፨ ወአፍጠና ሐቲተ ሰሎሞን ንጉሥ ዘእንበለ የሀብ አምኃሁ ወመልእክቶ ወይቤሎ ቦኑ ዘርእከ ሰብአ ኢትዮጵያ እንዘ ይግዕዙ እምህየ፨ ወአውሥአ ወይቤሎ መልአክ ፈርዖን ለንጉሥ ሕያው አንተ ንጉሥ ለዓለም ፡ ለእከኒ እግዚእየ ንጉሥ ፈርዖን እምእስክንድርያ ኀቤከ ወነዋ አየድዐከ ዘከመ መጻእኩ ፡ ወሰብ መጻእኩ እምእስክንድርያ ቦእኩ ቃህራ ውስተ ሀገሩ ለንጉሥ ወበጽሐትየ በጽሑ ህየ እሉ ሰብአ ኢትዮጵያ ዘትብል ፡ በጽሑ እንተ ኀለፈት ሠሉስ ውስተ ተከዚ ፈለገ ምስር እንዘ ይንፍሑ በዕንዚራት ወይረውጹ በሰረገላት ከመ ኂይለ ሰማያዊያን ፡ ወእለ ርእይዎሙ ይቤልዎሙ እሉ እንዘ መሬታዊያን ኮኑ ሰማያዊያን መኑኬ ይጠብብ እምሰሎሞን ንጉሠ ይሁዳ ወእትኒ ኢሐረ በሰረገላ ነፋስ ከመዝ፨ ወእለ ሀለዉ ውስተ አህጉር መጋነፍድ ስምዐ ኮኑ ከመ ሰብ ቦኡ እሉ ውስተ ብሔረ ግብጽ ወደቁ ወተሰብሩ፨

አማልክቲነ ወአማልክተ ነጉሥ ወማኅፈደ ጣዖታትኒ ከማሁ ተቀጥቀጡ ወሐተቱ ገነውተ አማልክት ማርያን ግብጽ በእንተ ዘወድቁ አማልክቲነ ወይቤሉነ ታቦተ አምላክ እስራኤል እንተ ወረደት እምሰማይ ሀለወት ምስሌሆሙ ወትነብር ውስተ ሀገሮሙ እስከ ለዓለም፡ ወበእንተዝኬ ሶበ ትበውእ ብሔረ ግብጽ ተቀጥቀጡ አማልክቲነ፡ ወአንተሰ እንጉሥ አልቦ ዘይመስላ ለጥበብከ እምታሕተ ሰማይ ወለምንት ወሀብከ ታቦተ ሕጉ ለእግዚአብሔር አማላክከ ዘአንጽሑ ለከ አበዊከ፡ እስመ ንሰምዕ ከመ ይእቲ ታድኅነከሙ እምእደ ፀርከሙ ወመንፈሰ ትንቢትኒ ባቲ ይትናገረከሙ ወአምላክ ሰማይኒአ የነድር ውስቴታ በመንፈሱ ቅዱስ ወትሰመይ ሰብአ ቤቱ ለእግዚአብሔር፡ ወለምንት ዘወሀብክሙ ክብርክሙ ለባዕድ። አውሥአ በጥበብ ሰሎሞን ወይቤ በአይቲ ይክል ኖኂታ ለእግዝእትነ እስመ ሀለወት ጌቤነ።

BIBLIOGRAPHY

Abir, Mordecai. *Ethiopia: The Era of the Princes.* New York: Praeger, 1968.

Ahlstrom, G.W. "The Travels of the Ark: A Religio-political Composition." *Journal of Near Eastern Studies* (43) 1984, 141-149.

Ahroni, Reuben. *Yemenite Jewry: Origins, Culture, and Literature.* Bloomington: Indiana University Press, 1986.

Aläqa Tayyä Gäbrä Maryam. *History of the People of Ethiopia.* Translated by Grover Hudson and Tekeste Negash. 2nd print. Uppsala, Sweden: University of Uppsala, 1988.

Albright, W.F. *The Archaeology of Palestine.* Harmondsworth: Penguin Books, 1949.

Al Jasir, Sheikh Hamad. *Al-Mug'am algugrafi li'l bilad al- Arabhyah al-Sa 'udiyyah* [Gazette of Saudi Arabian Place Names] (3 volumes). Riyadh, Saudi Arabia: Government Publications, 1977.

Arnaiz-Villena, Antonio Nagah Elaiwa, Carlos Silvera, Ahmed Rostom, Juan Moscoso, Edfizardo Gomez-Casado, Luis Allende, Pilar Varela, and Jorge Martinez-Laso. "The Origin of Palestinians and their Genetic Relatedness with Other Mediterranean Populations." *Human Immunology* 62, (2001), 889-900.

Arafat, W.N. "New Light on the Story of Banu Qurayza and the Jews of Medina." Journal of the Royal Asiatic Society of Great Britain and Ireland (1976), 100-107.

Armstrong, Karen. *Muhammad: a Western Attempt to Understand Islam.* London: Victor Gollancz, 1991.

_____. *A History of God* London: Heinemann, 1993.

_____ *A History of Jerusalem: One City, Three Faiths.* London: Harper Collins, 1997.

Barr, James. *Comparative Philology and the Text of the Old Testament.* Winona Lake, Indiana: Eisenbrauns, 1987.

Bezold, Carl. *Kebra Nagast: Die Herrlichkeit der Könige* [*Kebra Nagast:* the Glory of the Kings] Abhandlungen der Königlich Bayerischen Akademie, Band 23, Abth. 1, [Band 77 of the Denkschriften], Munich, 1909.

Bonné-Tamir, Batsheva. *Genetic Diversity among the Jews: Diseases and Markers at the DNA Level.* New York: Oxford University Press, 1992.

Briant, Joseph. *L'hebreu à Madagascar.* [Antananarivo, Malagasy Republic], 1946.

Bruce, J. *Travels to Discover the Source of the Nile in the Years 1768, 1769, 1770, 1771, 1772 and 1773.* [Edinburgh and Dublin], 1790.

Bulliet, R.W. *The Camel and the Wheel.* Cambridge, Mass: Harvard University Press 1975.

Buxton, David. *The Abyssinians.* New York: Praegar, 1970.

Cavalli-Sforza, Luigi Luca, Paolo Menozzi, Alberto Piazza. *The History and Geography of Human Genes.* Princeton N .J.; Princeton University Press, 1994.

Cerulli, Enrico. *Storia della letteratura etiopica.* [Milano]: Nuova accademica editrice, [1956].

Chatterji, Suniti Kumar. *India and Ethiopia from the Seventh Century B.C.* The Asiatic Society: Calcutta, 1968.

Clapp, Nicholas. *The Queen of Sheba.* Boston, Massachusetts: Houghton Mifflin, 2001.

Conti Rossini, Carlo. *Storia d'Etiopia.* [Bergamo, Italy] 1928.

Dawood, N. J. (Translator). *The Koran.* London: Penguin Books, 1997.

De Prorok, Byron. *Dead Men do Tell Tales.* London: Harrap, 1944.

Dever, William G. *Who Were the Early Israelites and Where Did They Come From?* Grand Rapids: Eerdmans, 2003

Dillmann, August. *Ethiopic Grammar.* Amsterdam: Philo Press, 1974. Reprint [London] 1907.

Doresse, Jean. *Ethiopia.* London: Elek Books, 1959.

Dothan, Trude Krakauer. *People of the Sea: the Search for the Philistines.* New York: Macmillan, 1998.

Dozy, Reinhart. *Die Israeliten zu Mekka von Davids Zeit.* [The Israelites of Mecca in David's Time] Leipzig: Engelmann, 1864.

Drewes, A.J. *Inscriptions de l'Ethiopie Antique.* Leiden: E .J. Brill, 1962.

Edelman, Diana V.(ed.). The Fabric of History: Text, Artefact and Israel's Past. *Journal for the Study of the Old Testament, Supplement Series 127.* Sheffield: Sheffield Academic Press, 1991.

Eisenman, Robert. *The Dead Sea Scrolls and the First Christians: Essays and Translations.* Shaftesbury, England: Element Books, 1996.

Encyclopaedia Judaica. Jerusalem: Keter Publishing House, 1971-2.

Fattovich, Rodolfo. Karim Sadr, Silvana Vitagliano. "Societa e tettirorio nel Delta del Gash (Kassala, Sudan Orientale) 3,000 a.Cr - 300/400 d.Cr.Africa." [Rome] 43, 1988, 394453.

_____. "Remarks on the pre-Aksumite Period in Northern Ethiopia." *Journal of Ethiopian Studies.* Vol. 23, 1990.

_____, Lorenzo Petrassi, Kathryn Bard, and Vincenzo Pisano. *The Aksum Archaeological Area: A. Preliminary Assessment.* Naples, Italy: Instituto Universitario Orientale Napoli, 2000.

Fiennes, Ranulph. *Atlantis of the Sands - the Search for the Lost City of Urbar.* London: Bloomsbury,1992.

Finkelstein, Israel and Neil Silberman. *The Bible Unearthed.* New York: Free Press, 2001.

Francis, Leslie J. "Is psychoticism really a dimension of personality fundamental to religiosity?" *Personality individual differences* Vol. 13, No.6, 1992, [Pergamon] 1992.

Gadd, C .J. "The Harran Inscription of Nabonidus." *Anatolian Studies,* 8, 1958.

Gamst, Frederick C. *The Qemant, a Pagan-Hebraic Peasantry of Ethiopia.* New York: Holt, Rinehart, and Winston, 1969.

Gilbert, Martin. *The Dent Atlas* of *Jewish History from 2000 B. C. to the Present Day.* London: Dent, 1993.

Ginzberg, Louis. *Legends of the Jews. [7 vols]* Philadelphia: Jewish Publication Society, 1967.

Goitein, S.D.(ed) *The Land of Sheba: Tales of the Jews of the Yemen.* New York: Schocken Books, 1947.

Guidi, I. *(Breve) storia della letteratura etiopica.* [Rome], 1932.

Greenfield, Richard. *Ethiopia, A New Political History.* London: Pall Mall, 1965.

Hammerschmidt, Ernst. *Athiopien: Christliches Reich zwischen Gestern und Morgen.* Wiesbaden, Germany: Otto Harrassowitz, 1967.

Hancock, Graham. *The Sign and the Seal a Quest for the Lost Ark* of *the Covenant*. London: Mandarin, 1993.

Haran, M. "The disappearance of the Ark." *Journal of the Israeli Exploration Society* 13, (1963), 46-58.

Harris, Joseph E. *Pillars in Ethiopian History*. Washington D.C.: Howard University Press, 1981.

Heine, Bernd. "Some linguistic observations on the early history of Africa." *Sprache und Geschichte in Afrika,* Cologne, Germany (1979), 37-54.

Hetzron, Robert (ed.). *The Semitic languages.* London: Routledge, 1998.

Hoyland, Robert G. *Arabia and the Arabs from the Bronze Age to the Coming of Islam.* London: Routledge, 2001.

Hubbard, David. *The Literary Sources of the Kebra Nagast.* Ph.D. diss., St. Andrews University, Scotland, 1956.

Hudson, Grover. "Language Classification and the Semitic prehistory of Ethiopia." *Folia Orientalia* Tome 18, 1977.

Huntingford, G.W.B. *The Historical Geography of Ethiopia from the First Century A.D. to 1704.* London: The British Academy, 1989.

Iliffe, John. *Africa, The History of a Continent.* Cambridge: Cambridge University Press, 1995.

Isaac, Ephraim and Cain Felder. "Reflections on the origins of the Ethiopian civilization." Paper presented at the Eighth International Conference of Ethiopian Studies, Addis Ababa, November 1984, 71-83.

Isenberg, Shirley Berry. *India's Bene Israel.* Bombay: Popular Prakashan, 1988.

Jagaer, Otto A. and Ivy Pearce. *Antiquities of North Ethiopia.* Stuttgart: University of Stuttgart, 1976.

Jones, Steve. *In the Blood God, Genes and Destiny.* London: Flamingo/Harper Collins, 1997.

Josephus, Flavius. *The Works of Flavius Josephus* (Translated by W.Whiston). Peabody, Massachusetts: Hendrickson, 1987.

Jubber, Nicholas. *The Prester Quest.* New York: Doubleday, 2005.

Kaplan, Steven. *The Beta Israel (Falasha) in Ethiopia from Earliest Times to the Twentieth Century.* New York: New York University Press, 1992.

Katz, Nathan and Ellen S Goldberg. *The Last Jews of Cochin: Jewish Identity in Hindu India.* Columbia: University of South Carolina Press, 1993.

Keller, Werner. *The Bible as History: Archaeology Confirms the Book of Books.* London: Hodder and Stroughton, 1956.

Kenyon, Kathleen. M. *Archaeology in the Holy Land.* London: Benn, 1979.

Kessler, David. *The Falashas, the Forgotten Jews of Ethiopia.* New York: Africana, 1982.

Kirk, John William Carnegie. *A grammar of the Somali language with examples in prose and verse; and an account of the Yibir and Midgan dialects.* Cambridge: University Press, 1905.

Kirtley, Michael and Aubine. "The Inadan, Artisans of the Sahara." *National Geographic:* August 1979.

Kitchen, K.A. "Punt and how to get there." *Orientalia, 40,* fasc.2, (1971), 184-207.

Knauf, Ernst Axel. *Midian. Untersuchungen zur Geschichte Palästinas und Nordarabiens am Ende des 2. Jahrtausends v. Chr.* [Midian. Searching for the History of Palestine and North Arabia at the end of the Second Millennium B.C.E.] Wiesbaden, Germany: Otto Harrassowitz, 1988.

_____. *Ismael. Untersuchungen zur Geschichte Palästinas und Nordarabiens im 1. Jahrtausend v. Chr.* . [Ismael. Searching for the History of Palestine and North Arabia in the First Millennium B.C.E.] Wiesbaden, Germany: Otto Harrassowitz in Kommission, 1989.

Kobishchanov, Yuri M. *Axum.* Philadelphia: Pennsylvania State University, 1979.

Kodar, S. S. *History of the Jews of Kerala.* Cochin, 1974.

Korotayev, Andrey. "Ancient Yemen: Some General Trends of Evolution of the Sabaic Language and Sabaean Culture." *Journal of Semitic Studies Supplement No.5,* Oxford: Oxford University Press, 1995.

_____, Vladimir Klimenko, and Dimitri Proussakov, "Origins of Islam: Political-Anthropological and Environmental Context *Acta Orientalia Academiae Scientiarum Hung.,* 52 (3-4), (1999): 243-276.

Lambdin, Thomas O. *Introduction to Classical Ethiopic (Ge'ez).* Cambridge, Massachusetts: Harvard, Scholars Press, 1978.

Lassner, Jacob. *Demonizing the Queen of Sheba: Boundaries* of *Gender and Culture in Postbiblical Judaism and Medieval Islam.* Chicago: University of Chicago Press, 1993.

Lecker, Michael. *Jews and Arabs in Pre- and Early Islamic Arabia.* Aldershot, England: Ashgate Variorium, Variorum Collected Studies, 1998.

Leeman, Bernard. "The Queen of Sheba and Africa: A Reassessment of the *Sheba-Menelik Cycle* of the *Kebra Nagast* in the light of the Salibi hypothesis." African Studies Association of Australasia and the Pacific, 15 July 1994, at La Trobe University, Melbourne, Australia.

_____. *The Ge'ez text of the Kebra Nagast.* Asmara, Eritrea: University of Asmara, 1997.

Leslau, Wolf. *Falasha Anthology.* New Haven, Conn.: Yale University Press, 1951.

_____. *Ethiopic and South Arabic Contributions to the Hebrew Lexicon.* Berkeley and Los Angeles: University of California Press, 1958.

_____. *Hebrew cognates in Amharic.* Wiesbaden, Germany: Otto Harrassowitz, 1969.

_____. *Comparative Dictionary of Ge'ez.* Wiesbaden, Germany: Otto Harrassowitz, 1991.

Levine, Donald N. "Menelik and Oedipus: Further Observations on the Ethiopian National Epic." Proceedings of the First United States Conference on Ethiopian Studies, Michigan State University, 2-5 May 1973, 11-23.

Littmann, Enno, D. Krencker, and Th. Von Lüpke. *Deutsche Aksum - Expedition.* (4 Vols). Berlin, 1913.

Marassini, P. "Ancora sulle 'origini' etiopiche" in S.F. Bondi, S. Pemigotti, F. Serra, A. Vivian, eds. *Studi in Onore di Edda Bresciani.* Pisa: University of Pisa, 1985, 303-314.

Marcus, Harold. *The life and times of Menelik II: Ethiopia 1844-1913.* Oxford: Clarendon Press, 1975.

Margoliouth, D.S. *The relations between Arabs and Israelites Prior to the Rise of Islam.* Schweich Lectures (Oxford), 1921. London: Oxford University Press, 1924.

Marsden, Peter. The *Taliban: War, Religion and the New Order in Afghanistan.* London: Zed Books, 1998.

McGovern, Patrick E. *The Late Bronze and Early Iron Ages of Central Transjordan: The Baq'ah Valley Project.* Philadelphia: University Museum, University of Pennsylvania, 1986.

McKinnon, Michael. *Arabia. Sand, Sea, Sky.* London: BBC Books, 1990.

Marshall, Sarah. "Myrrh: magi, medicine and mortality," *The Pharmaceutical Journal (UK)* 18/25 December 2004, 919-921

Masliyah, Sadok. "The Bene Israel and the Baghdadis: Two Indian Jewish Communities in Conflict" *Judaism* Issue No. 171/Vol43/Number 3, Summer 1994, 179-193

Mazar, Benjamin, *Biblical Israel: State and People.* 1992, Jerusalem: Israel Exploration Society, 98.

Mazrui, Ali. *The Africans.* New York: Little Brown, 1986

Miller, J.M. and J. Hays, *A History of Ancient Israel and Judah.* London: SCM,1986.

Moberg, Axel (ed.). *The Book of the Himyarites: Fragments of a Hitherto Unknown Syriac Work.* Lund-London-Paris-Leipzig. Skrifter utgivna av Kungl. Humanistiska Vetenskapssamfundet i Lund 7/ Acta Reg. Societas Humaniorum Litterarum Lundensis 7, 1924.

Modrzejewski, Joseph. *The Jews of Egypt*. Philadelphia: The Jewish Publication Society, 1995.

Morrisby, Edwin. "Socatra-Sinbad's Island." Collingwood, Australia: *Quadrant Magazine,* September 1986.

Mosley, Leonard. Haile *Selassie, the Conquering Lion*. London: Weidenfeld and Nicolson, 1964.

Munro-Hay, Stuart. *Aksum, an African Civilisation of Late antiquity*. Edinburgh: Edinburgh University Press, 1991.

Musil, Alois. *The manners and customs of the Rwala Bedouins*. Czech Academy of Sciences and Arts and of Charles R Crane. New York: American Geographic Society, Oriental Explorations and Studies, no. 6, 1928.

_____. Northern *Nadj - A Journey from Jerusalem to Anaiza in Qasim*. London: The Argonaut Press, 1930.

Newby, Gordon Darnell. *A History of the Jews of Arabia from Ancient Times to their Eclipse under Islam*. Columbia: University of South Carolina Press, 1988.

Nibbi, Alessandra. *Ancient Egypt and Some Eastern Neighbors,* Park Ridge New Jersey: Noyes Press, 1981.

Nöldeke, Theodor. "A review of Bezold's *Kebra Nagast*." *Vienna Oriental Journal*, 19, (1905). Oxford University Press, 1924.

Noth, Martin. *Das System der zwölf Stamme Israels*. Stuttgart, Germany: University of Stuttgart, 1930.

Obermeyer, Gerald. "Civilization and Religion in Ancient South Arabia". Amman, Jordan: *Bulletin of the Royal Institute for Inter-Faith Studies, 1,* No. 1, (Spring 1999), 35-64.

Oliver, Roland. *The African Experience*. London: Weidenfeld and Nicolson, 1991.

Osman, Ahmad. *Moses, Pharaoh of Egypt: the Mystery of Akhenaton Resolved*. London: Grafton Books, 1990.

Pagels, Elaine. *The Gnostic Gospels:* London: Weidenfeld and Nicolson, 1979.

Pankhurst, Richard. *An Introduction to the Economic History of Ethiopia from Early Times to 1800*. London: Lalibela House, 1961.

_____. (ed.) *The Ethiopian Royal Chronicles*. Addis Ababa: Oxford University Press 1967.

Parfitt, Tudor. *The Thirteen Gate: Travels Among the Lost Tribes of Israel*. London: Weidenfeld and Nicolson, 1987.

_____. *Journey to the Vanished City: the Search for a Lost Tribe of Israel*. London: Hodder and Stroughton, 1992.

_____. *The lost tribes of Israel the History of a Myth*. London: Weidenfeld and Nicolson, 2002.

Philby. H. St John. *The Queen of Sheba*. London: Quartet Books, 1981.

Phillipson, D.W. "The excavation of Gobedra Rock-Shelter, Axum." *Azania, 12,* 1977, London and Nairobi, Kenya: The British Institute in Eastern Africa, 53-82.

Praetorius, F. *Fabula de Regina Sabaea apud Aethiobes*. Halle, Germany: Halle University, 1870.

Pritchard, James (ed.). *Solomon and Sheba*. London: Phaidon, 1974.

Prosperi, Franco. *Vanished Continent an Expedition to the Comoros:* The Adventurers' Club, London: Hutchinson, 1957.

Quirin, James. *The Evolution of the Ethiopian Jews: a History of the Beta Israel (Falasha) to 1920.* Philadelphia: University of Pennsylvania, 1992.

Rabin, Chaim. *Ancient West Arabian.* London: Taylor's Foreign Press, 1951.

_____. "Loanword evidence in Biblical Hebrew for trade between Tamil Nad and Palestine in the first millennium B.C." Second International Conference Seminar of Tamil Studies, Madras, India, 1968.

Rapoport, Louis. *The Lost Jews, last of the Ethiopian Falasha.* New York: Stein and Day, 1981.

Retsö, Jan. *The Arabs in Antiquity: Their History from the Assyrians to the Umayyads.* London and New York: Routledge Curzon, 2003.

Reusch, Dr R. "Kilimanjaro and its ascent." *Tanganyika Times,* 10 February 1928.

Robinson, James M., (ed.). *The Nag Hammadi Library.* New York: Harper-Collins, 1990.

Rodinson, Maxime. "Sur eth. tabot, ar. tabut, et les noms semitiques de 1' Arche." *Groupe linguistique d'Etudes Chamito-Semitiques* 9 (1962): 64-68.

Sachar, Howard M. *The Course of Modern Jewish History.* London: Weidenfeld and Nicolson, 1958.

Saenz- Badillos, Angel. A History *of the Hebrew Language.* Cambridge: Cambridge University Press, 1993.

Sagan, Eli. At *the Dawn of Tyranny - The Origins of Individualism, Political Oppression and the State*. New York: Vintage Books, 1993.

Salibi, Kamal. *The Bible came from Arabia*. London: Jonathan Cape, 1985.

_____. *Secrets of the Bible People*. New York: Interlink, 1988.

_____. *Who was Jesus? A conspiracy in Jerusalem*. London: I.B.Tauris, 1998.

_____. *The Historicity of Biblical Israel - Studies in 1 & 2 Samuel*. London: NABU, 1998.

Schneider, R. "Deux inscriptions subarabiques du Tigre." Leiden, Netherlands: *Bibliotheca Orientalis,* 30,1973, 385-387.

_____. *Les debuts de l'histoire éthiopienne. Doc. Hist. Civ. Ethk.-Trav.* R.C.P. 230 (CNRS), 7, 1976, 47-54.

_____."Documents epigraphiques de l'Ethiopie." Paris: *Annales d'Ethiopie,* 10, 1976, 81-93.

Sellassie, Sergew Hable. *Ancient and Medieval Ethiopian History to 1270*. Addis Ababa, Ethiopia: Addis Ababa University, 1972.

Shah, Tahir. *In Search of King Solomon's Mines*. London: John Murray, 2002.

Shahid, Irfan. "The Martyrs of Najran: New Documents." *Societe des Bollandistes,* Brussels, 1971.

_____."The *Kebra Nagast* in the Light of Recent Research" *Le Mus'eon,* Louvain, Belgium, 1976,133-178.

Shanks, Hershel et al. "The Rise of Ancient Israel." Symposium at the Smithsonian Institution, October 26, 1991, Biblical Archaeology Society, Washington D.C., 1992.

Sharma, Arvind, ed. *Women in World Religions.* New York: State University of New York Press, 1987.

Sperling, Harry and Maurice Simon (translators). *Zohar.* London and Bournemouth: Soncino Press, 1949.

Shepherd, Naomi. *Ploughing Sand: British Rule in Palestine 1917-1948.* London: John Murray, 1999.

Shelemay, Kay Kaufinan. *Music, Ritual and Falasha History.* East Lansing: Michigan State University, 1986.

Silberman, Neil A. "Who were the Israelites?" *Archaeology,* 45, no.2. March/April 1992.

Simpson, St. John (ed). *Queen of Sheba: Treasures from Ancient Yemen.* London: British Museum Press, 2002.

Spencer Trimingham, J. *Christianity among the Arabs in Pre-Islamic Times.* London and New York: Longman, 1979.

Stothers, R.B. "Mystery Cloud of AD 536". *Nature,* 307, January 1984, 344-5.

Swadesh, M. *The Origin and Diversification of Language.* London: Routledge and Kegan Paul, 1972.

Tamene, Getnet. "Features of the Ethiopian Orthodox Church and the Clergy." Bratislava, Slovakia: *Asian and African Studies,* 7, 1998, 87-104.

Tamrat, Taddesse. *Church and State in Ethiopia 1270-1557*. Oxford: Clarendon, 1972.

Thompson, Thomas L. *Early history of the Israelite people from the Written and Archaeological Sources*. Leiden, Netherlands: E J.Brill, 1992.

_____. *The Bible in History: How Writers Create a Past*. London, Pimlico, 1999.

Timberg, Thomas A.(ed). "Social stratification among the Jews of Cochin", in *Jews in India*. New York: Advent Books,1986, 61-120.

Tobi, Yosef. *The Jews of the Yemen: Studies in their History and Culture*. Leiden, Netherlands: Brill, 1999.

Torrey, Charles Cutler. *The Jewish Foundation of Islam*. New York: Ktav Publishing House, 1967.

Ullendorf, Edward. "Hebraic Jewish Elements in Abyssinian (Monophysite) Christianity." In: *Journal of Semitic Studies, 1*, no.3, (1956), 216-256.

_____. *The Ethiopians*. London: Oxford University Press, 1960.

_____. *Ethiopia and the Bible*. London: Oxford University Press, 1968.

_____. *Is Biblical Hebrew a Language?* Wiesbaden, Germany: Otto Harrassowitz, 1977.

A. Vivian, eds., *Studi in onore di Edda Bresciani*, Pisa: Giardini Editori (1985) 303-14.

Von Wissmann, Hermann. *Die Mauer der Sabäerhauptstadt Maryab/ Abessinien als Sabäische Staatskolonie im 6.Jh. vChr*. Nederlands Historisch Archaeologisch Instituut te Istanbul, 1976.

Wallis Budge, Sir EA. *A history of Ethiopia (2* vols). London: Methuen, 1928.

_____. *The Queen of Sheba and her only son Menyelek I.* Oxford: Oxford University Press, 1932.

White, William. Chinese *Jews. A Compilation of Matters Relating to the Jews of K'ai feng.* New York: Paragon, 1966.

Whitelam, Keith W. *The invention of Ancient Israel: the silencing of Palestinian history.* London: Routledge, 1996.

Wilson, Ian. *Jesus: The Evidence.* London: Weidenfeld and Nicolson, 1984.

Winckler, Hugo. *Arabisch-Semitiusch-Orientalisch.* Berlin, Germany: Mitteilungen der Vorderasiatischen Gesellschaft, W. Peiser, 1901.

Zoltenberg, H. *Catalogue des manuscrits ethiopiens de la Bibliotheque Nationale.* Paris, 1877.

INDEX

'Umarah, 90
'Abesa, 121
Aaron, 7, 11, 149, 239, 242
Abha, 190, 205, 231
Abraham, viii, 2, 4, 5, 36, 44, 67, 70, 81, 102, 105, 146, 149, 179, 181, 184, 202, 204, 226, 228, 229, 232, 263
Abreha, 153
Abu Arish, 190
Abu Lahab, 177
Abu Talib, 177
Abun, 135
Abuna, 90, 111, 126, 252
Acropolis, 42
Acts of Solomon, 55, 92
Adam, 142, 146, 147, 149, 221, 263
Adde Kawerh, 126, 128
Addis Ababa, 251, 254, 293, 299, 302
Adigrat, 128
Adrami, 147
Adulis, 79, 88, 132, 133, 221
Adwa, 88, 128
Afghan women, 21
African Americans, 4
Africans, 186
Afrikaans, 186
Afro-Asiatic, 4
Afwerki, 251
Agaw, xv, 63, 127, 155, 237, 245, 246, 264
Ahasuerus, 193
Ai, 34, 36

Akhdam, 89
Akhenaton, 9, 200, 299
Akkadian, 9, 44
Aksum, vi, 14, 61, 75, 76, 79, 86, 87, 88, 89, 90, 95, 112, 116, 130, 131, 132, 133, 134, 135, 136, 138, 140, 141, 142, 143, 144, 146, 147, 148, 149, 150, 151, 152, 154, 155, 156, 171, 172, 215, 224, 234, 235, 236, 242, 245, 247, 249, 250, 259, 290, 296, 298
Al Junaynah, 193, 205
Al Luhayyah, 215
Albright, 32, 33, 34, 198, 260, 287
Albright Institute, 198, 260
Alexander III, 23, 265
Alexandria, 125, 134, 137, 156, 213, 214, 222, 244
Algeria, 2
Aliyeh, 21, 58, 71, 72
Alla Amidas, 151
Allah, 84, 230
Almaqah, 84
Alt, 32
Amalekites, 160, 185
Amda Seyon, 144, 156
American University of Beirut, 190
Amhara, 5, 127, 238, 241, 245
Amharic, 63, 187, 189, 237, 296
Ammon, 45, 168
Ammonites, 10
Amorites, 82

An Nimas, 192, 206
Anastasius, 137
Anatolia, 138, 140
Andaman Islands, 89
Anthony of Egypt, 150
Antigonus, 25
Antipater, 25
Antiquities of the Jews, 93
Antseba, 252
Aphek, 36
Apocalypse of Baruch, 139
Apocrypha, 55
Appleyard, viii, 258, 264
Aqaba, 42
Arab traditions, 81, 82, 87, 160, 182, 221, 228
Arabia, iv, v, vi, 1, 4, 5, 6, 13, 14, 26, 37, 44, 51, 61, 67, 70, 72, 75, 76, 77, 81, 82, 83, 85, 87, 88, 90, 91, 110, 115, 116, 117, 118, 125, 127, 130, 131, 132, 134, 136, 138, 139, 140, 144, 152, 153, 154, 155, 157, 159, 160, 162, 163, 164, 165, 166, 167, 169, 171, 172, 173, 174, 175, 180, 182, 183, 184, 185, 186, 187, 189, 190, 191, 193, 194, 196, 197, 198, 199, 200, 202, 205, 206, 214, 215, 216, 217, 221, 224, 226, 229, 232, 237, 240, 242, 244, 247, 249, 250, 253, 256, 259, 262, 292, 294, 295, 297, 298, 299, 301
Arabian Gulf, 14, 86
Arabic, iv, 5, 30, 64, 68, 70, 83, 94, 97, 107, 108, 111, 114, 116, 122, 135, 141, 156, 159, 160, 173, 185, 186, 187, 188, 197, 200, 206, 207, 217, 232, 234, 239, 244, 249, 264, 296
Arabic dialects, iv, 5, 185, 186
Arabs, 6, 28, 67, 76, 81, 97, 148, 153, 154, 159, 160, 161, 177, 178, 180, 181, 182, 183, 185, 226, 229, 230, 232, 292, 295, 296, 301, 303
Aramean, 13, 17, 166, 191
Arameans, 13, 17, 76, 257
Aramaic, 8, 17, 23, 48, 56, 63, 64, 66, 67, 68, 95, 106, 182, 223, 232, 239, 249
Ararat, viii, 70, 192
archaeological evidence, 18, 32, 35, 37, 39, 40, 45, 75, 166, 185, 195
archaeologists, 30, 31, 33, 34, 37, 38, 39, 40, 41, 44, 47, 48, 50, 80, 83, 157, 192, 197, 203, 206, 222, 253, 254
Archaeology, 34, 36, 40, 42, 49, 76, 107, 198, 257, 260, 287, 293, 294, 302, 303
Archangel Michael, 123
Argentina, 28, 170
Arian, 61, 136
Aristobulus II, 25
Arius, 136, 148
Ark of Noah, 70, 146, 149
Ark of the Covenant, ii, 8, 11, 53, 71, 87, 105, 109, 114, 118, 119, 121, 123, 128, 142, 146, 147, 150, 151, 157, 216, 219, 222, 224, 226, 227, 229, 230, 231, 232, 234, 235, 252, 292
Ark of Zion, 236
Armenia, 26, 138, 139, 140, 141, 144, 145, 241

Armenians, 49
Armstrong, 172, 288
Arthur, 2
Artxerxes I, 20
Arwe, 87, 100
Asa, 204
Ashdod, 219, 230
Asherah, 14
Ashkenazi, 49, 243
Asia Minor, 107
Asir, 82, 110, 171, 190, 191, 193, 195, 199, 200, 202, 205, 207, 215, 217, 226, 231
Asmara, vii, 78, 133, 236, 250, 252, 254, 266, 295
Assyria, 19, 35, 53, 162, 166, 168, 232
Assyrians, 8, 13, 16, 17, 37, 123, 145, 166, 168, 184, 231, 301
Astar, 133
Aswan, 132, 223
Atang, 235
Atbara, 215, 216
Atlas of Jewish History, 125, 169, 291
Augustus, 25
Austro-Hungarian Empire, 27
Awash, 75
Awgi, 264
Azariah, 88, 102, 119, 120, 121, 122, 125, 130, 132, 223, 235, 242, 244
Azd, 186, 188
Azqir, 139
Azvar-nahara, 22
Ba'al, 9, 10, 14, 227, 263
Babylon, 7, 17, 18, 19, 21, 53, 58, 59, 61, 62, 64, 65, 66, 70, 72, 96, 106, 108, 148, 162, 169, 170, 172
Babylonian inscriptions, 169, 174
Babylonians, 13, 17, 18, 123, 168, 184
Badr, 177
Baghdad, 4, 155
Bahn, 40
Bala Zadisareya, 116
Balfour Declaration, 29
Bani Yusuf, 206
Banu Hillal, 82
Banu Salaim, 82
Bar Kokhba, 26, 31
Barbaria, 132
Barre, 129
Baruch, 44
Barya, 129
Bathsheba, 11, 147
Bayna Lekhem, 78, 116
Bede, 65
Bedouin, 82, 154, 160, 173, 175, 176, 181, 229, 230
Beher, 133
Beitin, 34
Beja, 133, 134
Belontos, 210, 213
Belshazzar, 18
Ben Asher, 69
Ben Gurion, 33, 174, 262
Ben Sira, 113
Benaiah, 101, 117, 120
Ben-Dor, 47
Bene Israel, 132, 293, 297
Benin, 165
Benjamin, 10, 13, 161, 192, 257
Beowulf, 23, 89
Berbers, 153

Berenson, 62, 258
Bet Israel, 12
Beta Giyorgis, 76
Beta Israel, 8, 57, 63, 224, 237, 238, 239, 241, 244, 246, 248, 250, 251, 252, 253, 255, 264, 266, 293, 300
Beth Shan, 36
Bethel, 14, 17
Beth-shemesh, 231
Bezold, vii, 114, 214, 215, 288, 298
Bible, vi, 33, 35, 38, 42, 47, 49, 55, 66, 157, 191, 192, 194, 196, 198, 199, 202, 253, 255, 265, 291, 293, 301, 304
Biblical Hebrew, 9, 47, 67, 68, 186, 195, 259, 300, 304
Bilen, 264
Bilqis, 87, 89, 90
Black Jews, 12, 63, 237
Black Stone, 229
Blessings of Jacob, 23, 48, 65
Blessings of Moses, 23, 48, 65
Blue Nile, 155, 187
Book of Esther, 105
Book of the Himyarites, 130, 297
Boswelli, 85
Britain, 89, 152, 167, 258, 288
British, 29, 30, 31, 33, 46, 49, 165, 186, 254, 292, 300, 303
Britons, 2
Bronze Age, 3, 8, 10, 34, 36, 37, 45, 81, 87, 108, 201, 292
Buddhism, 176
Buddhist missionaries, 150
Bushmen, 74
Cain, 146, 263, 293
Cairo, 125, 164, 213, 214, 222

Caleb, v, 10, 63, 86, 130, 136, 138, 141, 143, 144, 145, 146, 147, 148, 149, 151, 152, 153, 154, 156, 178, 234, 245
Caleb Cycle, 130, 141, 142, 143, 144, 145, 146, 147, 148, 156
Caligula, 26
Camel, 208, 288
camel trains, 205
Camelot, 2
Canaan, 5, 8, 10, 12, 34, 44, 49, 54, 57, 146, 257
Canaanite language, 160
Canaanites, 9, 16, 42, 56
Canada, 4, 170, 257
Caucasus, 187
Cedars of Lebanon, 205
Cerulli, 114, 289
Chaldeans, 257
Chapel of the Tablet, 235
Charles I, 108
Chaucer, 65
Cherubim, 193, 235
China, vii
Chinese, 90, 189, 305
Chosen People, 59, 69, 121
Christ, 1, 20, 59, 61, 80, 83, 100, 106, 131, 135, 136, 142, 147, 149, 150, 152, 171, 176, 178, 179, 180, 204, 241, 249, 250, 252
Christianity, 27, 59, 60, 61, 131, 134, 135, 136, 140, 141, 142, 143, 146, 154, 155, 156, 173, 175, 176, 178, 197, 238, 241, 242, 245, 249, 250, 251, 252, 303, 304
Christians, 26, 32, 59, 61, 77, 113, 139, 140, 148, 152, 179,

203, 234, 239, 240, 242, 248, 290
Chronicles, 45, 55, 56, 80, 185, 204, 231, 299
Church of Mary, 235
Circumcision, 240
City of David, 70, 192, 206, 219, 231
Clube, 257
Cochin Jews, 132
Code of Hammurabi, 108
Cohaito, 79
coinage, 134
Coins, 134
Colchis, 145
colonies, 11, 28, 200
Commiphora, 85
Comoros, 243, 300
Constantine, 60, 134, 136, 145, 241
Constantinople, 137, 152, 156
Copper, 42, 166
Coptic Church, 235
Copts, 137
Council of Chalcedon, 135, 136, 144, 148
Council of Nicaea, 60, 135, 136, 143, 145, 146, 148
Cretans, 49
Culture, 150, 287, 295, 304
Cush, 163, 193, 215, 217
Cushites, 16, 170, 204
Cushitic languages, 4
Cushitic speakers, v, 81, 127
Cyrus the Great, 18
D'mt, 76, 126, 132, 155, 218, 240
Da Bassano, 254
Dabra Makeda, 76

Dahlak archipelago, 217
Dahlberg, 196
Dahomey, 165
Damascus, 29, 155, 175, 249
Damot, 155, 187
Dan, 14, 44, 192, 203
Danakil, 134
Daniel, 18, 56, 102, 193
Darius, 23, 193
Darius III, 23
David, viii, xiv, 8, 10, 11, 13, 14, 27, 33, 34, 36, 37, 40, 41, 47, 49, 54, 116, 117, 121, 147, 163, 166, 174, 185, 192, 231, 240, 255, 258, 261, 262, 264, 289, 290, 292, 294
David of Ethiopia, 240
Day, 1, 147, 194, 240, 291, 300
Dead Sea, 41, 43, 55, 58, 66, 202, 290
Dead Sea Scrolls, 55, 58, 66, 290
Death of Moses, 256
Debra Bizen, 252
Debra Damo, 140
Delilah, 148
Demographic change, 245
Denmark, 203
Der Judenstaat, 27
Deuteronomist, 54
Deuteronomy, 2, 17, 48, 54, 55, 56, 57, 58, 65, 109, 113, 141, 223, 227, 235
Dhat Ba'adan, 133
Dhat Himyam, 133
Dhofar, 86
Dhu Nuwas, 138, 173
Dhu Sharkh ibn Hudad, 90, 97
Diaspora, 26, 49, 172, 175
Dibon, 43

Dillmann, 114, 289
Djibouti, 74, 155
DNA, 13, 39, 89, 242, 244, 264, 288
Domitius, 156
Dozy, 181, 185, 290
Dragon Princess, 106
Dreyfus case, 28
Dutch, 126, 186
East Africa, 75, 85, 186
Eban, 30
Eben, 219, 230
Ecclesiastes, 56, 109
Esdras, 20
Egypt, 5, 6, 7, 9, 10, 13, 14, 15, 16, 23, 36, 37, 39, 43, 45, 56, 57, 66, 71, 82, 85, 87, 94, 107, 123, 124, 125, 130, 134, 138, 140, 152, 155, 162, 166, 168, 169, 170, 192, 199, 200, 204, 208, 209, 210, 212, 213, 214, 215, 216, 220, 223, 226, 227, 231, 236, 239, 298, 299
Egyptians, 6, 9, 17, 38, 44, 45, 75, 87, 162, 166, 174, 191, 199, 200, 244
Ekeye Azeb, 88
Ekron, 230
El, 9, 10, 14, 206
El Elyon, 206
El Sabaoth, 206
El Shaddai, 206
El Shalom, 206
Elephantine, 223
Elijah, 67, 97, 102
Ella Amida, 134
Elmeyas, 121, 125
Elohist, 54
Emerton, 194

England, vii, 108, 203, 290, 295
English, vii, 4, 49, 65, 68, 126, 163, 185, 186, 195
Enoch, 55, 113, 255
Eritrea, vii, 5, 55, 74, 77, 79, 83, 111, 113, 115, 123, 125, 127, 130, 132, 133, 210, 212, 213, 217, 220, 224, 236, 241, 245, 250, 251, 254, 264, 295
Esau, 148, 175
Esperanto, 69
Esther, 65, 95, 97, 101, 106, 193
Estifanos, 241
Ethiopia, v, vii, xv, 5, 7, 8, 12, 42, 55, 61, 63, 71, 72, 75, 76, 77, 82, 83, 86, 90, 94, 111, 112, 115, 117, 118, 119, 122, 123, 125, 126, 127, 128, 129, 130, 132, 146, 151, 155, 156, 170, 180, 187, 192, 194, 204, 207, 208, 209, 210, 211, 213, 214, 215, 217, 220, 223, 224, 226, 231, 233, 234, 236, 237, 241, 242, 244, 245, 247, 251, 254, 261, 263, 265, 266, 287, 289, 290, 291, 292, 293, 294, 296, 299, 302, 303, 304, 305
Ethiopians, 76, 78, 110, 127, 176, 204, 211, 213, 215, 236, 237, 238, 251, 255, 304
Etruscans, 39
Euphrates, 22, 205
Europe, 3, 8, 27, 28, 29, 46, 64
Europeans, 4, 246
Evagrius Scholasticus, 152
Eve, 202, 263
Ewostatewos, 241, 251, 252
Exilarchs, 60

Exodus, 2, 6, 7, 10, 15, 40, 41, 48, 49, 55, 56, 63, 65, 82, 99, 113, 169, 191, 200, 201, 221, 227, 235, 240
Ezana, 134, 135, 143, 242
Ezekiel, 18, 21, 56, 70
Ezra, 2, 10, 20, 21, 22, 23, 48, 54, 55, 56, 62, 66, 70, 71, 109, 130, 131, 135, 142, 161, 171, 172, 174, 183, 184, 206, 244, 247, 250, 252
Fadak, 173
Faisal, 29, 190
Falasha, 237, 258, 265, 266, 293, 296, 300, 303
Famine, 249
Farasan, 217
Fatimid, 155
Fattovich, viii, 126, 259, 261, 290
Fertile Crescent, 175
Fetha Nagast, 239, 240
Finkelstein, 49, 50, 291
Flad, 246
Flemish, 186
Frankincense, 85
French, 2, 29, 126, 165
Frumentius, 134, 242, 248, 254
Fulani, 165
Fundamentalism, 74
Gabra Maskal, 156
Gadd, 169, 262, 291
Gafat, 187
Galil, 249
Galilee, 25, 64, 66, 70, 139, 141, 172, 249
Gamst, 238, 245, 265, 291
Garden of Eden, 193
Gath, 219, 230

Gaul, 152
Gaza, 117, 123, 125, 208, 209, 212, 213, 214, 217, 220
Gazette of Place Names, 190, 203
Gdrt, 138
Ge'ez, iii, v, vii, 32, 55, 66, 76, 80, 94, 111, 112, 114, 122, 130, 135, 156, 187, 189, 207, 208, 214, 215, 217, 232, 233, 237, 254, 255, 263, 274, 275, 276, 295, 296
Gebes, 209, 211, 214, 216
Gentiles, 59
German, vii, 29, 32, 49, 54, 55, 64, 195, 232, 246
Germanic tribes, 61
Gezer, 35, 36, 198
Ghana, 164, 165
Gibeah, 219, 231
Gibeon, 35
Gilbert, 125, 169, 174, 291
Glanzman, viii, 88, 110
Glock, 111, 260
Glory of the Kings, 112, 146, 288
Gnostic Gospels, 299
Gnostics, 62
Gobedra, 75, 76, 300
God the Father, 61
Gojjam, 133, 264
Gold, 42, 133, 165
Golden Calf, 9, 103, 105, 227
Goliath, 40
Gomorrah, 41, 193
Gondar, 245, 248
Goren, 219, 231
Gran, 150
Greece, 5, 24
Greek language, 134

Greeks, 13, 23, 50
Greenfield, viii, 196, 291
Gregory of Nyssa, 113
Gregory Thaumaturgus, 156
Gregory the Illuminator, 143, 145
Grendel, 89
Grierson, 128, 234, 235
Guidi, 114, 291
Gulo Makeda, 79, 88
Gurage, 5, 127
Habas, 133
Hadiyya, 194
Hadramawt, 139, 243
Hadrian, 26
Hagar, 6, 81, 226
Haile Selaisse, 77, 79, 113, 150, 251, 254
Haiti, 108
Hajar, 229
Hamasien, 190, 250, 251, 252
Hamdani, 88, 116
Hammond, 195, 196, 197, 198
Hancock, 128, 222, 292
Hasel, 43
Hashim, 176
Hasmoneans, 25, 175
Hassan, viii, 139
Hayes, 46
Hazega, 251
Hazor, 35, 36
Hebraic, 8, 44, 64, 111, 115, 130, 155, 221, 223, 224, 226, 237, 238, 239, 240, 241, 242, 243, 245, 252, 265, 291, 304
Hebrew, v, xiii, 2, 3, 4, 5, 6, 7, 8, 9, 10, 12, 15, 23, 24, 27, 30, 34, 41, 43, 44, 45, 46, 48, 53, 54, 55, 56, 59, 63, 64, 65, 66, 67, 68, 76, 82, 86, 87, 88, 92, 95, 101, 115, 118, 127, 128, 129, 130, 135, 155, 174, 180, 182, 183, 184, 186, 187, 189, 191, 192, 194, 197, 199, 200, 201, 204, 215, 217, 221, 226, 227, 228, 229, 232, 233, 239, 243, 245, 253, 255, 258, 263, 265, 268, 296, 301
Hebron, 5, 36, 195
Helena, 60
Hellenism, 23, 25
Hellenized Jews, 26
Henoticon, 137
Herod, 25, 26, 70, 71, 175
Herod the Great, 175
Herod, son of Antipater, 25
Herodotus, 145, 172, 205
Hertzog, 48
Herzl, 27, 28, 30, 50
Hezekiah, 16, 41, 43
Hijaz, 42, 81, 98, 141, 160, 161, 170, 171, 172, 173, 175, 180, 182, 183, 185, 186, 191, 192, 193, 199, 200, 201, 202, 249
Hilkiah, 17, 54, 242, 244
Himbirti, 250
Himyar, 61, 72, 87, 133, 138, 141, 143, 144, 148, 151, 153, 173, 186, 234
Himyarites, 138
Hinzat, 79, 88
Hiram, 205
Hittites, 3, 6, 15
Holiness Code, 109
Holocaust, 33
Holy Land, 33, 61, 175, 257, 260, 294
Holy Spirit, v, 59, 136, 180

Holy Writ, 2, 22, 31, 58, 61, 181
Homo sapiens, 74
Horn of Africa, v, 77, 251, 252, 256
Horns of the Altar, 149
House of David, 44, 54, 58, 60, 135, 142, 147, 249, 250
House of God, 237
House of Herod, 25, 175
House of Judah, 19
House of the Forest of Lebanon, 42
House of Zadok, 11
Hubbard, viii, 255, 261, 292
Hungary, 108
Hussein, 230
Hyksos, 200
Hyrcanus II, 25
H-yrdn, 70, 192, 201
Ibrit, 63
Ibro, 129
Idumeans, 175
Ilmuqah, 133
Inadan, 8, 294
India, 12, 85, 86, 89, 99, 108, 132, 133, 134, 154, 159, 190, 194, 259, 289, 293, 300, 304
Indian Ocean, 179
Indo-European, 15, 69, 189
Instructions for Merikare, 199
Internet, 198
Iranians, 49
Iraq, 13, 29, 145, 229
Iron, 3, 8, 13, 14, 15, 34, 37, 45, 46, 47, 81, 87, 91, 131, 133, 149, 162, 163, 166, 297
Iron Age, 3, 13, 15, 34, 46, 87, 163
Isa, 180, 250

Isaac, 5, 67, 146, 156, 226, 293
Isaiah, 16, 19, 43, 56, 140, 239
Ishmael, 6, 81, 226
Islam, 6, 7, 27, 30, 61, 86, 91, 129, 154, 155, 164, 165, 173, 175, 176, 178, 179, 180, 181, 184, 185, 227, 228, 230, 245, 246, 259, 261, 262, 288, 292, 295, 296, 298, 304
Islamic traditions, 8, 95, 97
Ismenie, 88
Israel, vi, 1, 2, 6, 8, 10, 12, 14, 15, 16, 21, 29, 30, 31, 33, 34, 35, 38, 41, 43, 44, 46, 49, 50, 51, 53, 54, 62, 63, 70, 79, 93, 115, 117, 119, 121, 123, 128, 131, 142, 146, 148, 151, 161, 162, 165, 167, 168, 171, 173, 174, 182, 191, 194, 195, 198, 199, 201, 206, 209, 210, 214, 222, 223, 227, 231, 237, 238, 244, 246, 247, 248, 252, 253, 257, 258, 262, 264, 290, 291, 297, 299, 301, 302, 305
Israelis, 50, 251
Israelite religion, 10, 12, 115, 119, 131, 161, 184, 199, 206, 227, 242, 245, 247, 252, 255
Israelite states, xiv, 13, 184
Israelites, 6, 8, 10, 11, 18, 21, 43, 46, 54, 95, 107, 110, 126, 131, 138, 160, 161, 170, 175, 181, 182, 183, 185, 192, 198, 201, 204, 206, 217, 228, 230, 231, 239, 246, 250, 262, 263, 289, 290, 296, 303
Italian, 77, 78, 126, 251, 252, 254
Italians, 251

Italy, 152, 259, 289, 290
Ithiopis, 76
Ivrit, 63, 69
Iyo'as, 248
Jacob, 6, 137, 146, 203, 262, 295
Jacob Baradaeus, 137
Jalil, 249
Jamaica, 108
James, viii, 35, 55, 194, 241, 246, 258, 263, 266, 288, 300, 301
Jane Eyre, 23
Japan, 108
Jashar, 55
Jawf, 43
Jebel Fayfa, 159
Jebel Hadi, 207
Jeddah, vi, 163, 168, 192, 202
Jehoiachin, 17, 19, 60, 249
Jehoiada, 101
Jehoiakim, 17, 60
Jehovah's Witnesses, 61
Jeremiah, 44, 56, 237
Jericho, 34, 36, 49, 228
Jeroboam, 13, 17
Jerusalem, iv, 1, 2, 10, 12, 14, 15, 16, 17, 19, 20, 21, 23, 24, 25, 32, 35, 36, 39, 41, 42, 45, 47, 48, 54, 55, 58, 66, 69, 70, 71, 72, 85, 93, 94, 98, 114, 115, 116, 117, 119, 122, 123, 124, 125, 130, 138, 146, 155, 168, 171, 172, 175, 180, 181, 192, 195, 199, 206, 208, 212, 216, 217, 219, 223, 231, 232, 238, 246, 249, 257, 260, 262, 288, 290, 297, 298, 301
Jerusalem priesthood, 54, 249
Jesus, 20, 59, 199, 262, 301, 305
Jethro, 8, 221, 263

Jewish sources, 113
Jewish traditions, 106, 179
Jews, 23, 25, 26, 27, 29, 31, 33, 35, 39, 46, 47, 48, 49, 50, 55, 59, 61, 62, 64, 66, 69, 71, 72, 91, 112, 142, 147, 149, 150, 160, 169, 170, 171, 172, 173, 174, 175, 177, 179, 181, 182, 183, 184, 185, 206, 226, 232, 240, 241, 243, 245, 248, 251, 252, 253, 262, 266, 287, 288, 291, 293, 294, 295, 298, 300, 304, 305
Jizan, vi, 82, 159, 190, 191, 193, 199, 202, 217, 222
John Hyrcanus, 24
John the Baptist, 59
Jordan, viii, 29, 32, 37, 43, 47, 49, 71, 163, 192, 197, 201, 259, 299
Joseph, 6, 9, 18, 40, 59, 89, 139, 178, 197, 202, 206, 250, 265, 288, 292, 298
Josephus, 66, 71, 80, 87, 92, 93, 95, 99, 100, 107, 113, 114, 122, 143, 205, 215, 263, 267, 293
Joshua, 8, 10, 12, 34, 36, 38, 40, 45, 47, 53, 56, 63, 70, 191, 228
Josiah, 16, 17, 54, 58, 141, 223
Jubber, 265, 293
Jubilees, 55, 255
Judaea, 25, 60, 175
Judaeans, 18, 20
Judah, 1, 10, 11, 12, 14, 15, 16, 17, 20, 21, 22, 23, 40, 41, 44, 45, 54, 60, 63, 79, 91, 118, 123, 141, 161, 162, 167, 168,

170, 171, 179, 182, 183, 184, 192, 194, 204, 206, 216, 217, 231, 242, 249, 253, 258, 262, 263, 297
Judaism, 10, 21, 24, 25, 26, 47, 48, 50, 51, 60, 61, 62, 80, 131, 139, 142, 154, 161, 165, 171, 172, 173, 174, 175, 179, 180, 183, 199, 237, 239, 240, 241, 242, 244, 245, 246, 247, 248, 250, 262, 295, 297
Judas Maccabeus, 24
Judges, 48, 56, 65
Julian, 144
Julius Caesar, 25
Jurhum, 228, 234, 242
Just Master, 149
Justin I, 144
Justin II, 137, 144
Justinian, 137, 144, 152
Ka'bah, 6, 181, 228, 230, 234
Kansha, 250
Kaplan, 246, 247, 266, 293
Karaites, 62
Karnak, 168
Kassala, 75, 76, 290
Keall, viii, 201
Kebra Nagast, ii, iii, v, vii, 32, 80, 84, 92, 93, 95, 99, 100, 107, 108, 110, 111, 112, 113, 114, 116, 118, 122, 123, 124, 125, 126, 130, 136, 138, 142, 143, 144, 145, 146, 156, 159, 178, 207, 215, 216, 217, 220, 221, 222, 236, 254, 261, 263, 276, 288, 292, 295, 298, 302
Keller, 42, 293
Kenites, 263
Kenya, vii, 28, 86, 161, 300

Kenyon, 34, 35, 197, 228, 257, 294
Keren, 264
Keturah, 263
Khadijah, 176
Khamis Mushait, 82, 193, 200, 205, 215, 226
Khamtanga, 264
Khartoum, 163
Khaybar, 82, 173, 174, 182, 183
Khoury, 198
Kings, 12, 19, 42, 45, 55, 56, 80, 92, 193, 239, 267
kingship, 11, 29, 147, 157, 204
Kitor, 98
Knauf, viii, 203, 262, 294
Knights Templar, 128
Korean, 189
Korotayev, 259, 261, 295
Krauss, 204, 263
Krauthammer, 31
Ku'bar, 155
Kunama, 129
Kureishi, 74
Kush, 76, 133, 163, 193, 205, 215
Kushi, 12
Kushm, 221
Kuthah, 194
Kws, 71, 193, 205, 215, 216, 231, 239
Lachish, 36
Ladino, 64
Lake Hayq, 155
Lalibela, 155, 156, 214, 246, 299
Latin, 66, 114, 135, 227
Latos, 224, 250, 251
Law of Moses, 4, 53

Lebanon, 29, 49, 94, 191, 205, 267
Lemba, 8, 132, 224, 242, 243
Lemche, 38, 257
Leslau, viii, 187, 189, 258, 296
Lesotho, 108
Levant, 15, 37, 162, 166, 199, 232
Levi, 7, 192, 222, 250
Levites, 18, 94, 227, 229
Leviticus, 2, 55, 57, 108, 240, 269
Libya, 138, 178
Libyans, 13, 166
Lihyanic, 82
Liliths, 98
Linguistic evidence, 82, 185
Luke, 1, 80
Luxor, 7, 43, 168
Maasai, 186
Madagascar, 75, 170, 243, 265, 288
Mahoza, 60, 61, 72, 145
Mahrem, 133, 134, 136
Mai Bela, 78, 79, 80, 116, 236, 252
Maimonides, 8
Makari, 121
Makeda, 87, 88, 114, 116
Malagasy, 243, 265, 288
Malawi, 242
Malaysia, 89
Mali, 164, 165
Manasseh, 16, 244
Mansa Musa, 164
Manuel Comnenus, 265
Mapungubwe, 243
Mar Zutra II, 60
Marcian, 144

Margoliouth, 183
Marib, 79, 81, 82, 84, 85, 86, 110, 153, 193
Marsden, 21, 257, 297
Mary, 146, 161, 178, 180, 222, 241, 249, 255
Masoretes, 64, 66, 67, 69, 70, 192, 195
Masoretic scholars, 64, 206
Masruq, 151, 234
Mattathias, 24
Matthew, 1, 61, 80, 113
Maxentius, 60
May Qoho, 76
Mazar, 257
Mazber, 76
Mazrui, 247
McGovern, 47, 163, 297
Mdyam, 210, 213
Mecca, 6, 98, 153, 162, 164, 173, 176, 177, 181, 182, 185, 189, 191, 217, 228, 229, 231, 234, 290
Medina, 86, 160, 169, 173, 177, 182, 183, 185, 200, 217, 231, 232, 233, 287
Mediterranean, 13, 15, 26, 49, 59, 85, 133, 152, 167, 172, 175, 176, 190, 202, 205, 257, 287
Medyam, 148
Megiddo, 35, 45
Mekele, 90, 111, 116, 126, 187
Menelaus, 24
Menelik, ii, iii, iv, v, vi, vii, 79, 88, 92, 93, 108, 109, 111, 113, 114, 115, 116, 117, 118, 119, 120, 121, 122, 123, 124, 125, 126, 128, 130, 132, 135, 141, 142, 143, 146, 147, 148, 149,

156, 157, 159, 179, 207, 208, 209, 213, 214, 215, 216, 217, 220, 222, 231, 233, 234, 235, 236, 237, 238, 240, 242, 243, 244, 245, 247, 251, 252, 253, 256, 263, 266, 267, 276, 295, 296
Menelik II, 251, 296
Meroe, 39, 163, 170
Meroitic, 39
Mesopotamia, 4, 5, 18, 24, 37, 38, 60, 70, 82, 86, 139, 152, 162, 169, 202
Mesr, 125, 212, 214, 215, 216
Mesrin, 123, 208, 209, 213, 214, 216
Messiah, 16, 20, 69, 102, 139, 141
Metera, 79, 133
Micah, 19, 56
Michael of Fuwa, 223
Midgan, 129, 261, 294
Midianites, 263
Midrash Mishle, 101, 105
Midrashim, 113
Miller, 46, 258, 297
Milvian Bridge, 60
Minaen, 159, 183
Miriam, 7, 250
Mizpah, 20
Mkrb, 127
Mlk, 126
Moab, 43, 148, 194
Moabites, 37, 43, 63
Modern Hebrew, 63, 68
Monarchy, 257
Mondale, 31
Monophysites, 137, 141
Mormah, 36

Mormons, 48
Morocco, vii, 164
Moses, 2, 6, 7, 8, 9, 10, 11, 22, 40, 44, 53, 56, 57, 63, 65, 70, 72, 149, 154, 155, 160, 169, 179, 183, 191, 200, 201, 202, 205, 207, 221, 227, 239, 242, 246, 257, 263, 299
Mot, 9
Motu, 203
Mount Sinai, 210
Msrm, 71, 124, 193, 205, 217, 226
Muhammad, 84, 98, 151, 173, 176, 177, 178, 179, 180, 181, 183, 185, 221, 226, 229, 288
Munro-Hay, viii, 234, 235, 298
Myrrh, 85, 259, 297
Nabataeans, 262
Nabodinus, 18, 169
Nabopolassar, 17
Nadab, 102, 231
Nadir, 173
Najran, 86, 139, 151, 180, 205, 222, 234, 250, 302
Napata, 170, 231
Napoleon, 39
Nasirah, 249
Nazarenes, 56, 135
Nazareth, 249
Nazarite, 238
Nazret, 156
Nebuchadnezzar, 17, 18, 40, 167
Necho, 244
Negev, 37
Negus, 250
Nehemiah, 20, 56
Nestorian, 135
Nestorius, 148

New Jerusalem, 58, 171
New Kingdom, 9
New Testament, 31, 61, 80, 113, 135, 143, 149, 178, 180, 239, 249, 250, 255
New York Times, 42, 264
Newby, 160, 298
Nicaea, 136, 138, 149, 178, 236
Nicaean Creed, 61, 113
Nigeria, 165
Nikaule, 87
Nile, 4, 6, 15, 75, 123, 132, 152, 166, 168, 170, 190, 199, 204, 205, 214, 215, 216, 223, 231, 288
Nine Saints, 136, 140, 143, 233, 245
Nisibis, 139, 148
Noah, 70, 146
Nöldeke, 114, 232, 298
non-Jews, 59
North Africa, 61, 153, 154, 170, 175, 178
North Yemen, 186
Noth, 55, 191, 298
Noural Rouz, 88
Nubia, 6, 190, 200, 201, 204
Octavian, 25
Ofer, 36
Old Testament, ii, v, vi, xiii, 1, 2, 3, 7, 8, 10, 14, 18, 22, 23, 27, 30, 32, 34, 35, 36, 37, 39, 40, 41, 43, 44, 45, 46, 48, 50, 51, 53, 54, 55, 56, 63, 64, 65, 66, 67, 68, 69, 70, 71, 72, 80, 83, 92, 95, 97, 99, 100, 105, 108, 110, 111, 113, 114, 115, 126, 130, 135, 142, 143, 146, 147, 149, 157, 159, 160, 161, 162, 165, 167, 169, 170, 171, 178, 182, 184, 185, 186, 187, 190, 191, 192, 194, 196, 197, 200, 201, 202, 203, 204, 205, 206, 215, 221, 222, 224, 226, 227, 228, 230, 231, 232, 234, 237, 238, 243, 245, 246, 247, 252, 253, 254, 255, 256, 257, 258, 288, 290
Oman, 86, 159
Omri, 14, 37, 41, 43, 161, 162, 169, 184
One True God, 67, 84, 97, 109, 221, 229
Oniads, 24
Oracles of Baarlam, 48, 65
Origen, 113
Oromo, 127
Orthodox Church, 77, 128, 135, 226, 233, 235, 236, 237, 238, 239, 247, 250, 251, 254, 303
Oxus, 178
Palestine, iv, v, vi, 5, 6, 18, 24, 25, 26, 27, 28, 29, 30, 32, 33, 36, 37, 38, 40, 41, 42, 43, 44, 45, 46, 50, 51, 58, 59, 67, 70, 71, 110, 124, 127, 130, 131, 138, 140, 152, 157, 159, 162, 163, 166, 167, 168, 169, 171, 172, 173, 175, 182, 183, 186, 191, 199, 200, 203, 204, 206, 223, 232, 234, 235, 238, 249, 253, 259, 262, 287, 294, 300, 303
Palestinians, 30, 49, 50, 72, 257, 287
Palmyra, 107, 148
Papua New Guinea, 89, 203
Parfitt, viii, 194, 264, 299

Paul, 26, 40, 59, 61, 71, 143, 175, 241, 249, 250, 303
Pearl, 142, 147, 259
Pemba Island, 161
Perez, 148
Persia, 58, 61, 65, 75, 133, 139, 141, 148, 154, 159, 232
Persians, 18, 20, 21, 60, 90, 137, 144, 155, 169, 170, 172, 178, 223
Petra, 86, 148, 262
Pharisees, 25, 62
Philby, 82, 299
Philippines, 89
Philistines, 8, 10, 103, 148, 205, 228, 230, 289
Phillip, 265
Phoenicia, 15, 35, 167
Phoenicians, 9, 167, 172
Pirenne, 128
Poem of Moses, 48, 65
Poles, 29
Pompey, 25
Portuguese, 161, 248
Praetorius, 114, 300
Prester John, 246
priesthood, 7, 10, 11, 16, 18, 20, 21, 22, 23, 25, 54, 57, 58, 62, 71, 91, 106, 107, 109, 122, 125, 130, 131, 140, 152, 157, 161, 172, 180, 193, 203, 239, 242, 243, 263
Pritchard, 35, 37, 38, 263, 300
Procopius of Caesarea, 152
Promised Land, iii, v, xii, 2, 5, 8, 9, 12, 13, 16, 27, 30, 31, 36, 38, 40, 41, 45, 47, 53, 54, 56, 63, 69, 70, 72, 201, 202, 204, 205, 206, 228, 257

Psalm 68, 48, 66
Psamtik II, 170
Ptolemy I Soter, 23
Punt, 75, 252, 294
Qades, 210, 213
Qarmatians, 229
Qemant, 224, 238, 241, 245, 264, 265, 291
Qemanteney, 264
Qes, 250
Qosh, 88
Quaraiza, 173
Queen of Sheba, v, 1, 51, 73, 76, 79, 80, 82, 83, 88, 90, 92, 93, 95, 100, 107, 108, 114, 115, 118, 126, 128, 131, 138, 148, 157, 204, 205, 216
Quiran, 246, 247, 248
Qumran, 58, 68
Qur'an, 80, 96, 97, 99, 107, 113, 143, 163, 178, 180, 181, 185, 207, 227, 230, 249
Qwarenya, 63, 258, 264
Rabaul, 152
Rabbinical Judaism, 62
Rabin, xiii, 86, 160, 186, 189, 191, 197, 217, 233, 259, 261, 300
Racism, 128
Rahman, 84, 221
Ramses I, 201
Ramses II, 6, 9
Ramses III, 15
Raydan, 139
Rechabites, 263
Red Sea, 4, 42, 75, 77, 79, 81, 85, 86, 87, 88, 123, 125, 132, 133, 134, 138, 153, 155, 163, 172, 174, 179, 192, 199, 201, 204,

210, 214, 215, 217, 221, 232, 237, 244
Reds and Blacks, 127
Rehoboam, 14, 110, 119, 142, 147, 168
Reuben, 192, 287
Riddles, 101, 105
Rift valley, 75
Robin Hood, 2
Robinson, 30, 231, 301
Rod of Moses, 149
Rodinson, 233, 247, 264, 301
Roman Catholicism, 251
Roman Empire, 26, 27, 60, 61, 133, 136, 137, 138, 139, 140, 143, 153, 175
Roman women, 63
Romans, 24, 25, 26, 60, 71, 72, 148, 172
Rome, 24, 107, 134, 136, 137, 146, 290, 291
Rosetta Stone, 39
Ruah, 180
Rub al Khali, 86
Russia, 28, 29
Ruth, 11, 40, 43, 56, 113
Rwala, 160, 298
Saadiah, 89
Sab, 127, 130
Saba, 81, 84, 139, 263
Sabaea, xiii, 80, 82, 84, 85, 91, 100, 110, 118, 127, 132, 138, 167, 171, 172, 190, 192, 193, 300
Sabaean alphabet, 83
Sabaean inscriptions, 90, 115, 116, 118, 126, 130, 151, 203

Sabaeans, 76, 77, 81, 82, 83, 84, 85, 87, 90, 92, 107, 118, 126, 127, 133, 138, 170, 187, 217
Sabbath, 34, 57, 212, 233, 241
Sadducees, 25, 56
Saho, 127
Salibi, iii, vi, viii, xii, xiii, 47, 157, 190, 191, 192, 193, 194, 195, 196, 197, 198, 199, 200, 201, 202, 203, 204, 205, 206, 207, 215, 216, 217, 219, 221, 222, 224, 231, 247, 253, 262, 295, 301
Salome, 25
Samaria, 15, 20, 25, 41, 194
Samaritans, 4, 12, 17, 20, 23, 56, 63, 244
Samson, 103, 105, 148, 238
Samuel, 10, 55, 56, 301
San, 74, 89
Sana'a, 88
Sarah, 6, 226, 259, 297
Sarwat, 201
Sasu, 132, 133
Satan, 149, 238
Saudi Arabia, vi, 32, 82, 163, 190, 194, 200, 262, 287
Saudi Arabian government, 195, 202
Saul, 10, 26, 47, 59, 160, 192
Sayhut, 243
Schneider, 126, 127, 128, 261, 302
Sea of Eritrea, 210
Sea Peoples, 13, 15, 166
Seleucids, 24
Semien Mountains, 248
Semites, 5, 81, 127, 147

Semitic languages, 5, 32, 44, 67, 68, 187, 189, 261, 264, 292
Semitic speakers, 4, 76, 127
Senna, 243
Sennacherib, 16, 19, 80, 167
Septuagint, 66, 215
Serai, 5
Sesostris III, 199
Seti I, 6
Shabaka, 16, 80, 231
Shahid, 197, 302
Shams, 84
Shar Habil, 88, 90
Sharahbil Yakkuf, 139
Sharakh ibn Sharahil, 90
Sharia, 181
Sheba, ii, iii, v, vi, vii, xiii, 1, 11, 14, 40, 42, 51, 72, 74, 76, 78, 79, 80, 81, 82, 83, 85, 87, 88, 89, 90, 91, 92, 93, 95, 96, 97, 98, 99, 100, 101, 105, 106, 108, 109, 110, 111, 112, 113, 114, 115, 116, 117, 118, 119, 120, 121, 122, 123, 125, 126, 127, 128, 130, 131, 132, 135, 138, 139, 141, 142, 143, 146, 147, 148, 149, 150, 151, 156, 157, 159, 179, 181, 183, 184, 192, 193, 203, 204, 205, 207, 208, 216, 217, 222, 227, 231, 233, 234, 235, 236, 237, 240, 242, 244, 245, 246, 247, 252, 253, 256, 262, 263, 267, 276, 289, 291, 295, 299, 300, 303, 305
Sheba-Menelik Cycle, vi, 92, 93, 108, 111, 113, 114, 115, 116, 118, 122, 130, 135, 142, 144, 147, 148, 149, 156, 157, 179, 207, 216, 218, 231, 235, 236, 242, 256, 263, 295
Sheba-Menelik tradition, 138
Sheban kings, 126
Shebans, 77, 81, 84, 96, 110, 127, 129, 217
Shelemay, viii, 246, 247, 265, 303
Sheshonk, 13, 45, 80, 167, 206
Shiloh, 216, 219, 230, 231
Shishak, 13, 45
Shurab el Gash, 76, 77
Shusha, 193
Sibley, 195
Sidon, 231
Silberman, viii, 49, 50, 204, 263, 291, 303
Siloam, 41, 43
Sinai peninsula, 4, 227
snakes, 87, 100
So Chieluo, 106
Socotra, 87, 89, 159
Sodom, 41, 193
Solomon, iii, v, xiv, 1, 2, 4, 8, 10, 11, 12, 13, 14, 15, 22, 34, 35, 37, 40, 41, 42, 45, 46, 47, 49, 51, 53, 54, 56, 57, 58, 63, 65, 69, 70, 71, 72, 79, 80, 82, 86, 92, 93, 94, 95, 96, 97, 98, 99, 100, 101, 103, 105, 106, 107, 109, 110, 112, 113, 115, 116, 117, 118, 119, 120, 121, 122, 125, 126, 130, 131, 132, 135, 138, 141, 142, 147, 149, 157, 161, 162, 163, 166, 167, 168, 169, 179, 183, 184, 192, 194, 202, 204, 205, 207, 209, 210, 211, 213, 216, 218, 222, 227, 228, 230, 231, 235, 236, 237,

238, 242, 243, 246, 252, 255, 263, 267, 268, 300, 302
Solomonid dynasty, 156, 254
Somalia, 8, 85, 111, 115, 129, 130, 132, 174, 240, 246
Somalis, 129
Song of Deborah, 23, 48, 65
Song of Moses, 23, 48, 65, 109
Songhai, 164, 165
South Africa, 2, 242, 243
South Arabia, 5, 184
South Korea, vii, 91
Southern Africa, vi
Spain, 61, 153, 154
Station of Abraham, 229
Suakin, 75
Sudan, 71, 74, 76, 163, 204, 215, 232, 237, 290
Sumerian, 9, 189
Susa, 193
Swadesh, 187, 303
Swahili, 186, 203
Syria, 5, 6, 13, 15, 29, 37, 38, 49, 107, 118, 138, 140, 152, 177
Syriac, 136, 145, 232, 233, 239, 297
Syrians, 172
Tabot, 236
Tabotat, 236
Taif, 169, 170, 173, 177, 192, 201, 206, 249
Taima, 11, 14, 15, 18, 82, 86, 167, 168, 173, 174, 181, 183, 193
Takezze, 123, 214, 216
Taliban, 21, 257, 297
Talmud, 21, 62, 113
Tamar, 103, 105, 106, 148
Tamil, 86, 259, 300

Tamrin, 115, 117, 118, 121
Tanis, 166
Tanzania, v, vii, 89, 161, 243
Targum, 95, 97, 99, 101, 105, 106, 113
Targum Sheni, 96, 97, 99, 101, 105, 106
Tarim, 243
Tayyi' dialect, 189
Teacher of Righteousness, 25
Tehama, 163, 192, 201, 204
Tel Aviv, 34, 36, 49, 262
Tell Abu Hawan, 36
Tell Mor, 36
Ten Commandments, 8, 53, 108, 121, 227
Tesfamariam, viii, 266
The Bible came from Arabia, 301
The Sign and the Seal, 222, 292
Thebes, 43, 45, 166, 199, 200
Theodora, 137
Thompson, viii, 47, 48, 69, 70, 196, 203, 247, 253, 304
Thutmose III, 6
Tiban Asad Abu Karib, 139
Tigre, 126, 222, 241, 246, 251, 302
Tigré, 5, 126, 127, 261
Tigrinya, 5, 78, 127, 186, 237, 238, 245, 246, 250, 251
Tirzah, 14
Tobiah, 24
Torah, 4, 8, 9, 16, 17, 21, 22, 25, 54, 55, 56, 57, 62, 63, 69, 92, 99, 108, 119, 121, 122, 125, 132, 180, 207, 222, 239, 240, 244
Torrey, 84, 180, 182, 183, 185, 259, 304

Towner, 195
Trade, iv, xvi, 85, 259
Trimingham, 182, 197, 303
Trinity, 136, 148
Tsa'edakristyan, 78
Tse'azega, 251
Tubba, 139
Tuck, 2
Tumal, 129
Tunisia, 164
Turkey, 5, 15, 28, 70, 139, 145
Turkish Empire, 29
Turks, 29, 31, 49
Tuscany, 15
Tuwa, 207
Tyre, 205, 231
Ullendorf, viii, 215, 245, 265, 304
United Nations, 30, 34
University of Asmara, 78, 295
University of Pennsylvania, 47, 266, 297, 300
Unknown God, 12
Upper Nile, 6, 170
Ur, 4, 70, 232
Van der Graaf accelerator, 228
Vietnam, vii, 170
Vietnamese, 189
Vulcan, 7
Wadi Bishah, 191, 205, 215, 217
Wahb ibn Munabbihi, 91
Wales, 89
Ward, 196
Weizmann, 29
Wellhausen, 54
West Africa, 165, 167
West Arabian language, 233
West Bank settlement, 50

Western Arabia, ii, iv, 159, 168, 188, 222
Whitelam, 38, 258, 305
Wilkens, 203
Winckler, 185, 305
Women, 22, 91, 229, 302
World War, 29, 33, 77, 254
Writing on the Wall, 18
Wuqro, 126
Xi Wang Mu, 91
Y chromosome, 243
Ya'fur, 99
Yabika Egzi, 156
Yadin, 35
Yadir, 173
Yahweh, 206, 263
Yahwist, 54
Yanuf Dhu Shanatir, 139
Yathrib, 160, 173, 174, 177, 182, 183, 200
Yeha, 76, 79, 88, 128, 240
Yehud, 171
Yekunno Amlak, 156, 236
Yemen, vi, 5, 7, 11, 71, 79, 81, 83, 84, 86, 88, 90, 99, 110, 118, 139, 140, 141, 145, 154, 159, 160, 170, 172, 173, 178, 183, 185, 186, 188, 189, 190, 191, 192, 193, 199, 201, 204, 205, 215, 218, 221, 227, 234, 243, 244, 259, 291, 295, 303, 304
Yemeni traditions, 100
Yersina pestis, 152
Yeshu, 250
Yhwh, 7, 9, 10, 14, 24, 93
Yibir, 8, 44, 129, 130, 174, 222, 240, 246, 252, 261, 294
Yiddish, 64

Yudit, 155, 187, 245
Yurco, 43
Yusuf, 86, 138, 139, 141, 145, 148, 151, 152, 153, 154, 173, 234, 245
Za Besi Angabo, 87
Za Sebado, 88
Zadok, 4, 11, 16, 53, 54, 58, 119, 121, 122, 140, 243
Zadokites, 4, 12, 18, 22, 25, 54, 56, 57, 58, 62, 106, 141, 171, 242, 244
Zafar, 139, 151
Zagwe, 155, 156, 223, 245, 246
Zar'a Ya'eqob, 241
Zechariah, 19, 56, 120
Zedekiah, 17
Zeno, 137
Zenobia, 107
Zephaniah, 56, 239
Zerah, 204
Zerubbabel, 19, 20, 58, 59, 71, 72
Zimbabwe, 242, 243
Zion, 19, 27, 28, 80, 119, 120, 142, 146, 192, 206, 210, 211, 235, 236, 242, 253
Zionism, ii, 1, 27, 29, 51
Zionist movement, 2, 33
Zionists, 48
Zipporah, 221
Zohar, 113, 302
Zoltenberg, 114, 305
Zoroastrianism, 91, 173

Made in United States
North Haven, CT
25 April 2024